D1064380

Science of Sports Training:

How to Plan and Control Training for Peak Performance

by Thomas Kurz, M. Sc.

STADION

Science of Sports Training:
How to Plan and Control Training for Peak Performance

by Thomas Kurz, M.Sc.

Published by:

Stadion Publishing Company
a division of Stadion Enterprises
Post Office Box 447
Island Pond, VT 05846, U.S.A.

Publisher's Cataloging in Publication Data:

Kurz, Thomas
Science of Sports Training:
How to Plan and Control Training for Peak Performance.
Bibliography: p. 243-246
Includes index
1. Sports—Physiological aspects. 2. Athletes—Physiology.
3. Sports sciences. I. Title.
GV711.K967 1991 796.015 87-061430
ISBN 0-940149-00-1 (library binding)
ISBN 0-940149-01-X (paper trade)

Editing by Lisa A. Costello
Cover and Book Design by Ryszard Korczynski
Cover Photograph by Jim Johnson
Drawings by Mikolaj Zagorski

Printed in the United States of America

Prawilnym wspanialcom.

Acknowledgments

I would like to thank Jozef Drabik, Ph. D., who provided materials on developing endurance, coordination, children's sports training, and control of the training process; Stanislaw Klosowski, M. Sc., who provided materials on developing strength; Maciej Mierzejewski, M. Sc., who wrote the sections on psychosomatic training and means of recovery; Edward Pawlowski, M. Sc., who helped with the chapter on principles of methodology; and Krystyna Zareba, M. Sc., who did proofreading.

Thomas Kurz

TABLE OF CONTENTS

Warning—Disclaimer

The author and Stadion Publishing Company are not liable or responsible to any person or entity for any damage caused or alleged to be caused directly or indirectly by the information contained in this book.

Consult your physician before starting any exercise program.

I. INTRODUCTION

The period of life, when a talented and motivated person has the ability to train and compete in sports today and in the future, lasts only a few years. Some athletes shine in international competition for, at most, a couple of years.

The first few years of training allow for nearly normal overall education because in these years, less time and energy is dedicated to training than later. As the degree of mastery grows, the athletes must work harder and longer to compete at the international level. That leaves no time for work, normal studies, or procreation. Fortunately, the period of life when one can enjoy success at any of these occupations lasts much longer than the period of the highest athletic ability. It is obvious that an activity that can realize one's full human potential, teach useful skills, set one for life money-wise, bring great honor to one's family, and satisfy one's national pride,[*] but only if pursued with total commitment and only in a short, strictly defined period in one's life, should have a priority over everything else.

Everything—environment, activities, human contacts, all should be subordinated to the demands of athletic training. One should live where there are the most favorable training conditions and surround oneself only with people that are conducive to success. The people with no goals and with a negative attitude drain energy, have the mentality of cattle and must be avoided.

The purpose of athletic training is to achieve the highest possible sports result (for a given individual). Training is efficient if this result is achieved with a minimal expenditure of time and energy.

---

[*] What a delight it is for Byelorussian, Georgian, Lithuanian, Polish, Ukrainian, Uzbek athletes, as well as athletes of other captive nations, to defeat Russians!

I have tried to describe and explain all means of athletic training that lead to reaching peak performances without resorting to illegal ways because most of the illegal methods of enhancing performance are harmful in the long (and in the not so long) run.

If you choose to use the means of enhancing performance that are illegal or considered unethical, it is not enough to find the medical personnel that are willing to participate in the scheme. The physicians, the sports scientists, and the coaches, all have to have the highest level of qualifications, an extensive knowledge and experience with using the given type of dope (since methods of detection are constantly improving, the dope is constantly changing, so not many specialists have much experience with any of it). Doping cannot be a substitute for a proper methodology of training. If it is, instead of athletic success, it will cause embarrassment and harmful side effects. The use of anabolic steroids and of electrostimulation causes a disproportion between the development of muscle strength and of the mechanical strength of the joints and ligaments, which leads to injuries.

The coach that did not study anatomy, biomechanics, sports physiology, biochemistry, sports psychology, pedagogy, and methodology of sports training, knows only his/her sport but is not proficient in the standard techniques of other sports (such as all ball games, gymnastics, aquatic sports, and track and field), such a coach means big trouble for the pupil, even if that coach does not introduce illegal doping.

Apart from doping, I will also omit the recruitment and selection of athletes. This issue belongs in a manual of methodology of children's sports training because recruitment and selection take place at the early stages of training. At the advanced stages of training, what usually happens is elimination rather than selection. This book deals only with the issues having to do with increasing the effectiveness of sports training for already selected, committed athletes.

The examples illustrating the principles of training and the methods of controlling it, were taken from sports (track and field, swimming, boxing, wrestling, gymnastics, and ball games) that most people are familiar with. Further, these examples are presented in such a way as to make it easy to apply the conclusions to any other sport.

The methods of controlling the training process that are described in this book do not require complicated equipment and bunches of technicians to make this information applicable in training. The data provided by the most sophisticated scientific equipment is worth only as much as the coach's understanding of it, and the ability to apply it for desired results. A well educated coach or sports researcher does not need sophisticated exercise and testing equipment. A sound knowledge of the human organism lets him/her decipher relevant information and efficiently control the training process on the basis of simple measurements.

Several books on the methodology of physical education and sports training deal with general pedagogical issues such as moral education and aesthetic education (especially Soviet books). I believe that these two issues can be left out of this book. It is not because moral or aesthetic education is not important in sports, but because it happens mostly through the personal example of parents, coaches, and teachers (but mostly parents). The athletes, influenced by their work, the coach, and their home background, develop an appreciation of the beauty of the athletic effort in all sports, not only in their own. They learn to like the mastery of the body and mind, the efficiency in action, the brilliance and simplicity of technical and tactical solutions. Aesthetic and moral education are closely related. What is immoral is also in bad taste. A lack of disgust for immoral actions leads to such non-athletic and non-aesthetic behavior as the rapes and acts of vandalism committed by some representatives of boxing and various team sports.

Another reason I do not want to write about moral or aesthetic education is that stressing it in Soviet manuals and in programs for training their coaches does not seem to help.

The Soviet manuals on the theory of sports training list aesthetic education as an important factor in the development of an athlete. Yet, their practice contradicts that. Just look at how their gymnasts perform. Their choreographers must always insert some purely ornamental, and thus disgusting moves, into an otherwise impressive routine. These vulgar ornamentations serve no physiologic or biomechanic purpose in the exercise. They make the poor girls wear glued smiles in between evolutions on the balance beam. The smiles disappear anyway as soon as the next big move starts because there is nothing funny about a somersault on a balance beam. The few gymnastic events that have been left alone by the bourgeois and proletarian urge to decorate and ornament, are the parallel bars, the uneven bars, the high bar, jumps, and the horse. There, and in the sports to which these "aesthetes" have no access (track and field, races, games, contact sports), the austere beauty of difficulty still exists. The body-building contests, just as any beauty contests, are the epitome of bad taste. There is nothing wrong with building up and rebuilding the body, especially if it has a functional application. However, the artificial poses, the emphasis on the looks and not on the efficiency in action, the body being treated not as a tool— but as a decoration, and the vulgar reactions of spectators, give away the social origin of this sport.

II. PRINCIPLES OF METHODOLOGY OF SPORTS TRAINING

The principle of conscientiousness and activity.

The athletes and the coach are a team, and together they realize their goals. Athletes cannot remain ignorant about the rationale behind every aspect of their training and be motivated to properly carry out the coach's orders. Depending on their age and the stage of training, athletes should be increasingly involved in evaluating and planning their training. This does not mean that the coach has to talk him/herself to death explaining everything and answering every question. The coach merely makes learning materials available and points out the relevance of some information for successful training. He/she also does it in a way that corresponds to a given stage of intellectual development in the athletes.

The principle of sensualization.

The richer the sensual image (visual, tactile, auditory, kinesthetic) of the motor task, the quicker and better this task is learned. Since humans rely mostly on their sense of sight, visual aids and examples should be used most in athletic training. Great care has to be exercised when using any visual aids though. Because we are so dependent on visualization, an improper visual demonstration, for example in slow motion, will leave a long lasting memory that may prevent a learning of the skill at the proper speed. While visualizing or doing ideomotor training, the athlete should almost always imagine performing the skills at the real speed or faster. Visualization should be done in advance, before actually performing the skill. Mistakes in techniques or combinations of techniques are usually accompanied by an inability to imagine them properly. The repetition of an incomplete technique in physical training may lead to the establishment of this image of interrupted technique as dominant. Later, it will be difficult to perform this technique without interruption because even thinking about it, the athlete will not have the real image of continuous technique. An athlete that consistently repeats a technical mistake (in physical action) is probably making the same mistake in imagination or is completely unable to imagine the movement, at the point at which the mistake occurs.

It is obvious that the athlete that performs a technique better knows more about this technique. Apart from knowing the external form of the technique (spatial and temporal structure), the athlete may develop a "coded" image of this technique. This is the set of images, involving various senses, that an athlete associates with the desired form for this technique. This coded image or set of images does not need to resemble the external structure of the technique it is associated with. A coded form of technique is a record of sensations and images accompanying and associated with the peak performance of it. It is related to the external structure in such a way that recalling this image mobilizes the athlete to move in such a manner as to duplicate this structure. For example, having an image of glancing at a target, having relaxed shoulders, and then an explosion going off on the surface of the target (bag) accompanied by a short rapping sound, associated with a boxing punch, helps to consistently throw fast punches. The rapping sound of proper loudness immediately informs the boxer about the correctness of his/her technique.

The principle of accessibility and individualization.

Knowledge should be served in portions and in a form digestible to the student.

Athletes should be trained and educated taking into account their individual abilities, health, age, and sex. The coach's job is to know each individual athlete in his/her team or section and to adjust the means of training so each athlete develops his/her fullest potential. The exercises used in training should be accessible, i.e., possible to execute at the athlete's level of development. The accessibility of the exercises changes in the course of athletic training with the increasing abilities of the athlete.

The principle of gradual increase of loads.

The degree of changes the athlete's body undergoes as a result of exercises, depends on the volume and intensity of the work done. If the loads do not exceed the limits of body's adaptability (at a given stage of training), then there is direct relation between the loads and the adaptation. The greater the volume of the loads, the stronger and more lasting are the adaptations. The more intensive the loads, the more powerful are the processes of recovery and greater are the supercompensation phases following the workouts, however, the adaptations are less stable.

The organism needs time to adapt to the stressing stimuli. This adaptation may involve morphological (structural), physiological (functional), and psychological (learning) changes.

If the training load is not increased (the load remains standard), the performance resulting from using this load will initially improve, then plateau, and then gradually get worse. The effect of the standard load gradually diminishes as the organism gets used to it. As the organism adapts to this load, it handles the load more and more efficiently, with less energy expenditure. This puts less of a demand on the systems of the body so the functional changes in these systems diminish.

As long as the athlete needs to improve his/her performance, the volume and the intensity of training has to gradually increase. This has to be a long-term trend. In certain periods or phases of training the loads can be decreased, but this is usually only temporary. This principle also applies to developing the skills. The exercises for developing the skills, and in certain cases the skills themselves, have to be changed to more difficult ones as the athlete progresses.

The pace at which the training loads are increased must be correlated to the pace at which the body adapts. The body adapts itself to each new load with a certain delay. The delay depends on the volume and intensity of the load, and on the individual's ability to adapt to the load. This ability depends on age and other factors. An abrupt increase of the load may surpass the organism's ability to adapt. The resulting loss of physiological, and especially psychological balance, may lead to overtraining or injuries.

There are three methods of gradually increasing the loads: the ascending rectilinear method, the stepped method, and the wavy method.

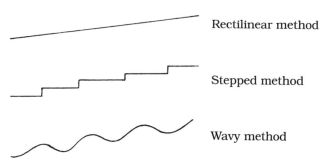

Rectilinear method

Stepped method

Wavy method

In the ascending rectilinear method, the loads are continuously and uniformly increased within a mesocycle (a monthly cycle of workouts) or macrocycle (a yearly cycle of workouts).

In the stepped method, the load is sharply increased in some workouts or microcycles (weekly cycles of workouts) and then stabilized at a constant in the following workouts or microcycles. The stepped method allows one to master higher loads than the rectilinear method.

In the wavy method, the loads are gradually increased in the first microcycles of the mesocycle. This is then followed by microcycles with a lower load. The waves of increasing, and then of relatively decreasing loads (the long term trend is toward an increase of the load), depend on the rhythm of biological processes in the athletes body and also by the life regime accepted by the society i.e., weekly, monthly, and longer rhythms (which also have a biological basis). The wavy method is the most rational because, if correctly applied, it takes advantage of the natural rhythm at which adaptive changes occur in the body's organs and systems. This method of increasing the training loads applies to all the time units into which the training is divided (microcycle, mesocycle, macrocycle). Actually, the division of athletic training into microcycles, mesocycles and macrocycles is a result of the cyclic character of the processes of adaptation. The loads should be changed in response to symptoms of adaptation, and not only for the sake of change. The first two methods, rectilinear and stepped, are occasionally used in training with low intensity loads and when the reactions of the body justify doing so. When it is done, the wavy method still serves as a main background.

The principle of specialization.

To fully develop and realize one's potential, one has to con-centrate on a single sports discipline. Today, competing in more than one sport prevents a successful performance even well below national team level.

As far as developing athletic form goes, it is inexpedient to strive for a maximum in all the motor abilities. An athlete does not compete in all sports. There is no such thing as an absolute versatility in nature. Think about animals, or cars. You cannot have maximum power with maximum economy. The key to success is in deciding what your priority is, and finding the right proportion for the development of supporting abilities so that none lags behind the main one so much as to hurt your performance. In sports, speed and endurance need a certain amount of strength, which varies depending on the sport, for their basis. The same is true of techniques because without a sufficient level of endurance, speed, and strength, you cannot do them properly.

The morphological and functional changes caused by exercising specifically prepare the organism to the same type of exercise that causes these changes. This means that to achieve success in a sport, one has to perform exercises that mimic the actions (techniques and tactics) of this sport. In some cyclical sports, long distance running for example, most of the training consists of running. In other sports, particularly acyclical, the number of repetitions of the main activity of the sport is limited by the intensity of effort going into one repetition (shot put, track and field jumps, boxing round). To help with the development of specific adaptation, where repeating the event or a part of an event is not enough, there are exercises that isolate and develop to a various degree the physical abilities needed in that event. The ratio of exercises from the sport (competitive actions/exercises), to the exercises that develop the specific physical abilities needed in this sport, varies depending on the type of sport, the stage of athletic development of the athlete and the period of the (yearly) training cycle they are in.

The principle of providing a general and versatile foundation for future specialization.

Specialization in athletic training as well as in any other human activity should be based on a wide foundation of general development. A lack of versatility and good general development limits the progress that is possible in specialization. Special endurance (aerobic or anaerobic) has to be based on general endurance (also aerobic or anaerobic). Special exercises do not develop every system, organ, or muscle in the same measure. As the level of training increases, the parts of the body that lag behind become weak links, limiting the athlete's progress. To prevent this, general exercises that ensure an all-round development of physical abilities, and especially the abilities neglected by special exercises, are used. The general exercises are not the same for every sports discipline. All exercises, in any sports discipline, can be divided into four groups: general exercises, directed exercises, special exercises, and competitive exercises. Each sports discipline may put different exercises in any of these four groups. The repertoire of the exercises belonging to any one of these four groups changes depending on the needs of the athletes (their ability, age, stage of training). To find out what exercises ought to be used in which group (general, directed, special, and training forms of competitive exercises) in the course of the macrocycle, the coach has to find out what exercises best prepare his/her athletes for the final task/goal of this macrocycle. Knowing what shape the athletes are in, the coach then finds the exercises that build a sufficient functional and morphological foundation for the special exercises. The general preparation must ensure steady progress and high achievements in the future. The content of special preparation depends on the basis provided by general preparation, and the content of general preparation depends on requirements of special preparation. The athlete's general preparation is also getting "specialized" as the athlete's training is becoming more specialized in the course of an athletic career. This does not mean that general exercises are more similar to the special ones. This means that general preparation is being differentiated in this or that component as applied to the specifics of a given sports discipline (that it reflects more closely the particular needs of a given discipline). The essence of specialization in general preparation is to more fully use the positive transfer of a level of training and to limit the effect of any negative transfer. This is why general preparation differs in various sports.

Long distance runners, at the beginning of their training cycle, lift weights, and weightlifters do some endurance exercises. Endurance exercises result in an increased speed of recovery thus making it possible, for example, to intensify strength training in the case of weightlifters. Runners, by doing various weightlifting exercises, strengthen all muscles, among them those that affect the efficiency of movement but are not the prime movers in running; for example, the muscles of the upper body. Consequently, we can see that the same exercise that is special in one sports discipline can be general in another discipline.

Coaches that want quick success make their athletes specialize early, developing mostly the physical abilities necessary in their specialty. In such a system, a shot putter practices the technique only by putting shot, develops the strength by standard weightlifting exercises, and the speed by short sprints and starts. Such an approach results initially in a considerable improvement of special performance in shot put but a stagnation of it in only a few years, after which permanent progress of the athlete is limited to the strength as measured by standard weightlifting methods and the speed measured by the standard 20 meters sprint from low start (starting blocks).

The complex motor skills are formed on the basis of the forms of movement coordination learned earlier. This basis is widened in the process of learning various new skills and so, increases the ability to further perfect the motor skills.

The richer his/her treasury of various athletic skills, the faster the athlete masters new special skills, and the more flexible is his/her application of these skills. The knowledge of techniques and tactics in a variety of sports gives better insight into one's sports discipline.

The so called "secondary movement illiteracy" is a result of reducing the variety of exercises. If new more difficult exercises are not added to the ones an athlete has mastered, and especially if the technical exercises are replaced with some simpler movements (such as basic endurance or strength exercises), the athlete loses the old skills and overall coordination.

The degree of athletic perfection depends also on the general cultural level of the athlete and his/her development of intellectual abilities.

The general and special training need to be well balanced. An excessively great volume of general training causes a reduction of the necessary volume of special preparation and results in a lowering of the special form. An excessive reduction in the volume of general training for the sake of special training narrows down the basis of sports specialization and restricts the growth of achievements. When determining the correlation of general training to special training it is necessary to take into account the level of preparedness, individual peculiarities, and the age of the athlete; as well as specific features of the sports discipline and the training period because the inter-influence of various components of the athlete's training changes at different stages of the process of development of an athlete.

Initially general exercises (strength, endurance, etc.), done concurrently with technical training improve the level of technical skill. They then cease to be effective, and for more improvement, so called directed exercises, that are closer related to the techniques, must be introduced. After some time even these exercises lose their effect on the technical proficiency of the athlete, and even more specialized exercises are needed for further progress. If continued throughout the athletic career, the general exercises (strength, endurance, coordination, etc.) will show gains in the abilities they are designed to develop, but only if measured by general tests. In other words, performing general exercises will increase proficiency mostly in performing these general exercises. No matter how much mass and strength one gains from performing general strength exercises, if the neuromuscular patterns of these exercises are not resembling those of the competitive technique, little or no strength gain will show in specialized technical tests or in competition. The same is true for any other physical ability such as endurance, coordination, speed, agility, etc. If specialized exercises are introduced too early in the athlete's career, at the expense of the general exercises, the initial pace at which the technical skills are developed is high. Later though, the athlete hits a plateau because the skills were developed without a foundation of general development. The lack of general coordination makes improving special technical skills difficult. The weakness of the muscles, ligaments and bones also limits technical skills. Special endurance is difficult to develop because the morphological and functional foundation (developed by general endurance training) needed for special exercises is missing. Improving performance at the stage of specialization by resorting to general exercises is difficult if not useless. The neuromuscular patterns of the techniques are already formed and the general exercises can't alter them.

The following are some typical exercises used in the training of a 110 meter hurdler as an example of versatility:

Exercises with weights; snatch, jerk and clean, press, half squats, step ups, calf exercises.
Back extensions, twists, sit ups and other abdomen exercises.
Hamstring exercises on machines.
Throws of light and heavy balls and shots from various positions, with one or both hands.
Jumps on one leg and on two legs with weights.
Running with weights.
Skips A, B, C.
Running with maximal speed.
Running with set speed on distances from 40 meters to 120 meters.
Running distances longer than 120 meters on the track and off the track for developing speed-endurance.
Cross-country continuous runs.
Running uphill.
Flexibility exercises.
Ball games.
Various technical exercises without using the hurdles.
Various technical exercises teaching and perfecting technique of running hurdles.

The principle of systematicness and continuity in the training process.

Any athletic form achieved is not permanent. Every interruption of the training process causes a regression of the form. Stabilization of morphological and functional changes requires a continuity of the training. The training process must be also systematic, i.e. have a goal or a set of goals, be controlled and planned according to results of the control tests, new material must be based on the previously done material, and the training process must be rhythmical and not sporadic.

The athletic training is planned as a long-term process requiring training stimuli to constantly affect the athlete so the form may be acquired, maintained, and further developed. In today's sports, working out every day and often several times a day is needed to compete even below the national level. However, the interval between workouts must guarantee restoration and improve work efficiency. This is accomplished by arranging various types of workouts in proper sequence (microcycle) and alternating training loads so that athlete recovers fully before the next main workout in a cycle. The connection between the workouts is ensured by the continuity of the immediate, delayed and cumulative training effects.

The principle of the cyclic character of the training process.

All things develop in cycles. Human life can be considered one big wave with its climbing, peaking, and declining phase. Several smaller waves are superimposed on our life wave. Some last years, some days, some hours, and some last even less than a second.

Rational athletic training takes this cyclical character of life into account and is planned in cycles. There are small cycles called microcycles and lasting about one week, average cycles called mesocycles lasting usually one month, and large cycles called macrocycles that last one year or six months. Each subsequent cycle partially repeats the proceeding one, but at the same time, to ensure progress in the training process, differs in content, loads, and sometimes methods.

The main theses of the principle of cyclic character of the training process:
— The main elements of training must be systematically repeated, but at the same time, training tasks must also change according to the changed needs of the athletes in subsequent cycles.
— Each phase of the training cycle, and each subsequent cycle, requires the use of adequately chosen training methods. Any training exercises or methods lose their effectiveness if they are used at the wrong time or in the wrong proportions.
— The wave-like changes in training loads must correspond with microcycles, mesocycles, and macrocycles.
— Any part of the training process is related to larger and smaller structures.

III. BASIC CONCEPTS IN ATHLETIC TRAINING

Athletic training leads to morphological, physiological, biochemical, and psychological changes. The character of these changes depends on the volume, intensity, duration, and density of workouts. The values of these components of training vary depending on the sport, period of training, and needs of the individual athlete.

Setting the training tasks for the athlete must take into account the basic proprieties of the organism:

1) trainability depends on the age of the individual,

2) increase of the training effect depends on the frequency of workouts,

3) recovery of the ability to work after the effort depends on quality and quantity of rest,

4) achieving athletic form depends on the intensity of work, and maintaining it depends on the volume of work.

Volume. Volume refers to the sum of physical work performed by the athlete in a workout, or in any period of time (microcycle, mesocycle, macrocycle etc.). It is measured in minutes or hours, miles, tonnage, heart beats, kGm, or number of repetitions. When talking about the volume of work in a training period, the number of workouts, total number of hours of a given type of work, and the number of days with workouts should be specified. If expressed in time units, the volume of a workout (V_w) is the total time of the work and necessary rest between efforts, not counting the time spent on organizational matters and the preparation of apparatus and equipment.

The relation between the volume of training work and an increase of ability is not rectilinear. With the increasing sum of the above-threshold training effort, the increase of trained ability is relatively decreasing. This means that the degree of effectiveness of training, or the increase of ability to the volume of training work ratio, constantly decreases. This ratio can be described by a parabola.

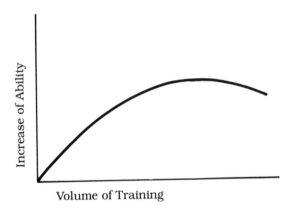

This shows that an untrained individual can, with a little training effort, experience a great increase of ability. As the level of ability grows, training that affects the organism similarly will produce progressively smaller increases in ability. Eventually, increasing the volume of training work alone without changing the intensity will cease to increase the ability at all.

Every athlete has individual critical value of training load, in workout and in cycles of workouts that he/she should not exceed. Beginning runners reach maximal oxygen uptake after 80-100 minutes of workout and then the oxygen uptake declines. Highly trained runners reach that point after 3 hours. Some athletes respond to increased training loads with a proportional increase in the results. Some respond with a very small increase in the results with a great increase in the load, and some others have a greater increase in the results than in the load. The athlete's ratio of result increase to training load increase should be compared often so as to find optimal load increases for the athlete and to avoid overtraining.

Intensity. Volume of work, performed by the athlete, per time (duration) of this work is called intensity. The term "intensity" may also be used in reference to a single exercise. Intensity depends on the strength of the nervous stimuli, which depends on the load, speed of movement, work to rest ratio, and the mental effort accompanying the exercise. The intensity can be measured in meters per second, repetitions per minute, or percentage of maximal intensity. When using percentage of maximal intensity, the intensity of the exercise is compared to the best performance of the athlete in that event. If measured by this method, the relative intensity of some exercises can exceed 100%. For example, a long distance runner can do interval training with a speed, and thus intensity, greater than the race speed. Weightlifters, using different types of muscle contractions, holding or lowering the weight, can handle greater loads than the ones they lift normally.

The intensity of an exercise (with exception of speed or strength exercises) can be roughly estimated by dividing the heart rate in this exercise (HR_e) by the maximum heart rate for a given athlete (HR_{max}).

$$I_e = HR_e \div HR_{max}$$

An article by Nikiforov, in Sport Wyczynowy number 8, page 26, 1972, describes a simplified method of estimating the intensity of a workout in boxing. By measuring the heart rate during typical boxing exercises and emotional tension (measured by electric resistance of the skin), researchers assigned values of intensity, represented by points. Exercises with the lowest intensity had one point. Exercises with the heart rate slightly higher than that of the previous group had one point more. Control competition and fighting in target competition had two points for each increment of heart rate.

Exercises	Heart rate	Intensity in points
Games, cross-country runs	140-165	1
Strength exercises, swimming	140-165	1
Jumping rope, shadowboxing	160-170	2
Exercises on apparatus	165-175	3
Techniques with partner	170-180	3
Sparring	175-185	5
Free sparring	175-190	6
Selection fight	180-200	8
Fight in target competition	185-220	10

Definitions:

Sparring is conducted according to a set scenario; one boxer attacks in a assigned manner, the other defends himself. If the task of the sparring is not properly realized the coach stops it.

Free sparring is conducted according to the normal rules. The boxer is responsible for carrying out the previously designed strategy and must justify all deviations from it. The coach mostly watches and between the rounds listens, and then, after the free sparring, discusses it with the boxer.

A selection fight is conducted according to the normal rules and its goal is selection for the main competition.

The values of intensity expressed in points were used to calculate the intensity of the workout using the following equation:

$$I_w = \sum(I_e \text{ in points} \times T_e) \div \sum T_e$$

I_w— intensity of the workout

I_e— intensity of an exercise in points

T_e— duration of the same exercise

Because athletes can have the same heart rate when performing work of various intensities, it is more precise to calculate it by dividing the volume of work in exercise by its duration.

$$I_e = V_e \div D_e$$

Yet another way of estimating the intensity of an exercise is to divide the actual power (P_a in kGm/sec.) developed in the exercise by the maximal power (P_{max}.) that this athlete can develop in the same period of time.

Index of intensity: $iI = P_a \div P_{max}.$

Intensity of a workout is arrived at by dividing the sum of results from multiplications of values of intensity of every exercise (%I_e) by the volume of each exercise (V_e), and then dividing by the total volume of exercises (V_E).

$$I_w = \sum(\%I_e \times V_e) \div \sum(V_E)$$

Intensity of a workout can be also estimated by adding up the heart beats during the workout (all exercises and all rest breaks) and during the first stage of recovery (first five minutes of a cool-down) then deducting the average resting heart rate multiplied by the time of workout, plus the time of first stage of recovery. This method gives a better idea of the internal load i.e., how the workout affected the organism.

Work of low intensity but high volume leads to slow but steady progress and consistent performance. A high intensity of work brings quick but unstable progress because it can overstrain involved systems, and even if it does not, the total volume of work performed with high intensity is nearly always lower than the volume possible with low intensity. This means a smaller chance for the organism to gradually develop sufficient adaptation. High volume is needed for big enough changes in the organism, and low intensity ensures that the stimuli is developmental and not destructive. The increase of intensity of training usually happens at the expense of volume and vice versa.

A high intensity of training work, based on a previously done high volume of work, prepares the athletes for high sports results.

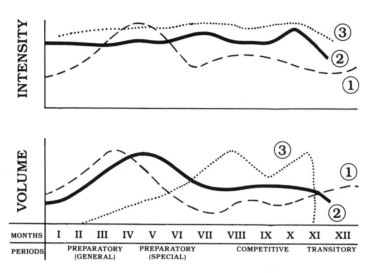

An example of training load dynamics in a yearly cycle.
1—general exercises; 2—special exercises; 3—competitive exercises (Reprinted from Zbigniew Naglak: Trening Sportowy, Teoria i Praktyka. 3d ed. 1979. Courtesy of PWN Warszawa.)

Examples of exercises/efforts of various absolute or physiologic intensities:
sprints 100 meter, 200 meter, 110 hurdles, 400 meter—maximal intensity;
800 meter, 1500 meter—submaximal intensity;
3000 to 10000 meters—high intensity;
20000 meter run, 5000 meter swim, majority of acyclic exercises—moderate intensity.

Zones of intensity and respective types of effort depending on energy sources according to Volkov[69] and Koriagin:
1) Moderate to high intensity, aerobic effort—heart rate 120-160/min. (average 140/min.) duration of an exercise; over 5 minutes.
2) Submaximal intensity, aerobic-anaerobic effort—heart rate 160-190/min. (average 175/min.) duration of an exercise; from 2 min. to 5 min.
3) Submaximal and maximal intensity, anaerobic-lactacid effort—

heart rate 180-190/min. (average 185/min.) duration of an exercise; 21 seconds to 2 minutes.

4) Maximal intensity, anaerobic-alactacid effort—heart rate 170-190 min. (average 180/min.) duration of an exercise; 1-20 seconds.

Types of effort and zones of intensity:

Pure aerobic effort; intensity 70-80%, (during variable training intensity may oscillate between 20% and 80%) prolonged work (in continuous training up to 180 minutes, in interval training 10 or more repetitions of 1-3 min. efforts with 30-90 seconds rest.) with heart rate up to 150/min. If rest breaks are used they end as soon as heart rate falls to 120/min.

Mixed aerobic-anaerobic effort; intensity 80% in continuous training, in variable training oscillates between 50% and 90%, to 95% in interval training, heart rate 170-180/min. up to 30 minutes in continuous training, in other types of training by the end of rest period heart rate falls to 140-120/ min. (shorter work periods have shorter rest and higher heart rate at the end of rest).

Anaerobic-lactacid-glycogen effort; intensity 95-100%, duration of exercise from 20 seconds to 3 minutes. Heart rate 190/min. Rest breaks over 10 minutes.

Anaerobic-phosphagen effort; work up to 15 seconds with maximum intensity. Rest between efforts 4-6 minutes.

Anabolic (strength) effort; intensity 40-70%, duration of exercise either to failure with 3-4 minutes of rest between sets of repetitions of an exercise, or the duration can be set at 1.5 min. to 2 min. with rest break of the same length.

Motor density. This refers to the amount of time that the athlete is exercising in a workout (not counting rest periods between exercises), per total time of the workout. A workout may have a high motor density and a low intensity if light exercises are done continuously. A gymnastic, or weightlifting workout, may be very intensive and have low motor density. Briefly; density means work to rest ratio in exercises or in a whole workout. Different types of training have a different optimal work to rest ratio. For example, in low intensity endurance training, the rest break varies from half to equal that of the time of work. In high intensity endurance training, the rest break is three to six times longer than the work.

The density of the workout is calculated by dividing the sum of exercise volume in time units (ΣV_e) by volume of the workout in time units (V_w).

$$D_w = \Sigma V_e \div V_w$$

Duration of a workout (T_w). The total time of the workout including the rest breaks between exercises and the time spent on organizational matters and the preparation of apparatus and equipment.

The above components of training (volume, intensity, motor density, and duration of the workout) constitute and characterize the external load which can be easily calculated using the already mentioned components of training. The index of external load in a workout can be calculated using workout intensity (I_w), workout density (D_w), and volume of workout (V_w).

$$EL_w = (I_w \times D_w \times V_w) \div 10000$$

The external load can be estimated by multiplying the volume of training work (V_w in kGm) by the coefficient of its intensity (cI).

$$L_w = V_w \times cI$$

It can be also estimated by multiplying duration of the workout (T_w) by index of intensity (iI)

$$L_w = T_w \times iI$$

The organism's reaction to the external load is called the internal load. The internal load can be defined as the degree of mobilization of the organism that is required for certain work. This is reflected by heart rate, volume of lung ventilation, oxygen uptake, lactic acid in the blood, or simply the type and magnitude of fatigue caused by the training. Although it is affected by each component of the external load, the internal load is difficult to assess. The same external load, applied even for the same athlete, but at different times, may cause a different internal load. Keeping a training diary for every athlete, with records of all exercises in every workout, an everyday self-evaluation, and frequently testing pertinent skills and abilities, facilitates evaluation of the internal load. Knowledge of both the internal and external load is necessary for planning training.

An increased intensity and volume of workout does not necessarily mean an increased internal load. When the increase in the level of fitness or athletic form is greater than the increase of the load, then the work will be done with lower effort in spite of the increase of objectively measured indicators of work. The internal load is increased when the amount of work increases more than the fitness or athletic form.

According to an article by N. Georgiev and K. Semov, the internal training load can be estimated on the basis of duration of work, average heart rate, and total amount of heart beats in a workout.

Duration of work	Average heart rate	Total heart beats in workout	Internal load
1-60 min.	130/min.	up to 10800	low
61-90 min.	131-145/ min.	10801-14400	medium
over 90 min.	over 145/min.	over 14400	heavy

Content of an exercise. Sometimes called function of the exercise. It refers to the motor task achieved and to the changes in the body resulting from this exercise.

Dynamic characteristics of exercise. It refers to the speed of movements and the character of muscular contraction in particular phases of movement (internal structure of movement).

The pace of movement. It is the measurement of the repetition of individual movements or cycles of movements per unit of time. "Free pace" or individually stable speed is the pace most convenient for an individual. "Forced pace", which is any pace that differs from free pace, is more difficult to maintain without an external driving stimuli (pace keeper) because energy has to be expanded both on work and on keeping the pace.

Spatial characteristics of exercise. In other words, the form of movement in space (external structure of movement).

Fatigue. Fatigue is when the homeostasis is disturbed and the ability to work is temporarily lowered as a result of performing this work. The changes (exhausting energy resources, lack of oxygen in the tissues, changes of activity of some enzymes and hormones, impaired thermoregulation, change in pH balance, accumulation of products of metabolism, changes in the central and peripheral nervous system) that occur during the work depend on the type of work and its intensity. All types of fatigue cannot be evaluated on the basis of only one biochemical indicator, for example, the amount of lactic acid.

Microtrauma. Gradual changes in the structure of tissues resulting from a disproportion between the strength/durability of the tissue and the too frequent application of even moderate stimuli are called microtrauma. Frequent exceeding the durability, no matter how minimal, of the links of the motor system or internal organs leads to an accumulation of the microtrauma and so called gradual overstrain/gradual onset injuries. For a long time the gradual changes do not interfere with performance and go unnoticed by the coach and even the athlete. Eventually, however, the wearing down will intensify and will cause such symptoms as greater fatiguability, pain after effort, and pain in lower temperatures. The aches or pains change their duration and intensity and may be neglected by the athlete. In the end, the tissue will come apart/diffuse, which means strain, sprain, or fracture. Microtrauma leading to gradual overstrain can be mechanical (static or dynamic), thermal (heat or cold), or toxic (protracted acidosis). Certain types of overstrain are characteristic for particular sports. Changes of wrist and hand bones, and elbow joint in boxing; knees in team handball; lumbar section of the spinal column in judo and weightlifting; trapezius muscle in track and field throws; biceps femoris in jumps; muscles of the foot, calf and Achilles tendon in running.

Overstrain. An abrupt worsening of health and "trainability" resulting from the application of physical loads exceeding the current ability of the athlete, is called overstrain. Physical overstrain can be acute or chronic and it does not usually involve the whole body. Overstrain can be limited to one organ, for example, the heart. A one time application of an excessive load causes the acute overstrain. Repeated application of excessive loads causes chronic overstrain resulting in changes in the athletes organism leading to diseases or illnesses of its various organs and systems.

Overtraining. An illness resulting from overstraining the central nervous system of the athlete is called overtraining. Such a breakdown of the higher nervous activity is also called neurosis. Overtraining can be caused by the following:
 − continuous application of intensive, monotonous loads/workouts combined with insufficient rest and restoration intervals,
 − repeated participation in a string of competitions with great personal responsibility,
 − difficulties of combining strenuous training with intensive studies (examinations, tests), with work in shifts, with interpersonal conflicts in the family and in the workplace (with complex family and work interrelations).

Situations that facilitate overtraining: chronic infections, systematic violations of the principles of nutrition, irrational training methods, frequent loss of great weight (making weight), abuse of toxic substances (tobacco, alcohol, etc.), physical overstrain.

Overtraining has more to do with the sequence of different kinds of efforts than with the total training load or the load to rest ratio. When workouts are arranged in weekly microcycles in the following sequence: speed, strength, speed-endurance, and endurance, it stresses the neuromuscular system on the first two days and the vegetative system on the following two days, and leads to overtraining.

One of the main causes of pathological occurrences and illnesses in athletes is an improper organization and irrational methods of training which leads to excessive overloading, and exceeding the functional abilities of a given athlete at a given stage of training.

There are three stages of overtraining:

1. The first stage. The sports results stop increasing or even decline. Processes of excitation dominate over processes of inhibition in the central nervous system. The athlete becomes irritable, offensive, complains about poor sleep, does not feel good, and loses weight. Sometimes after workouts, there are palpitations, possible changes in the rhythm of the heart, and the breathing is stronger than usual.

To stop the development of overtraining at this stage, it is necessary to change the methods/regime of training. Additional days of active rest (other sports disciplines) must be introduced into the microcycle. It is necessary to closely watch the nutrition, improve its quality, and carry out complex vitaminization. Taking these measures will restore the former trainability in 20-30 days. After an additional medical check up and the permission of the physician, the athlete can return to the normal training.

2. The second stage. If the proper measures are not taken, the second stage of overtraining may follow. In this stage the sports performance is clearly getting worse and the ability to handle training loads is also lowered. After workouts the athlete is unusually weak and tired. The athlete starts to avoid any physical effort. The irritability increases. Pain appears in the vicinity of the heart (feeling of squeezing, irregular beats), and also a heaviness on the right side, below the rib cage. The resting pulse rate increases and so does the pulse rate measured when the routine efforts are performed. Reaction to the functional/stress tests, as a rule, is atypical. Often, in this (second) stage the athlete gets

various illnesses and aggravates previous injuries (or the existing conditions are aggravated). In certain cases sports results get better (but for a short time, as a rule, the improvement is not lasting). This temporary improvement of result can deceive the coach and the athlete. To re-establish full athletic trainability, in addition to the measures used in the treatment of the first stage of overtraining, the athlete ought to stop any workouts of the special preparatory type for two to three weeks. Instead, workouts of the active rest type are recommended. The treatment is conducted by a physician. Usually trainability is regained after one to two months.

3. The third stage. If the violation of the proper methodology of training continues; the loads are further increased, the athlete participates in competitions without sufficient rest and without necessary preparation, or as in several cases— when ill; the over-training enters its third stage. The athlete is apathetic, lacks interest in his/her sports discipline, "loses heart", gets weak, depressed, and loses faith in his/her abilities. The trainability declines sharply. The athlete sleeps poorly at night and is sleepy at day. Small efforts cause profuse sweating. Physical efforts may cause a sharp increase in the pulse rate, a lowering of the systolic blood pressure, and an increase of the diastolic pressure (asthenic type of the reaction). The athlete that entered this stage of over-training, needs special medical attention and should be admitted to a hospital or sanatorium. The normal training is permitted after one and a half to two months.

In cases of overstrain and overtraining the athlete should be thoroughly examined by a physician because both the overstrain and the overtraining can result from acute or chronic illness or disease.

S. Israel, in his article "Das Akute Entlastungssyndrom", iden-tifies two types of overtraining: basedowic and addisonic.

The basedowic overtraining results from overstressing an athlete's emotional processes (overexcitation) by overemphasizing high intensity stimuli in training and great mental concentration. It is characterized by:
— increased metabolism,
— accelerated resting heart rate,
— sweating,
— sleepiness,
— weight loss,
— easy fatigue,
— headaches,
— slightly increased temperature,

— hypertension,
— longer reaction time,
— lowered technical skill,
— irritability,
— restlessness and other psychological problems.

It occurs mostly among inexperienced athletes in speed- strength sports.

The addisonic overtraining results from an excessively high volume of training work. It is characterized by:
— progressive anemia,
— hypotension,
— diastolic blood pressure increased over 100 mm Hg immediately after exercise,
— digestive disturbances,
— anorexia (loss of appetite),
— low resting heart rate and slight fatigued feeling.
— there is no increase in sleep requirements,
— no weight loss,
— no apparent (special) psychological manifestations (symptoms),
— the temperature and the metabolic rate are normal.

This type of overtraining occurs mostly among older, more advanced athletes.

The treatment for overtraining consists of a special diet, physiotherapy, and climatic therapy.

Special diet for basedowic overtraining: alkaline foods (milk, fruit, vegetables), vitamins (A, B, C), no stimulants (coffee, tea), alcohol in small quantities is permitted.

Special diet for addisonic overtraining: acidifying foods (cheese, meat, eggs, sweets), vitamins (B, C).

Physiotherapy for basedowic overtraining: swimming outdoors, warm baths 35-37 degrees Celsius, cold showers in the morning, light and rhythmical exercise, massage, no sauna!

Physiotherapy for addisonic overtraining: hot-cold showers, sauna of medium temperature alternated with short cold showers, dynamic exercise, vigorous massage.

Climatic therapy for basedowic overtraining: moderate ultra-violet irradiation, change of environment (alternate various altitudes).

Climatic therapy for addisonic overtraining: seaside and sea level altitude.

Professor Eric Newsholme[28], of Oxford University, a biochemist, explains overtraining as a result of depletion of glutamine, an amino acid needed in large quantities for normal operation of the immune system, namely the lymphocytes. Glutamine is processed in the large muscles, and is depleted after severe exertion. The lymphocytes cannot function if the concentration of glutamine falls to 80% of normal. Dr. Ken Kingsbury[28], one of the doctors conducting a study at the British Olympic Association's medical center at Northwick Park Hospital, says that athletes repeatedly get sore throats, swollen glands, ulcers in the mouth, and so on, which disappear rapidly after competition. These minor infection are symptom of lowered efficiency of the immune system which, if training loads are not lowered, may lead to more serious illness.

Dr. Lynn Fitzgerald[28], an immunologist at St George Hospital, Tooting, says "For the immune system, all stress is the same, whether it is physical or psychological stress. Whether it is a major life event, or training pressure, it all adds on, and there is a point where the whole system breaks down."

Rest. The type (content) and amount of rest must be adequate for the training task. The wrong type or the wrong duration (too short, too long) of rest adversely affects training effect. It may lead to detraining, overtraining, or at least to undesirable changes in the character of the exercise.

The length of rest and its type (active, passive, using special means of enhancing recovery) determines what will be the effect of the exercise preceding and following it. The greater the muscular tension during exercises, the longer the rest interval required. Unfamiliar exercises require more rest than familiar ones with the same mechanical load. Brief rest of rigidly set duration, not allowing full recovery, intensifies the effect of the next exercise. The rest sufficient for full restoration of work capability to the previous level, permits repetition of the exercise or workout without decreasing or increasing the amount of work performed. Rest between workouts long enough to permit supercompensation allows an increase in the amount of work in the next workout. Rest for too long, may cause the workout to occur past the supercompensation phase, when the level of ability is declining again. Similar is the situation with the rest between exercises during a workout. For example, in team ball games, after a period of intensive activity, 4-6 minutes of rest causes improvement in the quality of tactical actions when the player enters the game again, 9-12 minutes of rest is still beneficial, 15-20 minutes is detrimental to performance, and longer than 20 minutes is the most detrimental. One has to be careful in deciding the length of the rest. A rest interval allowing for supercompensation in one ability, may be too long or too short for other abilities.

Adaptation. Adaptation to a given type of effort can be measured by the speed of recovery of the system or organ affected by this effort. Evaluation of the level of adaptation ought to be based on several indicators, for example; function of the circulation, respiration, metabolism, central nervous system, and endocrine system. Often, an extreme concentration of metabolites, a maximal heart rate, or the attainment of maximal oxygen uptake do not mean inability to continue work. The adaptation may cause very specific form of compensation for a given individual. Conducting the training process according to general physiological or clinical norms limits learning about the capabilities of the athlete and interferes with individualization of the training process (violates the principle of individualization).

Training effect. Training effect varies, depending on the initial state of the organism, content of a workout, cumulative effects of consecutive workouts, and the rest interval between workouts. There are three types of training effect:

Immediate training effect— refers to the condition of the organism at the end of an exercise or workout. On one hand it is characterized by the degree of exhaustion of systems affected by the workout, on the other hand, it is characterized by the beginning of the recovery processes and by the skills just learned. To evaluate the immediate training effect, reactions of particular systems, biochemical changes, and the quality of exercises in relation to previous reactions to the same exercises are measured during the exercises, immediately after exercises and during rest breaks between repetitions. As a result of this control, intensity, volume, quality, and sequence of exercises in a workout can be corrected. An improper sequence of exercises may cause the opposite of the desired effect. For example, strength or strength-endurance exercises (anaerobic-glycolitic efforts) are more effective if preceded by speed or low repetition strength exercises (anaerobic-alactacid efforts) and are less effective after aerobic endurance exercises.

Delayed training effect is a continuation of the immediate training effect and refers to the rebuilding the body and increased hormonal activity. Depending on the time elapsed, gradually increasing degree of recovery of systems affected by the workout occurs. Some systems recover faster than others, so the abilities or skills that are based on their efficiency are back to normal or above normal earlier than others. If the next workout begins before rebuilding of energy stores is complete and the metabolism has returned to normal, the internal training load of that next workout will be increased. If the rest interval is long enough to allow complete recovery but not much more, the volume and intensity of work possible in the next workout will be the same as in the most recent workout. Such rest intervals are used when stabilization and consolidation of morphological and functional changes in the organism is desired. If the rest interval is long enough to permit recovery over and above the initial state, (or supercompensation), it allows an increase in the load of the next workout. To evaluate delayed training effect or changes in speed of recovery and type of fatigue, measurements are taken before a workout and a few hours after. The most important are; biochemical measurements of processes of protein synthesis, restoring energy sources, and measurements of abilities that, in an aggregate manner inform about the degree of recovery after a workout or a set of workouts. The evaluation of the delayed training effect lets coach compare the planned progression of loads to the actual progression and correction of their volume, intensity, and type in microcycles and mesocycles.

Cumulative training effect—it is the sum of functional and morphological changes in the organism, caused by and affecting the immediate and delayed training effects. When all goes well, the cumulative training effect means an increase of skills and abilities. If there are flaws in the training process, the cumulative training effect results in overtraining or undertraining. To evaluate cumulative training effect, the efficiency of organs and systems, and the level of abilities and skills is measured before and after each period of training (such as general preparatory period, competitive period, etc.). These measurements are compared with "a model of a master" and with a task for the period and then corrections are made in the plan of the period.

Indicators of desirable cumulative effect. When at rest, the following functional changes in the cardiovascular and pulmonary systems indicate a proper development of athletic form, and are most pronounced in exponents of endurance sports: frequency of heart beats and of breathing is lowered, volume of heart is increased, the periods and phases of the cardiac cycle are increased, time of bleeding is decreased. A lowered intensity of the metabolism permits the organism of the athlete to economically utilize it's resources accumulating energy. Endurance athletes experience a slowing down of processes of stimulation and an inhibition of their nervous system. The efficiency and endurance of the organism can be reliably assessed by maximal oxygen uptake. In speed-strength sports, such as sprints, an increase of maximal oxygen uptake indicates improved form only for athletes of lower classes. For top rated sprinters, or other athletes of speed-strength sports, after achieving the optimal level of development of aerobic endurance (maximal oxygen uptake), indicators of anaerobic endurance are of greater importance because the oxygen debt of first class sprinters reaches 25 liters/minute, and lactic acid concentration reaches 250-300 mg%. With improved form of speed-strength athletes the blood level of hormones participating in metabolism of proteins (androgenic hormones) and adrenal hormones regulating metabolism of carbohydrates, fats, and water and salt regulation, is raised. A fast mobilization of all abilities of the organism in speed-strength sports is accompanied by increased activity of the sympathetic nervous system, which leads to a raised level of adrenalin in the blood and to increased activity of the thyroid hormones. Athletes relying on quick reactions, experience quickening of the processes of stimulation and inhibition.

Concurrently, with the above functional changes, training causes morphological changes in the muscles and bones. Athletes concentrating on strength training (weightlifters, wrestlers, and throwers), should increase their muscle mass and bone density.

During all functional tests, the better prepared athletes show smaller (as compared to values at rest) functional changes than the worse prepared ones.

Classification of sport disciplines

Sports disciplines and exercises can be classified according to the structure of the movements (cyclic, acyclic, mixed), type of competition (individual, team), amount and type of contact (varying degrees of contact, non-contact), motor ability most stressed (speed-strength, endurance), use of equipment or apparatus, degree of standardization of exercises (standard, nonstandard), and methods of comparing results (points, points in a set time, time, weight, height, distance).

Standard exercises are those where there is a fixed routine of performing movements (track and field, gymnastics, figure skating, weightlifting).

Nonstandard exercises are performed in constantly changing circumstances (team games).

In cyclic exercises such as walking, running, cycling, and rowing the movements are rhythmically repeated.

In acyclic exercises such as the techniques of gymnastics, wrestling, boxing, and team ball games, each movement is performed one at a time and followed by different movements.

Mixed exercises such as long jump and high jump, have a cyclic phase (pre-run) and an acyclic phase (jump).

Contact sports are those that permit physical contact (hockey, soccer, team handball, rugby), or are based on physical contact (wrestling, boxing, fencing)

In non-contact sports athletes try to out-perform each other without physical contact, competing simultaneously or consecutively (races, gymnastics, archery, chess, tennis, track and field).

Speed-strength sports are those that rely mainly on speed and strength (sprints, jumps, throws, weightlifting).

Endurance sports are those where mainly endurance is stressed (middle-distance and long-distance running, swimming, bicycling).

Individual encounter sports are those where the contest is between only two individuals (chess, boxing, tennis).

Individual contact sports are the individual encounter sports that allow physical contact (judo, boxing, wrestling, fencing).

Methods of training

There are three groups of training methods:
1. Strictly regulated exercise methods
2. Competitive methods
3. Play methods

1. Strictly regulated exercise methods are the basis of the athletic training. The exercises used in these methods are easily measurable, depending on the type of exercise, and can affect either individual functions of the organism or have a more general effect. Repetition of techniques, or of their elements, in technical training also falls into this group of methods. The exercises are measured by their effects, amount of work performed, and their organization in time (rest periods). Examples of methods of this group are standard-repetitive, variable, interval, and continuous methods.

2. Competitive methods rely on participation in competitions of various quality depending on the needs of the athlete and the role these competitions have in building athletic form. Only these methods ensure full modeling of the conditions of competition. First class athletes allot 15% or more of their training time to competition. The training load in this method is regulated by the proper choice of opponents, number of starts, duration of bouts or games, and rest intervals. Extensive use of this method is recommended for athletes with many years of experience rather than for beginners (beginners use it too, but not as much). It develops the ability to control one's psychological reactions to the stress of competitions.

3. The play methods either create a favorable emotional background when developing ability (that otherwise would require monotonous work), or are used as a means of helping a restoration after heavy training or competition. Usually forms of mobile games are used in these training methods. They make high physical and mental demands on the organism but, because of the fun athletes have while exercising, they gladly participate in workouts and more quickly recover their ability to train. They are used in training for all sports, not only in ball games, because they require and develop initiative, team work, and flexible tactical thinking. The proportions of types of effort in exercises used in mobile games are difficult to predict.

The choice of training methods and the type of training depends on the specific demands of the sport, the training tasks for a given stage of the long-term training and for a given cycle, and the individual characteristics of the athlete.

Besides the above methods, which are exclusively used in sports training, general pedagogical and other methods are used in training.

The general pedagogical methods such as verbal (explanation, incentive, persuasion) and sensory (visual presentation, feedback) are modified to suit the special requirements of sports training. Only those verbal methods that allow for the maintenance of the high motor density of the workout are used in workouts. These are: verbal control (commands, instruction), figurative explanation (where verbal expressions rely on sensory and motor experiences to invoke a desired image of the action), and self-regulation (where the athlete thinks over the action and carries out orders that the athlete has given to oneself). Apart from traditional sensory methods (presentation of pictures, models, movies, personal demonstration) there are specialized methods directly influencing the athlete in the course of performing the movement. These are methods of visual or acoustical pacing (lights or sounds setting the pace), developing kinesthetic sensations that accompany proper a execution of the technique (performing exercises on simulators or with assistance), and methods of immediate feedback (where acoustic or visual signals inform about deviations from either the required mechanical parameters of movement or the vegetative functions accompanying exercise).

The additional methods of training such as ideomotor training, autogenic training, and psycho-regulating training (modification of the autogenic training), which also have uses outside sports training, are used in special sessions as well as in normal workouts.

In a process as complex as sports training there is no method of training that is the best. Only the optimal combination of various methods, selected by taking into account the requirements of the sport, stage of training, individual athlete, and other circumstances, can ensure the best results.

Types of workouts

Within the above methods, various types of workouts can be done. The types of workouts are classified according to the amount of exercises used and their sequence, intensity and duration of work, and rest intervals between exercises. When planning and conducting a workout one should regulate the amount of work and rest according to the needs of the athletes. Classification makes it easier to describe differences in the effects of various arrangements of exercises. The following are four types of workouts:
—continuous
—variable
—repetitive
—interval

A continuous workout is characterized by a constant low intensity of work and a relatively (to other types of workout) long duration of workout. It is recommended for developing general endurance, an increase in the economy of work, the ability to mobilize muscle groups for long efforts, self-control of the athlete during exhausting efforts, resistance to symptoms of fatigue, and to the results of a loss of fluids.

A variable workout has various durations for performing each exercise. The intensity of exercises varies and it is lowered when partial recovery is needed. This workout brings best results if the intensity of exercises is initially low, then gradually is increased to less than maximal values, and then gradually lowered. This type of workout is used for developing strength, endurance, as well as economy, coordination, and precision of movements. It is mainly used in the period of developing techniques and tactics.

A repetitive workout consists of repeating a certain type of exercise in a workout. It has a constant intensity of exercise, optimal (for a given task) rest periods, and a variable number of repetitions of the exercise. This type of workout is recommended for the beginning of the preparatory period in the macrocycle. It can be used for developing strength, speed, endurance, flexibility, as well as for learning new movements, learning the pace of exercises, and consolidating previously learned habits.

An interval workout has strictly regulated work and rest periods, training loads, intensities of work in exercise, and number of repetitions of the exercise. Rest periods should be of such a type and duration as to ensure that the new stimuli is applied while the effects of the previous one are still present. In other words, when the athlete has not yet recovered from the previous exercise. The athlete should not use maximal training loads in the interval workout. This type of workout is used for developing speed-endurance but, because of high intensity of work, it can be used only with well prepared athletes. A high intensity of work puts great demands on the organism and, in insufficiently prepared athletes, can destabilize form.

Types of exercises

In each training method, exercises are divided into the competitive, special, directed, and general exercises. The needs of an individual athlete, determined by peculiarities of his/her organism, decide what exercises should belong to each of the above groups. The long term process of athletic training should start with the most general exercises, and as the athlete progresses, the exercises should become more specific for a given sports event. If special form, as measured by specific tests or by sports results, is improving as a result of performing a particular exercise, then this exercise should be used as long as the results keep on improving. When the results stop improving, then it may mean that the exercise ought to be replaced by a more specific one. It does not necessarily mean that the exercise is no good any more. It only means that it is no good at improving the specific sports perfor-

III. BASIC CONCEPTS IN ATHLETIC TRAINING **45**

mance of a given athlete. It may still be useful for developing the general form of this athlete.

1. Competitive exercises are the actual competitive actions (techniques) of a given sport. They are performed in the same fashion as during competition. It is important to distinguish between the formal competitive exercises and their training forms. The former are performed under the real conditions of competition and according to the rules of the sport. The latter, in the composition of actions and their immediate goal, are similar to the formal competitive exercises, but the ultimate goal is to realize certain training tasks, not to compete. The organization of the efforts is subject, not to the rules of the sport, but to the rules of methodology of training.

Competitive exercises, formal and training, are the only method of fully recreating the requirements of a given sport and thus stimulate the development of special form. These exercises cannot be removed from the training regimen but, because of their intensity, their share in the total amount of exercises is very small. For example, within a year, high jumpers spend approximately two hours on jumps with full approach, pole-vaulters three hours, gymnasts (high bar combinations) six hours.

2. Special exercises consist of elements of the competitive actions and/or actions that are nearly identical in form and dynamic character to the competitive actions (techniques). For example, special exercises for ball players consist of techniques and tactical fragments of the game. For gymnasts these will be single techniques (technical elements) and connections that are parts of the competitive combinations. For javelin throwers these will be imitations of the throw, with the same dynamic character of work and the same sequence of engaging muscle groups (hip-shoulder-arm), using a pulley. Special exercises influence, more selectively than competitive exercises, the specific skills and abilities necessary in a given sport. For example, punching various kinds of bags develops punching skills more effectively than a boxing match, or performing parts of a lift helps to develop the strength of particular muscle groups and improve the skill of using them more than competitive lifts.

3. Directed exercises combine certain traits of the general and special exercises. They involve the muscle groups that are essential in the given sport and use the same energy source as in the actual sports action. Their dynamic characteristics are similar to the special exercises but the exact form of movement is different. For example, various jumps, other than the competitive one, are the directed exercises for jumpers, various throws with a medicine ball are directed exercises for a shot put, barbell and dumbbell lifts,

duplicating the dynamics of the judo pull or push (kuzushi), are directed exercises for judoka. Because they are more remote in form of movement from competitive exercises than the special exercises, they allow the athlete to do more work, in a more controlled fashion than special exercises, without any negative influence on the technique.

4. General exercises include both, exercises similar in certain elements to special exercises, and exercises that are very different, even contrary, from them. They must be diverse enough as to, in combination with special exercises, ensure an all-around development of physical abilities of the athlete and, their composition must reflect, to some extent, the specific features of the sport to make possible the positive transfer of the training effect.

General exercises are used in all periods of the macrocycle. In the first, general, stage of the preparatory period they are the main means of training. In the stage of special preparation their purpose is to stabilize the form. In the competitive period they are used as a means of active rest. General exercises reinforce the training effect of special exercises thanks to the variability of stimuli. They break the monotony of training, develop abilities that were underdeveloped by special exercises, or develop needed abilities in a different way; at the same time causing positive emotions in athletes. In all sports, prolonged practicing of the main competitive exercise strains the central nervous system and can lead to overtraining. To avoid these unwanted effects of specialization, one microcycle (5-8 days) of general exercises can be done instead of special exercises at the end of special preparatory stage. This is also done in cases of a prolonged competitive period.

General exercises are those that are nonspecific for a given sport that shape all systems of the body. The purpose of these exercises is to harmoniously develop the whole organism so it can withstand further specialization. Usually, the general exercises used in the period of general preparation have a work and rest arrangement during the workout similar to the competitive exercises.

General exercises that are designed to develop general endurance have an intensity or speed (individually stable speed) permitting a maintenance of heart rate at 150/min. for long periods of time. General strength exercises are done with a lower speed than is required in competitive exercises, with resistance that develops a different type of strength than that used in competitive exercises, and a higher number of repetition than in directed or specialized strength exercises.

Sports	Competitive and special exercises of the sport	Acrobatic exercises	Ball Games: Basketball	Ball Games: Volleyball	Ball Games: Other	Cycling	Gymnastic exercises without apparatus or equipment	Gymnastic exercises on apparatus	Gymnastic exercises with equipment	Jumps: High	Jumps: Long	Jumps: Other	Rowing	Running with Accelerations	Running up to 10,000 Meters	Running over 10,000 Meters	Skating	Skiing: Cross-Country	Skiing: Down Hill	Swimming	Throws: Hammer	Throws: Shot Put	Throws: Other	Walking	Weightlifting
Basketball	A	S	A	M	M	N	A	R	M	R	A	N	A	A	N	N	N	N	N	N	R	A	A	A	M
Boxing	A	R	S	R	S	N	A	M	A	R	R	A	S	M	A	M	R	R	N	R	N	R	R	A	S
Cycling	A	R	R	R	R	A	A	R	A	R	R	R	R	M	A	N	M	R	R	R	N	N	R	A	M
Decathlon	A	M	M	R	R	N	A	A	N	A	A	A	N	A	A	N	R	N	R	M	A	A	A	A	M
Discus Throw	A	M	M	R	R	N	A	A	A	M	M	M	N	A	A	N	N	R	R	N	S	M	A	A	A
Gymnastics	A	A	S	R	R	N	A	A	A	S	R	A	N	M	R	N	R	R	R	R	N	R	R	A	S
Hammer Throw	A	M	S	R	R	N	A	A	A	M	M	M	N	A	A	N	N	R	N	N	A	M	A	A	A
High Jump	A	M	R	R	R	N	A	M	A	A	M	A	N	A	A	N	N	R	R	R	R	M	M	A	S
Javelin Throw	A	M	M	R	R	N	A	A	A	M	M	A	N	A	A	N	R	R	N	R	S	M	A	A	A
Pentathlon	A	A	R	S	R	N	A	A	A	A	A	A	N	A	A	N	N	N	N	N	M	A	A	A	A
Pole Vault	A	M	R	R	R	N	A	M	A	M	M	A	N	A	A	N	N	R	R	R	R	M	M	A	S
Rowing	A	R	M	R	R	N	A	M	A	R	R	S	A	N	A	N	R	M	R	R	N	R	R	A	R
Running: 100M., 200M., 110M. Hurdles	A	M	R	R	M	N	A	M	A	M	A	A	N	A	A	N	R	M	N	R	M	M	M	A	M
Running: 400M., 400M. Hurdles	A	M	M	R	R	N	A	A	A	A	A	A	N	A	A	M	R	M	R	N	M	M	M	A	A
Running: 800 M., 1500 M.	A	R	R	R	R	N	A	A	A	R	M	A	N	A	A	A	R	M	N	N	M	M	M	A	N
Running: 3000M., 10,000M.	A	N	R	R	R	N	A	M	A	R	M	M	N	A	A	A	N	M	N	N	R	M	R	A	M
Running: Marathon	A	N	R	R	R	N	A	M	A	R	M	M	N	A	A	A	N	M	N	N	R	M	R	A	M
Shot Put	A	M	S	R	R	N	A	A	A	M	M	A	N	A	A	N	N	R	N	N	M	A	A	A	A
Skating	A	R	M	R	M	A	A	R	A	M	M	A	M	N	A	M	A	N	N	R	R	M	M	A	N
Skiing: Cross-Country	A	R	M	R	M	M	A	M	A	R	M	M	M	A	A	A	R	A	A	M	R	M	M	A	M
Skiing: Down Hill	A	S	R	R	R	M	A	M	M	M	M	A	R	S	M	N	N	A	A	R	R	R	R	A	R
Skiing: Ski Jumping	A	M	R	R	R	R	A	M	A	M	M	A	N	S	M	N	N	A	A	N	R	R	R	A	S
Soccer	A	S	R	R	A	N	A	M	M	M	R	A	N	A	A	R	N	N	N	N	R	R	A	A	R
Swimming	A	R	R	S	A	R	A	M	M	R	N	R	M	S	M	R	N	S	N	A	N	R	R	A	S
Tennis	A	S	R	M	A	N	A	S	M	R	R	A	N	A	A	N	N	N	N	N	N	R	A	A	N
Triple Jump	A	M	M	R	R	N	A	M	A	M	A	A	N	A	A	N	R	S	N	R	R	M	M	A	M
Weightlifting	A	M	R	R	R	N	A	M	A	R	M	M	N	M	A	R	N	R	N	R	N	R	M	A	A
Wrestling	A	M	M	R	S	N	A	M	A	R	R	M	N	M	A	R	N	R	N	R	N	R	M	A	M

Exercises used in training qualified athletes
A—*exercises used by all athletes in a given sports discipline,*
M—*exercises used by most athletes,* **N**—*exercises never used,*
R—*exercises rarely used,* **S**—*exercises used by some athletes.*

Exercises have two ways of influencing an organism. One way is through changes in the structures of the body, for example, strength exercises can change structure of muscles, tendons and bones, while endurance exercises change lung capacity, composition of blood, and structure and function of the heart. Another way, no less important, is through changes in the nervous system. We learn certain coordinations performing the exercises and this is why introducing general exercises in the period when special exercises are already used will not help to improve special skills.

The following are examples of general, directed, and special exercises in the strength training of a discus thrower, one or two years after the beginning of stage of initial specialization, in special preparatory period of a macrocycle:

1) General strength exercises: snatch (barbell), clean on chest, squats, half-squats, bench press, abdomen exercises.
2) Directed strength exercises: snatch for height, trunk twists with barbell across shoulders, trunk rotations with weights held in arms above head, abdomen exercises with twisting of the trunk, half-squats with toe raises, jumps with barbell, multiple jumps, inclined bench press, bouncing the barbell up from behind the neck.
3) Special strength exercises: various forms of throws using shot, medicine balls, elements of discus throw using elongated weights used to fix hurdles, discus throws with heavier equipment (weight plate 2.5 kg./5.5 lb.)

Factors affecting the ability to train and compete

1. Health. It determines the athlete's disposition toward training. An athlete must be in good overall health to fully benefit from training. Minor health problems, seemingly unrelated to performance, like tooth decay, can start a general infection when combined with the great stress of heavy workouts. Chronic sinus inflammation, often found in skiers and swimmers, lowers the quality of work done in a workout and affects the recovery. Proper breathing is difficult for boxers with neglected fractures of nasal bones (septum nasi). Boils are a sign of general infection and are a contraindication to working out for seven to ten days after the boil is gone.

2. Somatic type. The size and proportions of the body determine what sports one can succeed at, and what techniques and tactics one should employ. The length of an arm outstretched forward with a clenched fist decides on the choice of tactics most suiting a boxer. In basketball, not the body height, but the total height of reach (how high one can reach with one's arms), is a decisive factor. The amount of turnout in a hip joint, shoulder and lumbar mobility,

and the height projected on the basis of the parents height, are used in selecting children for gymnastics. The flexibility of legs and the amount of turnout in a hip joint determines in what types of throws (hand throws, hip throws, leg throws) one will specialize in judo and sambo.

3. Type of personality. Some athletes prefer to play in attack, some in defense. Some need a strict tactical plan, others do best if they can improvise. Individual preferences should be used in assigning athletes to their positions in team sports and choosing types of techniques and tactics most suitable for them.

4. Intellectual level (IQ). Ability to learn technique depends on the athlete's IQ. Ability to draw is related to the spatial and kinesthetic sense. An athlete that mastered the technique well can easily draw the crucial phases of it. Tactical skills of an athlete depend on his/her technical skills, rational thinking, concentration, and divisibility of attention. The ability to analyze the efficiency of a given tactic or technique and to make an adjustment in it, or discard it, regardless of any personal tastes, depends very much on mental flexibility, a component of IQ.

5. Will and motivation. No matter how suitable one's physique is for any given sport, if the person is not internally motivated to dedicate their whole life to it, the training time will be wasted. If other factors determining performance are not below a certain minimum level, strongly motivated people eventually prevail. "Unmotivated talent" will soon drop off, but before that happens, it will occupy the training space, the time, and the coach's energy that could be better used with the driven ones. "Blood will tell in the end." You can't keep a good person down or elevate a lousy one to a higher level.

IV. CYCLIC CHARACTER OF THE TRAINING PROCESS

Every system develops in cycles, yet so often we forget this and expect steady, gradual growth, in sports training, for example.

Human life consists of many cycles. The greatest one, life itself, starts with birth and ends with death. Its wave climbs up as we grow up, peaks, and then goes down until we die. Not all capabilities develop and decline at the same rate. In some of our capabilities we can perform very well nearly until the death. Others, mostly physical, have a relatively short peaking period, after which follows considerable decline.

There is no such thing as maintaining a maximum condition indefinitely. If there was, then we would not die. Human life can be considered one big wave with its climbing, peaking and declining phase. Several smaller waves are superimposed on our life wave. Some last years, some days, some hours, and some last even less than a second.

Rational athletic training should take this cyclical character of life into account. Nights follow days and seasons change because of the cycles of Earth movements. Monthly cycles are connected with the moon. It causes tides in oceans and lifts the earth's crust up to 16 inches. Cell divisions in the human epidermis are rhythmic and cyclic. It has been estimated that normal epidermal cells take about 27 days to travel from the basal layer to the surface.

Franz Halberg, Eugene Johnson, Walter Nelson, Walter Runge and Robert Sothern, in an article "Autorhythmometry: Procedures for Physiologic Self-Measurements and Their Analysis" published in Physiology Teacher, January 1972, have shown that the lung capacity, body temperature, heart rate, and grip strength rise and fall in a circadian cycle. Robert Sothern was interviewed by Susan

Perry and Jim Dawson, authors of the book "The Secrets Our Body Clocks Reveal", and informed them that he, for more than twenty years, three to five times a day, measured several of his body functions. It turned out that his lung capacity, grip strength, and speed at which hair grows, rise and fall in a monthly cycle. Nails and hair are both made of the protein keratin. The human hair of the scalp grows about 0.3 millimeter per day. Nails grow about 0.1 millimeter per day. Growth is slower in winter than in summer and slower in infants and elderly than in young adults. Nails grow from the matrix at the base of the nail root. Matrix cells multiply and move forward, synthesizing keratin. The nail-forming organ is particularly sensitive to physiologic changes; stress, long fever, and noxious drugs can make nails grow thinner, thicker, furrowed, or otherwise deformed. Any type of nail deformity should be checked with a physician to be sure of the athlete's good health.

Plants and animals have gradually developed genetically controlled daily cycles of activity that are of similar, but not identical, length as the twenty-four-hour earth cycle. For example, the human natural daily cycle is nearly twenty-five hours long. It governs the sleep and wake cycle, changes in temperature, blood pressure, hormone excretion, cell division, and other aspects of an organism's functions.

Thanks to many external cues, such as sunrise and sunset, our cycle can synchronize with the twenty-four-hour day. Changing the length of the day and the amount of sunlight influences our metabolism, slowing it down for winter and speeding it up for warm seasons. Children grow faster in summer than in winter. Our lungs and muscles are most efficient in the summer.

Week is a result of the weekly cycle of changes in blood pressure, pulse rate, body temperature, and hormone secretion. Certain illnesses develop in weekly cycles, for example, cold, pneumonia, and malaria. Transplanted organs (heart, kidney, pancreas) are in the most danger of rejection at weekly intervals. A United States Army study, quoted in the book "The Secrets Our Body Clocks Reveal", shows that it took a week, for the soldiers flown to Europe, to regain their ability to think clearly and logically.

We have cycles of activity that last 90 minutes, affecting concentration, dreams, and hunger. Our energy level and ability to concentrate follows a 90 minute cycle. We have dreams every 90 minutes. We get hunger pangs in 90 minute cycles. Under stress these cycles shorten to 60 minutes or less. This is why the optimal duration of workout is between one hour and 90 minutes. Of course, workouts of athletes training for an event that lasts longer than 90 minutes, for example, the marathon, have to be longer. Some long-distance runners workout for three hours.

Dr. Jurgen Zulley[77], a psychologist at the Max Planck Institute for Psychiatry in Munich, has found evidence for a four hour sleep-wake cycle with nap periods at approximately 0900, 1300, and 1700 hours (9 am, 1 pm, and 5 pm).

Biologically, "we are essentially rhythmic creatures," says psychologist Edward F. Kelly[15], president of Spring Creek institute in North Carolina. "Everything from the cycle of our brain waves to the pumping of our heart, our digestive cycle, sleep cycle— all work in rhythms. We are a mass of cycles piled one on top of another, so we are clearly organized both to generate and respond to rhythmic phenomena."

The studies conducted by Doreen Kimura[4], a psychology professor at the University of Western Ontario in London, Ontario, have demonstrated that there is a relationship between monthly fluctuation in the female sex hormones and a woman's ability to perform tasks involving verbal skill, motor (neuromuscular) coordination, and spatial reasoning. Motor coordination and verbal skills were better when the estrogen level was high. Tasks involving spatial reasoning were performed better when the estrogen levels were low.

The experiments were designed so that any mood changes linked to the menstrual cycle did not play a role.

Kimura said that the fluctuating hormones probably affect different sides of brain. Research has shown that the left side of the brain specializes in verbal and motor skills, while the right side specializes in spatial skills. On days of high estrogen levels, the general activity of the left side of the brain is probably increased. On days of low estrogen levels the right side is probably more active. Similar testing on men is more difficult because they do not have a comparable monthly hormone cycle. Levels of the male sex hormone testosterone are higher in the morning than in the evening, however, and Dr. Kimura is planning studies in which men would be tested.

Neurobiologist Jill Becker[44] of the University of Michigan has shown that the female rats trained to walk a narrow beam make fewer errors in that task during the portion of their menstrual cycle when their estrogen levels are high.

The wavelike oscillation of the training loads, in cycles of various length, and the periodization of the training process, all result from the periodical oscillation of the work capability, the various recovery times of various systems of the organism, the correlation between volume and intensity of work, and the fact that a low volume of high intensity training loads influences athletic form differently than training loads of high volume and low intensity.

It is possible to increase loads in a rectilinear-ascending fashion but only when the frequency of workouts is low, the intensity of work is low, and the volume of work is low. As soon as the volume and intensity reach values that are necessary for developing competitive form, the parameters of work must follow waves of increasing, stabilizing and decreasing values to prevent overtraining. The duration and amplitude of these waves is decided on the basis of reactions of the athlete's organism to the effort, and depends on the overall training load (mostly intensity) and the training level of the athlete.

The lowering of the training loads in microcycles directly preceding the main competition is conditioned by a lagging transformation of the cumulative training effect. The increase of the results appears, not when the training loads are at the highest values, but when the training loads have stabilized or decreased. Changes in the training loads have to be planned so as to ensure that the cumulative training effect will be greatest at the time of competition.

These are the general rules of changing the dynamics of training loads (work):
— the smaller the frequency and intensity of workouts, the longer may be the ascending phase of the wave, but the amount of improvement from workout to workout is very small;
— the higher the intensity of the workouts and the means of recovery used in the interval between them, the more frequent are the waves;
— volume of training load is inversely proportional to its intensity. A great volume of training loads, necessary to cause lasting morphological and functional changes in the organism, and a high intensity of work, necessary for accelerating the development of the special form, are mutually exclusive.
— To avoid overtraining or injury, the increase of intensity of work must be based on sufficiently great morphological changes, resulting from long training with a high volume of work.

Every cycle partially duplicates the previous one, and differs from it as much as it has to to satisfy the changing requirements of the training process.

Structure of a workout

A properly designed workout or physical education lesson plan includes the following parts:
1. The introduction, where the coach **briefly** explains the task.
2. The general warm-up, including cardiovascular warm-up and general stretching.
3. The specific warm-up; where movements resemble more closely the actual subject of the workout.
4. The main part of the workout; when the main task is realized.
5. The cool-down.

This general structure of workout is conditioned by the changes in the athlete's work capability when exercising. At first, the work capability raises, then oscillates around a certain optimal level and eventually declines.

Most workouts are dedicated to only one task. The high demands of sports training usually call for the full concentration of effort on each single task. For this reason high class athletes do 500 or more workouts in a year (several workouts per day). Workouts with more than one task occur in technically complex sports. The changing character of work in such a workout makes precise control difficult, but on the other hand, the workouts are less monotonous. The proportion of one-task to multi-task workouts depends on the particular sport. Sports with combined events (decathlon, gymnastics) have a greater number of multi-task workouts than the single event sports. Single task workouts are better for the development of a particular technique because such workouts allow for the arrangement of exercises in the most rational way and, for for keeping the proper sequence of types of effort during the workout.

The workout begins with a gathering of the athletes, taking attendance, and explaining the task or tasks. The duration of the whole introduction indicates the degree of professionalism of the coach and the motivation of the athletes. The shorter duration, the better. In the well run training program each task is based on the previous one. This makes lengthy demonstrations and explanations unnecessary. The warm-up follows the introduction.

Warming up has to prepare all systems of the body in order to perform at top efficiency. It has to affect the heart, blood vessels, nervous system, muscles and tendons, and the joints and ligaments. The goals of the warm-up are: an improved elasticity and contractibility of muscles, greater efficiency of the respiratory and cardiovascular systems, improved (shorter) reaction time, increased awareness, better concentration, an improved coordination, and regulation of emotional states, especially before competitions. All these changes occur when the body temperature is increased by muscular effort. The principles used in arranging the exercises of the warm-up are: from distant joints to proximal (to the center of the body), and from one end of the body to the other (top to bottom or vice versa), ending with the part of the body that will be used first in the next exercise. This last principle applies to all parts of a workout.

The whole warm-up before the main part of a workout should take 20-40 minutes. The length of the warm-up depends on the task, intensity, and/or duration of work that will follow it. The greater the intensity of the workout, the longer the warm-up should be. Speed, strength, and difficult technical workouts require the longest warm-up. A general warm-up should start with about five minutes of aerobic activity; for example, jogging, shadowboxing or any exercise having a similar effect on the cardiovascular system. Flexibility improves with an increased blood flow in the muscles so you can follow this with dynamic stretches, for example, leg raises to the front, sides and back, and arm swings. Leg raises are to be done in sets of ten to twelve repetitions per leg. Arm swings are to be done in sets of five to eight repetitions. Do as many sets as it takes to reach your maximum range of motion in any given direction. Usually, for properly conditioned athletes, one set in each direction is enough. Doing static stretches before a workout that consists of dynamic actions is counterproductive. The goal of the warm-up, which is to improve coordination, elasticity and contractibility of muscles, and breathing efficiency, cannot be achieved by doing the static stretches, isometric or relaxed. Isometric tensions will only make you tired and decrease your coordination. Passive, relaxed stretches, on the other hand, have a calming effect and can even make you sleepy.

The more intensive the effort and the lower the temperature, the more one has to warm-up the muscles. A high temperature environment does not make warming up unnecessary. It only requires a lowering of the intensity of exercises in the general warm-up.

Warming up should involve a gradual increase in the intensity of your exercises. Toward the end of a warm-up, when it becomes "specific", one should use movements that resemble more closely the techniques of one's sport or the task assigned for this workout. You may do easier forms of your techniques, but do not get sloppy! What you repeat, you learn, and then in a crucial moment of, for example, competition, you will do a substandard technique.

Example of a warm-up for an endurance workout:

1. Walk and march with jogging and light running.
2. Slalom between trees, bushes, etc.
3. Light jumps, running sideways and backward, and other exercises for legs done in motion.
4. Light running for 300-500 meters.
Points 1 through 4 take approximately 15 minutes.
5. Rest while marching.
6. Flexibility and agility exercises while standing, marching, and jogging (bends, twists, squats, lunges, arm swings, legs swings).
7. Light running for 300-500 meters.
Total length of the warm-up is 20-25 minutes.

Example of a warm-up for a strength workout:

1) Jogging, shadowboxing, or other light exercises (5 minutes).
2) Flexibility exercises while standing or marching (bends, twists, squats, lunges, arm swings, legs swings) interspaced with skips and various jumps in place (5 minutes).
3) Exercises with light dumbbells (bends, twists, squats, lunges, arm raises).
4) Running in place interspaced with jumps.
5) Exercises with heavy dumbbells (squats, lunges, bends and twists of the trunk).
6) Running in place interspaced with jumps.
7) Exercises with a barbell (squats, lunges, bends, twists, and jumps).
Total length of the warm-up is 20-25 minutes.
During the main part of the strength workout, each set of the exercise with a target weight has to be preceded by a shorter set of the same exercise with 60%-75% of the target weight.

Example of a warm-up for a speed workout (sprints):

1) Jogging 800 meters.
2) Relaxing exercises (shaking limbs, easy arm and leg swings) (3-4 minutes).
3) Jogging 200-300 meters.
4) Flexibility exercises (3-4 minutes).
5) Jogging 200-300 meters.
6) Flexibility exercises (3-4 minutes).
7) Rest while marching (2-3 minutes).
8) Sprints (3-4 repetitions) at 70%-90% of maximal speed.

Example of a warm-up for a technical workout:

1) Jogging 800 meters.
2) Relaxing exercises (shaking limbs, easy arm and leg swings) (3-4 minutes).
3) Jogging 200-300 meters.
4) Flexibility exercises (3-4 minutes).
5) Jogging 200-300 meters.
6) Flexibility exercises (3-4 minutes).
7) Rest while marching (2-3 minutes).
8) Technical exercises (15-22 minutes) starting with elements and ending with 2-4 repetitions (with lower intensity) of the whole technique that is to be perfected in this workout.

A pre-competition warm-up should begin 60-80 minutes before the start. It is much different that the warm-up in a workout. It consists of the following four parts:

1) First part begins with jogging or slow running until athlete starts sweating (10-30 minutes). Next, exercises that warm the muscles that running did not warm. Number of exercises similar to that used in the workout. This part can be preceded by massage, rubbing with liniments, or electrostimulation. These means of passive warm-up may permit shortening this part of the pre-competition warm-up (general warm-up) but not the second part (special warm-up).

2) Second part has to prepare central nervous system, setting proper rhythm and coordination of movements. The distribution of efforts in this part is crucial for performance. The choice of exercises depends on the type of effort in competition.

In sports that require a maximal speed of movement, this part of warm-up will usually include repetitions of single elements of a competitive exercise and then; joining them together, repeating the whole exercise with accelerations; attempts at performing the whole exercise with submaximal effort. Such attempts ensure precise and confident movements. The effort should not be maximal because such attempts lower the quality of performance in competition. If the skill has not become a habit and is not reliable, several careful repetitions of it in this part of the warm-up may bring good results in competition. In endurance sports, athletes do less exercises in the first part of warm-up and dedicate the second part to performing for longer time competitive actions with low intensity. The total time of the above two parts of the warm-up is 20-30 minutes.

3) Third part lasts 10-30 minutes until athletes are called out. This is the time athletes use for getting to rooms where they can get massages, change dress, prepare their gear, and relax.

4) Fourth part happens just prior to the start. Competitive exercises are performed in complete form to finally prepare for the start. Maximal efforts just before start are as useless now as they were in the second part of the warm-up. After a few repetitions, the athlete rests in motion and waits for the start.

If the long jumper changes the length of the pre-run and position of the markers during warm-up for competition then it means that there is something wrong with the training. A well trained athlete should know exactly what his/her best distance is for pre-run before jumping, how many steps it takes, and where to put the markers.

In the course of one competition, athletes can start several times with 10-60 minutes rest between starts. This makes it necessary to additionally warm up before each start. Each such additional warm-up lasts 8-10 minutes and consists of 5-8 minutes of low intensity exercises for raising the temperature of the body while the remaining time is dedicated to easy repetitions of the competitive exercise. These repetitions are done without a great amount of tension. These additional warm-ups are short because after one start, the organism warms up quickly.

Now—back to warming up for a workout. A good coach will rarely repeat the same sequence of warm-up exercises in different workouts. The tasks of the workouts change and the warm-up has to be built of the exercises that best prepare the athletes for the current task. Usually the "specific" part of the warm-up lasts five to ten minutes. A specific warm-up should blend with the main part of your workout.

The optimal sequence of tasks in the main part is:
a) learning a new technique or tactics;
b) developing speed and/or coordination (in this new technique perhaps);
c) developing strength (general or specific for the learned skill);
d) developing endurance (general or specific for the learned skill).

Short speed or strength efforts are usually introduced before long endurance efforts because the former create a favorable psychological background for the latter.

The techniques of such sports as weightlifting and the throwing events of track and field, may be performed after the speed exercises because these techniques require a lot of strength.

The above does not mean that a single workout should cover all these tasks. It means that as the workout progresses, its accent generally shifts toward exercises of lower intensity and longer duration, demanding progressively less coordination. A single workout can also be dedicated to the realization of only one of the above tasks, for example, endurance. Dedicating the whole workout to one task makes it more effective in the realization of the task than complex workouts and makes directing the training process easier.

Occasionally speed or technical exercises are done after strength or endurance exercises. This is done when athletes are nearing the competitive period, their mastery of the technique is good, and they need to learn using the technique in adverse conditions.

Generally, after the warm-up, all the exercises are arranged in the order of the descending intensity of effort. The exercises should not be grouped primarily by the body part or the form of movement, but by their intensity, i.e., dynamics. The more dynamic or more intensive exercises are to be done first.

When the main part is over, it is then time for the cool-down. The "cool-down proper" should include exercises that slow down the physiological functions of athletes bodies and enhance the recovery after the workout. It may start with a slowed down version of the last exercise of the main part or a low intensity ball game. The cool-down may be used for performing exercises that correct posture defects, resulting from the sports training or, of other origin. When the athletes breathe normally they can do some muscle stretching. Usually only static stretches are used here. You can start with the more difficult static active stretches that require a relative "freshness". After you have achieved your maximum reach in these stretches, move on to either isometric or relaxed static stretches (or both); following the isometric stretches with relaxed stretches. Pick only one isometric stretch per one muscle group and repeat it two to five times, using as many tensions per repetition (attempt) as it takes to reach the limit of mobility that you have at this stage of your training. The athletes that need a precise sense of time (duration of the round) or space (size of ring or mat) can use the cool-down for exercises perfecting these abilities. All athletes can walk around and each stops when he/she feels that the previously set amount of time has elapsed. To improve the feel of the ring or of the mat, blindfolded athletes can, either individually or in rows, move to assigned spots or lines, stopping when they believe they are on their mark.

After all these exercises, the coach should **briefly** evaluate the objectives fulfilled in this workout.

According to chronobiological research conducted by Charles Winget, Charles DeRoshia, and Daniel Holley, the best time to conduct a strength workout is between 14:00 and 20:30 hours because the hand grip strength is greater then. The best time for stretching is about 13:30, and for aerobic endurance workouts, it is the late afternoon and early evening hours because the heart and lungs are more efficient then. The precise control of fine movements is poor in the morning, especially around 11.00 hours, because the secretion of chemicals (dopamine and noradrenaline) that influence the brain's alertness peaks then. Physical discomfort, such as cold, is tolerated better in the late morning, but performance in strength and in endurance events (swimming, running, rowing, and shot put) is better in the evening. Physical effort is perceived to be easier in the late afternoon and in the early evening. Long-term memory is best formed in the late afternoon, so that seems to be the best time for the technical workout.

Y. V. Shcherbina has found out that the effect of an identical physical load varies depending on the time of the day when it was performed. Bioelectrical activity and muscular strength increases from 12:00 to 13:00, then declines from 14:00 to 18:00, then increases from 18:00 to 20:00, and then declines again. The best time to perform speed-strength efforts is in the periods when the muscular strength and the bioelectrical activity of the muscles is increasing.

Apart from regular workouts athletes usually participate in auxiliary (supplementary) workouts. Their purpose is to improve the athlete's weaknesses. Typically, auxiliary workouts are dedicated to improving aerobic endurance, strength (general or of specific muscle groups), or flexibility. They may consist of one type of exercises, for example, dynamic flexibility exercises. Auxiliary workouts are often done early in the morning, before breakfast. If their duration is more than 30 minutes, a light snack can precede them.

Soviet scientists, G. Kassil, V. Levandov, R. Suzdalnitsky, B. Pershin and S. Kuzmin[56], conducted research on the subject of the regulation of the immune system in athletes during strenuous workouts and competitions. They have found that during workouts with a moderate intensity, the content of antibodies in the blood was increased and, as a result, the immunity of the athletes improved. With the increasing intensity of workouts, the content of the antibodies was first reduced to the pre-workout level and then declined sharply, which weakened the immunity. These researchers then tested the blood of athletes immediately after major competitions, when extreme physical strain is accompanied by strong excitement. They found that in such a state the number of antibodies dropped to nearly zero. The duration of the period, when the immunity of the athlete is so dangerously low, varies individually and depends on many factors.

The scientists have also found the relationship between different types of exercises and the antibodies in blood. The short, intensive efforts, such as sprints, jumps, and throws, were followed by a short, powerful ejection of adrenalin into the blood. The time of these exercises was too short for the phenomenon of lowering the content of the antibodies to occur. In long lasting efforts, such as long distance running, this phenomenon of lowering the content of antibodies manifests itself fully.

It was also found that in sports where the athlete is subjected to protracted physical strain, different people react differently to stress. In some, adrenalin intensively enters the blood, while in the others it is insulin— a hormone that reduces the sugar content in the blood. With insulin, glucose is used to a better advantage in muscle tissue, while the athletes themselves endure lengthy strain worse. With the knowledge of such important facts about one's organism, every beginning athlete can be given recommendations for a particular type of sports where he/she can be successful.

Eating candies or cookies before exercising can impair your workout performance. The consumption of sugar triggers release of insulin that within 20-30 minutes lowers the body' blood glucose. This may cause premature fatigue. Simple sugars are easily digested by an organism so the level of glucose in the blood increases rapidly after eating them, which causes the pancreas to release a great amount of insulin. This results in removing more glucose from the blood than is necessary to maintain its normal level, explaining the sleepiness and lowered ability to work after eating candies. The presence of insulin prevents using fatty acids as a source of energy during physical effort.

In addition, most cakes and candies contain lots of fat which, because it requires a long time to be digested, remains in the stomach causing discomfort during a workout.

Fructose, also a simple sugar, is absorbed without releasing insulin.

Structure of a microcycle

Rational doses of effort, followed by adequate rest, cause the body to, not only compensate for the loss of energy sources and building materials used in the effort, but to compensate in excess (super-compensate). Through supercompensation it is possible to increase the work capability of the body. The frequency of workouts should be such as to hit the phase of supercompensation often enough to insure growth. If the rest breaks between workouts are too short or too long, the supercompensation phase is missed, and the next workout hits a phase of reduced work capability either before or after supercompensation.

The recovery of all systems affecting the functional abilities of the body does not proceed simultaneously. Various systems recover, and thus can reach supercompensation, in different lengths of time. This allows the athlete to workout daily or even several times a day, without overtraining, provided that the content of each consecutive workout stresses the system that has sufficiently recovered and does not adversely affect the recovery of other systems.

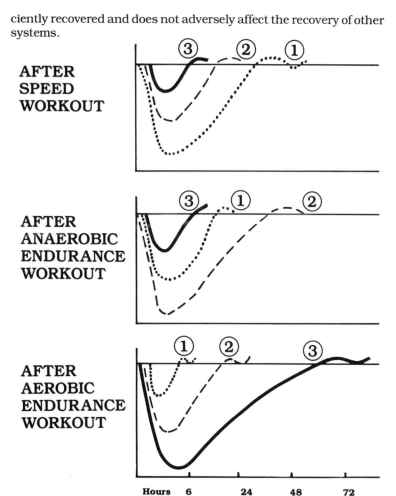

Diagram of recovery of speed (1), anaerobic capability (2), and aerobic capability (3) after speed workout, anaerobic endurance workout, and aerobic endurance workout, according to V. N. Platonov.

A microcycle consists of the training phase and the recovery phase. The training phase must have at least one workout, but may have several. The recovery phase may consist of a day of complete rest or of special restorative workouts (active rest). Theoretically, the shortest microcycle could last two days. In reality it hardly ever happens. Some microcycles last only two, three, four, or five days (microcycles lasting 4-5 days are used by some highly advanced athletes), but usually the microcycle lasts one week. The structure of the microcycle varies depending on specific features of the sport, current training tasks, and reactions of individual athletes. The workouts with maximal and close to maximal training loads determine how a microcycle is planned. For young athletes that have just entered the stage of initial specialization, loads of maximal intensity can be used once every 12-14 days and only 2-4 times during preparation for a competitive period. Usually 6-8 repetitions of the workout with a close to maximal load is enough to reach the desired level of ability, but older athletes of high class may need 12-15, such workouts done more often, thanks to their intensive means of recovery. A usual, weekly microcycle can contain one or two workouts with a close to maximal training load. These workouts are called "main workouts". The main tasks of the microcycle are realized in these main workouts. These workouts have a greater intensity and volume of work, which requires 40-60 hours of rest. Longer microcycles (hardly ever used and if at all, mainly in the special preparatory period) may even have three such workouts. To maximize the effect of the main workouts and to maintain continuity of the training process, additional workouts are held. The additional workouts, each dedicated to a different task, with training loads oscillating from small to big, are done in the periods between main workouts. Their function may be to either increase the effect of the main workout (this increases the amount of supercompensation), or to speed up the recovery after the main workout by means of active rest, and either to realize additional tasks (prevention of loosing flexibility after endurance workouts), or to realize tasks of secondary importance at this stage of training. In endurance oriented sports, more often than in speed-strength sports, main workouts may be done before full recovery is achieved. The main training phase and recovery phase are repeated twice in the course of the week, with the last recovery phase coinciding with the end of the week. An average of five to six workouts (minimum three to four) in a week allows for "co-influencing" between these workouts.

In planning the microcycle (or any period of the training process) one cannot only take into account the total workload in all exercises. The sequence of the types of effort has great importance. Studies of a recovery period have shown that the full recovery, after an endurance workout that was preceded by a speed workout, usually occurs after 48 hours. When the speed workout follows the endurance workout, the recovery takes 72 or even 96 hours. Recovery after anaerobic efforts takes 3-8 hours. After aerobic efforts, recovery may take a few days. After three days with workouts, incomplete recovery occurs, a cumulative effect of these three days. This adversely affects the results of subsequent workouts if continued without some form of rest for more than three days.

Soviet researcher N. G. Ozolin suggests the following sequence of workouts in a microcycle:
1) technical (learning or perfecting technique at medium intensity),
2) technical (perfecting technique at submaximal and maximal intensity),
3) speed,
4) anaerobic endurance,
5) strength with submaximal and maximal loads,
6) muscular endurance with medium and low loads,
7) muscular endurance with high and maximal intensity,
8) aerobic endurance with maximum intensity,
9) aerobic endurance with medium intensity.

N. J. Volkov, in the article published in "Sport Wyczynowy" number 2, 1971, suggests the following arrangement of intensity of work in a microcycle:
First day—workout of maximal intensity. Time of one exercise: 10-15 seconds. Pulse 190/minute.
Second day—workout of submaximal intensity (90-95% of maximum). Time of one exercise: 2-3 minutes. Pulse 190/minute.
Third day—workout of low to moderate intensity (20-80%). Long duration of the workout. Pulse 150/minute.
Fourth day—workout dedicated to active rest.
Fifth day—workout of submaximal intensity (50-95%). Pulse 170-180/minute, after rest periods the work is resumed when pulse is 130-140/minute.
Sixth day—workout of low to moderate intensity (20-80%). Long duration of the workout. Pulse 150/minute.
Seventh day—rest.

Types of workouts in a microcycle:

Speed. Intensity maximal. Time of one exercise 10-15 seconds. Pulse 190/min. Rest as long as it takes to regain top speed.

Technical. Intensity submaximal (50%-95%). Pulse 170-180/min. Rest between exercises till pulse falls to 130-140/min.

Strength. Intensity submaximal (90%-95%). Time of one exercise 2-3 min. Pulse 180/min.

Endurance. Intensity low (20%-80%). Time of one exercise—as long as needed. Pulse approximately 150/min.

Active Rest. Intensity low. Time of one exercise—as long as it is fun. Whole workout usually not longer than one hour. Pulse 120-150/min.

The following sequence: speed, strength, speed-endurance (anaerobic endurance), aerobic endurance, although it appears to follow the preferred sequence of workouts, may lead to overtraining. In this example the neuromuscular system is stressed in the first two days, and the next two days the vegetative system is stressed. Such an arrangement is one of the causes of overtraining.

The content of each workout of the microcycle depends on the previous workouts, on the workouts that will follow it, and on the type and amount of rest. This is especially clear in microcycles with many workouts in one day. In such a case, the effect of the first workout will influence the warm-up and the type and amount of work in the second workout. The planning of the third workout will depend on the combined effect of the two preceding workouts. The training load of each workout is smaller than if there would be one workout in a day. If the first of the two workouts in a day is very intensive and long, the second one ought to consist of simple and non-fatiguing exercises.

The ancient Greeks understood the connection between the volume, intensity of training, and the recovery processes. Their workouts were arranged in four day microcycles: first day—specialized calisthenics, second day— intensive workout, third day—rest, fourth day—moderate workout. The athlete was in good athletic condition when his movements were harmonious and he was not fatigued. Cold sweat and a pale face signaled the end of work.

The following factors have to be considered when planning a microcycle:

1. **The function of the microcycle and its place in larger structures, the mesocycles, and the macrocycles.** At the general preparation stage of the macrocycle, the microcycles include a wide variety of workouts for a well-rounded development of abilities and skills. This affects the number of main workouts, their sequence, and the work loads. At the special preparatory stage, before main competitions, the content of the microcycles narrows down to the perfection of the competitive activity, and the structure of the microcycles reflects the schedule of competitions.

2. **Requirements of the sport and the training level of the athlete.** As the level of abilities of the athlete grows, so does the load in the training phase. In endurance sports, workouts are often held before full recovery occurs.

3. **The individual reactions to training, depending on the preceding workouts and rest, as well as on phases of the**

athlete's biological cycles. Coordinating phases of the microcycle with a 5-7 day biocycle helps to increase the training level.

4. **The schedule of athlete's work (if an athlete holds a job in addition to sports training).** At the initial stages of a long-term training process, and in cases where athletes cannot afford not to work, the microcycle has to be planned on a weekly basis. This is not always best for sports results but it permits the coordination of workouts with everyday life.

Types of microcycles:

1. General Preparatory Microcycle (GPMI): this is the main type of the microcycle being used mostly at the beginning of the preparatory period of the macrocycle, and when it is necessary to increase the proportion of general training. Workouts in this microcycle have to develop the main physical abilities of the athlete. When the increase of the load (work) in the microcycle is gradual, uniform, with a big volume, but a less than maximal intensity in most workouts, it is called an ordinary microcycle (GPMIO). When the intensity of the load is increased suddenly, while maintaining considerable volume, it is called a shock microcycle (GPMIS).

Sample of General Preparatory Microcycle (GPMI):
Day #1—Speed, day #2—Technique, day #3—Strength-Endurance, day #4—Active Rest, day #5—Rest, day #6—Strength, day #7—Rest.

2. Special Preparatory Microcycle (SPMI): has a greater proportion of the special exercises for developing special form. The structure of the microcycle is determined by its task, to develop skills and abilities necessary for competing in the selected sport. This type of microcycle also has the ordinary (SPMIO) and shock (SPMIS) versions.

(Both GPMI and SPMI have ordinary and shock versions. In an ordinary microcycle, loads are increased uniformly and intensity is below the ultimate level. A shock microcycle has high intensity and a considerable volume of loads.)

Sample of Special Preparatory Microcycle (SPMI):
Day #1—Technique, day #2—Strength, day #3—Special Endurance, day #4—Active Rest, day #5—Technique & Tactics, day #6—Speed-Strength, day #7—Rest.

3. Introductory Microcycle (IMI): mimics the distribution of efforts and rest in the competition. The content of such microcycles depends on the athlete's condition, the results of tests, and the

selected method of bringing an athlete to competition level. (Introductory Microcycle (IMI) mimics the program of the forthcoming competition (distribution of loads and rest in accordance with the alternation of days of competition and intervals between them, the order of coming out on the field on the day, etc.) At the same time, the content of IMI depends on the athlete's shape. In some cases the last IMI may contrast the Competitive Microcycle.)

The efficiency of pre-competitive training can be increased by introducing the so called "contrasting microcycles" between introductory or special preparation microcycles (planning it according to the "pendulum principle"). The contrasting microcycles differ, in their loads and type of exercises, from the specialized microcycles. These differences grow as the competition nears. The specialized (introductory or special preparation) microcycles mimic more and more closely the efforts of the competition, while the contrasting microcycles are increasingly dissimilar to them, for example, they use exercises of general preparation and have a low intensity of work. The effect of the training loads is greatest in specialized microcycles but lower in contrasting microcycles. In certain cases, the so called "contrasting microcycle" may immediately precede competitions. Some of its workouts are the opposite of the typical pre-competitive workouts.

4. Competitive Microcycle (CMI): besides the participation in competition, this includes the activities preparing for the competition, maintaining form between days of competitions, and aiding with recovery after the competition. The number of days in CMI varies depending on the frequency of competitions. A rehearsal of a whole microcycle of forthcoming competition is called a model competition microcycle (CMIM). It can be used in the special preparatory period as a means of familiarizing athletes with competition and reducing the pre-start anxiety. Usually, the greater the training load in a model competition microcycle, the smaller the number of workouts in it.

Sample of Competitive Microcycle (CMI):
Day #1—Rest, day #2—Speed-Strength, day #3—Technique & Tactics, day #4—Technique & Tactics, day #5—Special Endurance, day #6—Active Rest, day #7—Competition.

5. Restorative Microcycles (RMI): used after a series of shock microcycles and after a series of important competitions. This type of microcycle has a relatively low volume and intensity of work and includes a greater number of days of active rest. The exercises and the environment are changed to help with the recovery processes.

Structure of a mesocycle

Several microcycles (between two and six) make one mesocycle. Usually a mesocycle lasts from two to four weeks. The types of microcycles making up the mesocycle, and the amount of work in them, depends on similar factors to those that are considered when planning a microcycle. In addition to the regularities determining the optimal structure of the microcycle, there are specific regularities in the development of athletic form in the series of microcycles. Various adaptive changes in the body, in response to training loads, occur at different times. Some systems respond with greater delay than others. One fine example of this is the marching fracture experienced by military recruits. Initially, the recruits improve their marching speed and distance and then, after about six weeks, if their complaints about painful feet are not heeded and the amount of marching is not reduced, they develop a stress fracture of the second metatarsal bone. Usually training loads in all types of mesocycles follow a curve that initially raises, then declines and reaches its lowest point in the last microcycle (it may be an ordinary preparatory microcycle or a restorative microcycle). Each subsequent wave of loads is 5%-10% higher than the previous one. Mesocycles, with their higher and lower phases of work loads, prevent the unwanted cumulative effect of a series of the microcycles. L. P. Matvyeyev, states that Soviets have certain research data that supports taking into account the so called "physical biorhythms", lasting 23 days, in planning mesocycles. The length of the mesocycle is also determined by the intensity of mental and physical efforts and, for mesocycles in the competitive period, by the schedule of competitions. The tasks of the macrocycle decide the number of each type of mesocycles and their sequence in the macrocycle.

Female athletes may need to plan the distribution of training loads in a mesocycle taking into account changes in work capability depending on their individual reactions to phases of their menstrual cycles. For example, female sprinters during premenstrual (3-4 days) and menstrual (3-5 days) phases do a light to medium volume of aerobic or mixed training loads. The same type of the load is done during the ovulatory phase (3-4 days). In the postmenstrual phase (7-9 days), and in postovulatory phase (7-9 days), a high to maximal volume of anaerobic work (speed-strength, speed) is done.

Types of mesocycles:

1. The Introductory Mesocycle begins the macrocycle (yearly or half-yearly cycle). Usually, it contains two to three general

preparatory microcycles with ordinary loads, and one restoration microcycle. The intensity of work is low, while the volume may reach considerably high values. The number of such mesocycles done at the beginning of the macrocycle depends on the athlete's condition before entering the new macrocycle. In normal circumstances (no injury, illness, or any other problems with maintaining good form), only one introductory mesocycle is done in the macrocycle.

2. The Basic Mesocycle is the main type of mesocycle used in both the general and special preparatory periods of macrocycle. This is the main type of mesocycle for developing abilities and forming skills. Special preparatory and general preparatory versions differ in the type of microcycles they contain. Depending on the dynamics of the training loads, this mesocycle can be either "developing" or "stabilizing". Basic developing mesocycles have great training loads, for example, in one mesocycle of the special preparatory period, the total volume for a high class long-distance runner may reach 600-800 kilometers, 200-300 kilometers for swimmers, and 1500-2000 lifts for weightlifters. The developing mesocycle is usually followed by a stabilizing mesocycle. In such a mesocycle, the training loads stabilize at the level reached and do not increase in the course of the mesocycle. This facilitates adaptation to the new training load. The stabilization of training loads affecting a given motor ability (strength, endurance, speed) is done when this ability is developed sufficiently for the current needs, and the increase of the loads (necessary for a further improvement of this ability) could limit the time and energy available for other abilities or skills that have greater priority, or this increase of the training load could lead to injury or overtraining. The number of basic mesocycles in a macrocycle depends on the amount of time available for preparation for major competitions. Depending on the current training needs, the basic mesocycle may include various combinations of microcycles, mostly of the preparatory (general and special) type, for example, three ordinary preparatory microcycles and one shock microcycle; or two shock microcycles alternated by two ordinary microcycles; or one ordinary microcycle, two shock, and one restoration microcycle.

3. The Test (Control-training) Mesocycle combines work for developing athletic form with competitions that are important for testing and training. The content of this mesocycle is determined by the results of these test competitions. In cases of athletes lacking special form it may mean intensifying the special preparation, or lowering the training loads in cases of chronic fatigue. The correction of serious flaws in skills and deficiencies in abilities that are detected in this mesocycle, may affect the plan of the following mesocycles. A test mesocycle may consist of two competition

microcycles, each followed by one preparatory microcycle. The test competitions are approached without necessarily bringing the athlete to competition level.

4. The Pre-competitive Mesocycle has the task of reproducing the conditions (climate, altitude) and schedule of the forthcoming competition and at the same time, fine tune the skills and abilities needed for the competition. The main types of microcycles are the model competitive microcycle and the preparatory microcycle. The total training load is reduced before main competition. The loads are reduced because the sports results are not highest when the training loads are highest, but after the loads stabilize or even drop. If there is more than one important competition in a yearly macrocycle, the pre-competitive mesocycle, modified to suit these competitions, may be used before each of them. For competitions of lesser importance, preparation may consist of just one microcycle of the introductory type.

In recent years, the mesocycle immediately preceding the main start (pre-competitive) is formed according to the so called pendulum principle. In such a mesocycle, the model microcycles with increasing training loads are alternated with contrasting microcycles that have an increasing proportion of the general and versatile exercises, decreasing training load, and increased amount of active rest. The rhythm of these altering microcycles is such as to ensure the phase of increased mobilization occurs at the time of competition.

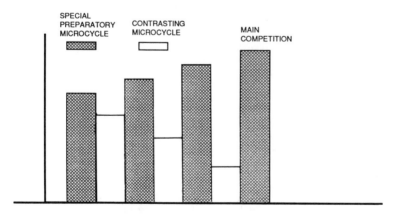

Mesocycle formed according to the pendulum principle

The pre-competitive mesocycle may also consist of several model competition microcycles with alternately higher and lower training loads (a model microcycle with a higher load usually has less workouts in it), ending with the introductory microcycle that has a lowered load and an increased amount of active rest which ensures the recovery and maintenance of athletic form for competition.

Examples of microcycles in a pre-competitive mesocycle according to L. P. Matvyeyev:
a) Preparatory, Model, Preparatory, Model, Introductory;
b) Model, Preparatory, Preparatory, Model, Preparatory, Introductory (this arrangement may be used even if an athlete has to perform big volume of work before the main competition).

5. Competitive Mesocycles are used during main competitions, when there are intervals of one month or less between important starts. They may consist of just two microcycles, one introductory and one competitive; or one introductory, one competitive, and one restorative microcycle. The structure of the competitive mesocycle depends on the number, importance, and sequence of competitions, and the laws of maintaining the athletic form.

6. Restorative (Intermediary) Mesocycles (preparatory or maintenance) are placed between competitive mesocycles, if many important competitions are spread over a long competitive period, and at the end of the macrocycle in the transitory period.

The restorative preparatory mesocycle has to restore and improve the training level after a series of competitions. It may consist of two restorative microcycles and two preparatory microcycles.

The restorative maintaining mesocycle only has to restore working capability and maintain it at a sufficient level. The form, content, and conditions of the workouts are changed to improve the recovery process.

Structure of a macrocycle

Athletic training is organized in yearly cycles, called macrocycles.

Developing and maintaining form requires an increase in training loads, but great efforts in training and competition cause mental and physical fatigue. Maintaining form for a prolonged time would mean a prolonged use of intensive training methods and a limited variety of exercises. However, because of the organism's adaptation response, these intensive and monotone exercises would have to be done with increasing loads which eventually could reach levels that, at this stage of development, are unsafe. For this reason, the form is allowed to temporarily drop at the end of the cycle after major competitions. This allows athletes to recover and forget certain elements of their skills, which will be re-learned at the new, higher level in the next cycle of training.

A great volume and low intensity of training loads (work), applied over long time, causes lasting, morphological changes in the athlete's organism, but the volume of training in any given period of time cannot be expanded indefinitely. High intensity training quickly raises athletic form but makes this form unstable. Athletic training that is intensive enough to develop competitive form, will eventually cause overtraining. The planning of a macrocycle is based on the laws of acquiring, maintaining, and temporarily losing competitive athletic form. For this reason it is divided into three main periods: preparatory, competitive, and transitory. The length of each period must ensure completion of its tasks and depends on the initial level of preparation, the demands of the sport, and the schedule of competitions. The yearly schedule of competitions ought to be planned taking into account the periodization of the training. Competitions of little importance should coincide with the preparatory period, while important ones should be planned for the end of the training cycle, in the competitive period.

In endurance sports, most of the year is spent preparing for one competitive period.

In speed-strength sports and in team games there are often two competitive periods in a yearly macrocycle, which divides the macrocycle into two halves. The semiannual cycles are characterized by a relatively fast increase of volume and intensity of work. The sports results also grow quickly, but the combination of a rapidly increasing volume with a high intensity of work, may strain the organism of the athlete. Semiannual cycles do not allow for gradual and sufficient increase of volume of work and eventually limit the development of the athlete. For these reasons, semiannual cycles should be used in conjunction with yearly macrocycles. The structure of the macrocycle should vary depending on the age, training experience, and training tasks of the individual athlete.

Yearly macrocycles with a prolonged preparatory period prepare an athlete well for greater loads, are good for introducing great and lasting changes in athlete's form, and renew the arsenal of technical and tactical habits. If preparing for record results is the goal, the semiannual cycles or the yearly cycle with a prolonged competitive period, are appropriate. Short training cycles may lead to overtraining or injuries. Cycles with too long a preparatory period, adversely affect the frame of mind of the athletes (unwillingness to work out, mental fatigue, irritability, and lack of concentration).

1. The Preparatory Period lasts from 3-4 months in a half-yearly cycle to 5-7 months in a yearly cycle. Its task is to develop abilities and skills that are the foundation of desired competitive results. It is divided into the general preparatory period and the special preparatory period. The results achieved in the preparatory period predict the level of competitive form that can be achieved in this macrocycle. As a rule, these results must exceed the results from the corresponding phase of the previous macrocycle.

a) The General Preparatory Period is longer than the following Special Preparatory Period, especially in the case of beginners.

General exercises occupy 50%-40% of the training time for advanced and 70%-60% for beginners. The higher percentages are at the beginning of this period and then the proportion of the general exercises declines to the lower values. The task of the general exercises in this period is to increase the general abilities (strength, speed, endurance, etc.), and to renew and increase the level, amount, and versatility of skills. Directed exercises and special exercises are used to develop the basics for special abilities and for mastering the skills and knowledge needed in the techniques and tactics of the sport. The competitive exercises are used sparingly, mostly as a form of modeling for future competitions, or in a simplified form. The competitive actions should not be repeated too frequently in their proper form, that in which they were mastered in the previous macrocycle, because this would only solidify the skills at the old level.

In the general preparatory period both the volume and intensity of work increase, but the volume grows more quickly. Intensity is increased only as much as it does not interfere with increase of the volume. A great intensity of work could cause a temporary, but unstable, improvement of athletic form. The stability of form depends on the volume of work and the length of time over which it was performed.

The training loads increase at this stage in different ways, both in general exercises and in special exercises. The volume of work in general exercises increases very quickly. High class athletes have already reached the maximal volume of work in a given macrocycle in the general preparatory period. The volume of work in special exercises increases more slowly, but its intensity right from the start raises to the ultimate set level. Athletes in poor shape require a very gradual introduction of intensive exercises. The lower the class of the athlete, the lower the intensity of the loads used for perfecting the technique. Introductory and basic mesocycles are used at this stage. The basic mesocycles are longer at this stage, lasting up to 6 weeks, than in later stages because the relatively low intensity of training loads permits using longer cycles.

b) The Special Preparatory Period, with the foundation of general fitness provided by the general preparatory period, prepares the athlete for achieving the goal set for this macrocycle. Exercises developing specialized forms of abilities, technical and tactical skills, as well as special psychological preparation for the target competitions, occupy most of the training time. The athletic form is built by exercises that progressively, and more accurately, reproduce the actual competitive actions. The competitive method of training is increasingly used at this stage of the macrocycle. General exercises occupy from about 30% to 40% of the training time. As the special preparatory stage nears its end, control-training and trial competitions become more frequent. Consequently, the test mesocycle, including a series of competitions with limited responsibility, is used at this stage.

The intensity of special exercises, and the volume of competitive exercises grow at the beginning of this period (intensity of competitive exercises is always high). The total volume of training loads stabilizes and then declines as their intensity grows. Increasing both the total volume and the intensity of work in this period would lead to overtraining. The morphological changes, necessary for specialization, are still present thanks to the great volume of work that was performed in the general preparatory period so the further increase of volume in special preparatory period is not needed. Initially, the total volume is reduced at the expense of the volume of the general exercises while the volume of the special exercises continues to grow. The volume of the special exercises then stabilizes and gradually declines. However, the volume of the competitive exercises and of these special exercises that are closely related to the competitive actions, continue to grow.

The increase in the total intensity of training loads causes mesocycles to become shorter, lasting from 3 to 4 weeks. Shock microcycles and restorative microcycles are used more frequently in mesocycles of this period.

In endurance sports, such as long distance running, the preparatory period is prolonged. The following arrangements of mesocycles are used in the preparatory period of the yearly macrocycle:
1) Introductory mesocycle
2) Basic (general preparatory and developing) mesocycle

3) Basic (stabilizing)
4) Basic (special preparatory and developing) mesocycle
5) Test mesocycle
6) Basic (special preparatory and developing) mesocycle
7) Pre-competitive mesocycle

In the speed-strength sports, the macrocycle has two competitive periods, each at the end of approximately a six months period. The following arrangement of mesocycles is used in the preparatory period:
1) Introductory mesocycle
2) Basic (general preparatory and developing) mesocycle
3) Test mesocycle
4) Basic (special preparatory with pre-competitive elements) mesocycle followed by the first competitive period with its mesocycles.
1) Basic (general preparatory and stabilizing) mesocycle
2) Basic (special preparatory, developing) mesocycle
3) Pre-competitive mesocycle followed by the second competitive period.

2. The Competitive Period may start with control-training competitions and end with major competitions. The competitive period lasts from six weeks to two months in a half-yearly cycle and 4-5 months in a yearly cycle (in such a case, the major competitions are organized in the last 4-5 weeks of this period). Its length is limited by the ability to maintain form without detriment to future progress. The main task is achieving optimal (maximal for a given stage of development, provided it does not preclude greater results in the future) competitive results. Skills and abilities that are essential for achieving the planned results are perfected, while the overall training load is stabilized. Separate components of the training may change to suit the requirements of a particular competition, but radical changes in the structure of the training loads cannot be made in this period because it would cause a loss of competitive form. General exercises occupy 30% of the training time, just enough to maintain the general athletic form. Special exercises are used to develop a maximum, (in a given macrocycle) level of special athletic form. Technical and tactical exercises renew the skills mastered earlier and alter them to suit the new, higher training level of the athlete and his/her opponents, as well as possibly changed requirements of the competitions. The adaptability of technical and tactical skills to various situations, the perfection of coordination in techniques, the perfection of efficient technical and tactical actions, and the development of tactical thinking are stressed here. The tasks of psychological training are to prepare the athlete for a particular competition, to develop the

ability to regulate emotions and mobilize will-power during competitions, and to develop the ability to deal with failures.

Competitions cause special psychological and emotional changes that help to mobilize the athlete for the highest of achievements. Such mobilization occurs at the cost of reserves of the organism and is difficult or impossible to achieve in normal workouts. For this reason, competitions play an important role in perfecting technique, and in developing specific competitive endurance and psychological stability. Once the necessary level of fitness is achieved, thanks to general preparatory and special preparatory periods, properly chosen competitions are the most important means for a further improvement of competitive form. To be an effective means of improving competitive form, the competitions have to be sufficiently frequent. In speed-strength sports and in ball games there are 20-40 competitions (of the preparatory character and the ones considered "main" together) in a competitive period, which means competing more often than once a week. In individual contact sports, multi-event sports, and endurance sports, the competitions are less frequent. The exact number and rank of competitions that an athlete enters depends on the individual characteristics of the athlete and on the sport. The majority of competitions in a macrocycle, including the competitive period, are actually just training for the main competitions. The intervals between such preparatory competitions are long enough to merely restore the work capacity after the previous competition. The series of starts with short, 2-3 day intervals between them, are effective in training high class athletes. The structure of the loads in such a series of starts is similar to a microcycle with some workouts performed without full recovery. This greatly stresses the athlete's organism and, if followed with the adequate type and amount of rest, further develops competitive form. The main competitions, usually 3-5 in the competitive period, are the focal point of all athletic training in a macrocycle. The interval between such major competitions is long enough for complete recovery.

Depending on the length of the competitive period, it is made of various types of mesocycles. When the competitive period is short, up to two months, it may consist of two to three competitive mesocycles, each including an introductory microcycle, the main competition, and a restorative microcycle (see competitive mesocycle). When the competitive period is longer, 3-4 months or more, the restorative and pre-competitive mesocycles are added. Restorative mesocycles are needed to maintain or even improve the level of general training that declines in competitive mesocycles. They also prevent the unwanted side-effects of repeated competitive loads and break the monotony of repeated starts. The ability to achieve high sports results temporarily drops in these mesocycles, but it does not result in a loss of athletic form.

Pre-competitive mesocycles are used when the particular conditions (climate, altitude) of the main competition require long adaptation.

Usually the mesocycles in a competitive period are arranged in the following versions:
a) Competitive, Competitive, Restorative (maintaining), Competitive;
b) Competitive, Competitive, Restorative (maintaining), Competitive, Restorative (preparatory), Competitive;
c) Competitive, Competitive, Restorative (maintaining), Competitive, Pre-competitive, Competitive.

The exact arrangement of mesocycles depends on the length of the competitive period, how the competitions of various importance are distributed within it, and on the conditions of competitions.

In the short (6-8 weeks) competitive period, the dynamics of the training loads continue tendencies that were found in the special preparatory stage. It usually means a slightly lowered volume and an increase or stabilization of intensity of work.

In long (over 2 months) competitive periods it is necessary, in the second half of this period, to increase the volume of work while continuing to increase the intensity of exercises. For example, in speed- strength sports, the monthly volume of work in the second half of the competitive period can reach 80-90% of the maximal monthly volume in the preparatory period. In endurance events, if the volume of work has to be increased, it reaches lower values than in the preparatory period and the rate of increase may have to be smaller than in the preparatory period. The reactions of the athlete, to work of increasing intensity and duration must be carefully monitored. If there is a threat of overstrain, the intensity of work must be lowered. The training loads in this period particularly must be individualized.

The intensity of training work preceding competitive starts increases in endurance events of long duration, while the frequency of the main workouts decreases. In sports like boxing, wrestling, or fencing, the intensity reached in the special preparatory stage is not increased later. In speed-strength events (weightlifting, throws, jumps), the intensity of training work in this period is decreased. Decreasing the intensity of work ought to cause a feeling of "freshness" or a lack of any of the discomforts associated with heavy training.

3. The Transitory Period lasts from three to six weeks, until the athlete has completely recovered from previous efforts. The task of this period is the prevention of overtraining through active rest, and to maintain a level of training that guarantees achieving a higher level of training in the forthcoming macrocycle than the level achieved in the previous one. In some cases, passive rest has to be used in the beginning of the transitory period. The intensity of work is low, and falls to about 50% or less of its highest values in this training cycle.

At the beginning of this period, a relatively high proportion of special exercises may be used to eliminate defects in techniques, and later, if it is necessary, some special exercises are used to maintain the level of special training. Eventually general exercises may occupy up to 90% of the training time.

The exercises are very diversified, the conditions of workouts are varied, and a repetitive use of the same type of exercises are to be avoided. The athlete is permitted to chose the subject of workouts to make sure they are not perceived as compulsory and boring. This is the time for such exercises as hiking tours.

The transitory period consists of two or three restorative mesocycles of either the maintaining or preparatory type. As the restoration process is completed, this period blends into the preparatory period of the next macrocycle. The sufficiency of recovery is determined by results of the joint control, by the coach and the sports physician, as well as by the subjective desire of the athlete to reach for new goals.

In instances when the athlete did little work in the preparatory period and participated in few, if any competitions, the transitory period may consist of a single mesocycle or even of a single microcycle.

As a rule, the more trained the athlete— the heavier the transitory period. Only beginning athletes may suspend training in this period.

Virtually no transitory period is used after the first competitive period of a year divided into two semiannual macrocycles. The preparatory period immediately follows the first competitive period.

There is an alternative way of naming periods of training. Knowing its terminology may make understanding the purpose of each period easier.

The three training periods: of accumulation, intensification, and transformation (corresponding to general preparatory period, special preparatory period, and competitive period) lead to the start in the main competition.

In the period of accumulation, the athlete accumulates morphological and functional changes performing a high volume of work with an intensity or speed of movements that is naturally easy for him/her to maintain while keeping the heart rate at 150-160 beats/min. This level of speed is called "individually stable speed".

In the period of intensification, the athlete uses specialized exercises with a speed and form of movement specific in his/her sport, where the speed of movements is increasingly greater than "the individually stable speed". That intensity or speed of movements, called "individually unstable speed", cannot be maintained for a prolonged time and requires longer periods of rest than the time of work in an exercise. The heart rate during exercises used in this period is between 170-190 beats/min. Older, more advanced athletes can increase the length of this period at the expense of the period of accumulation.

In the period of transformation, form accumulated and intensified previously becomes transformed into sports results. Exercises in this period are highly specific and increasingly important starts lead to the main start of the season. To prevent overtraining and a loss of general form, some work of the type used in the period of accumulation is used. Prolonging the period of transformation beyond 2-3 mesocycles leads to exploitation of the athlete.

The 4-6 weeks of the period of transformation, that precede the main start in a macrocycle are also called the "Immediate Start Preparation". The more endurance oriented the sport, the longer the "Immediate Start Preparation". It begins with a series of starts that inform about the current needs of the athlete. These starts are followed by 2-3 microcycles of accumulation. First two microcycles improve general athletic form by a high volume of work (some specialized work is also done). Then two microcycles of intensification follow. During these two microcycles, directed exercises with an increasing amount of special exercises are done for the development of special endurance or for the development of a feature characteristic for a given sport. During these microcycles special endurance is developed mainly by starts in competitions.

The final 1-2 microcycles of the "Immediate Start Preparation" are filled with the ultimate efforts of the main competition and with a recovery of competitive form.

The example of the "Immediate Start Preparation" given above (sequence of microcycles: 2xAccumulation, 2xIntensification, 2x-Transformation with the last Transformation microcycle including the main start) is typical for an athlete that has a low level of energy and starts infrequently. During competitions such athletes can mobilize beyond all expectations. An athlete that has a high level of energy and likes to start frequently will arrange the microcycles like this: Accumulation, Transformation, Intensification, Transformation, Accumulation, Transformation with the main start. The form here is developed by frequent starts. The main start is preceded by 10-14 days of accumulation.

The period of transformation and starts is followed by 4-6 weeks of detraining where general exercises of low intensity and increasing volume are done.

The ratio of mesocycles in each of these three periods may be 5:2:3 or 5:1:2.

Increasing intensity of exercises

	Accumulation	Accumulation	Accumulation	Intensification	Transformation
Sprints	march, jog, coordination exercises, special exercises without resistance	special exercises with light and medium resistance, technical exercises	speed exercises, work on rhythm, endurance runs (1–2 min.)	speed exercises, interval training, speed-endurance	tests and starts
Jumps	march, jog, coordination exercises, special exercises without resistance	special exercises with light and medium resistance, technical exercises	speed exercises, runs jumps with short and medium pre-run, finding the proper distance for the pre-run	speed exercises, interval training, jumps from a full pre-run	tests and starts
Throws	march, jog, coordination exercises, special exercises with light resistance	special exercises with medium resistance, various jumps, running	local strength-endurance exercises, technical throws, speed exercises (runs)	special strength exercises, speed exercises	strength training (max. loads) tests and starts
Middle distance runs	jog, aerobic endurance runs	aerobic-anaerobic endurance runs, big running play, work on rhythm	anaerobic endurance, interval training (extensive), repetitive training (long distances), big running play	work on pace, speed exercises, interval training (intensive)	tests and starts
Long distance runs	aerobic and aerobic-anaerobic endurance runs	big running play, circuit training, cross-country runs	anaerobic endurance, aerobic endurance (cross-country runs), interval training (extensive), big running play (intensive)	work on pace, interval training (intensive), big running play (intensive)	tests and starts

Typical exercises used in periods of accumulation, intensification, and transformation in track and field.

Olympic cycle

When applicable, the planning of macrocycles has to take into account their place in the plan of preparation for the Olympic Games.

One version of the four year Olympic cycle:
First and second year—macrocycles with expanded basic preparation for building a sufficiently strong foundation for high results in the Olympic year. Athletes that already participated in important competitions train lighter in the first year, with more emphasis on volume than on intensity, and compete less.
Third year—modeling and testing the training plan and the system of competitions planned for the Olympic year.
Fourth year—training according to corrected and approved plans. Mobilizing the full potential of the athlete for ultimate results.

This cycle can begin before the athlete reaches the stage of maximum results and is still at the stage of intensive training.

Athletes with relatively short training (six to eight years) increase the volume of work in the four year cycle in one of the following two ways:
1. 1st year—45% of total increase for the Olympic cycle; 2nd year—35%; 3rd year—15%, 4th year—5%;
2. 1st year—25%; 2nd year—35%; 3rd year—20%; 4th year—20%

The absolute value of workload increase for "veterans" is smaller than for those less advanced. The percentages of that increase in the four year Olympic cycle may look like this:
1st year—0%; 2nd year—50%; 3rd year—20%; 4th year— 30%.

V. DEVELOPING PHYSICAL ABILITIES

There are two sides of the motor function— skills and abilities. Teaching movements develops skills and is called "technical training". Developing physical abilities is called "conditioning". Technical training is often impossible without a sufficient level of development of the physical abilities. Psychological training is necessary for developing a high level of competitive form and even for developing physical abilities. All aspects of athletic training are closely related. Their singling out is done only for the convenience of describing the athletic training.

When developing one of our physical abilities, we influence all the other abilities. How much we influence other abilities depends on the kind of work used and the level of physical training. For people whose level of physical conditioning is low (they are in poor shape), exercises intended for the development of one specific physical ability will put considerable demand on other abilities. For example, for beginners, a 100-meter run will be a test of not only their speed, but also of their strength, endurance, and agility.

At the initial stages of training, the development of one physical ability will develop others. As the training goes on, a dissociation of physical abilities takes place and exercises, which before led to the development of all physical abilities, now will affect only some of them. Later on, even negative relations appear between some of the abilities. Thus, the tasks of simultaneously reaching the maximum indicators of strength and of endurance turn out to be mutually exclusive. However, the greatest degree of development for a specific physical ability may be achieved only if other abilities are also developed to a certain extent.

Developing strength

Strength, as a human motor ability, allows one to overcome external resistance through muscular contraction. Depending on how muscles contract and tense, muscular contractions are divided into static (isometric) contractions, where tension changes while the length of the muscle remains constant, and three kinds of dynamic contraction; isotonic contraction, where the muscle changes length while its tension remains constant; auksotonic contraction, where both the length and tension of the muscle change; and isokinetic contraction, in which the muscle contracts with a constant velocity (thanks to the servomechanisms in special types of exercise machines). The isokinetic resistance, just like the hydraulic resistance of water, severely hampers one's ability to move rapidly or train to improve quickness or agility. In reality, the most common is the auksotonic type of contraction.

Dynamic contractions can be further divided into concentric contractions, when the origin and insertion of the muscle get closer during contraction, or eccentric contractions, when the distance between origin and insertion increases during contraction, for example, when the contracting muscle is lengthened by the overwhelming load (most athletes can lower 40-50% more weight than they can lift).

Strength exercises cause both structural changes (increased number of mitochondria, capillaries, amount of muscle glycogen, size of muscle fibers, structure of connective tissue, and density of bones associated with the exercised muscles) and changes in the nervous system.

Changes, caused by strength exercises, in the neuromuscular system are specific for each type of exercise used. Only in the case of beginners can one type of exercise cause improvement in all forms of strength. A prolonged use of isometric exercises causes an increase of sarcoplasm in muscle cells, a rounding of the nuclei, a transverse expansion of motor plates, a meandering of capillaries, and a thickening of endomisium and perimisium. Dynamic exercises cause a thinning of the layers of endomisium and perimisium, an extension of motor plates along the length of muscle cells, the nuclei to become oval, and a sharp pronunciation of the transverse striations of the miofibrils.

Muscular contraction generates force ($F = ma$). An analysis of exercises used in sports and p.e. has shown that the force increases most often as a result of changing either the mass or the acceleration. In exercises where strength grows thanks to a gradual increase of the displaced mass, muscles tense harder while the speed of contraction is constant. A good example here is weightlifting. In exercises where mass is constant, better result is achieved by increasing acceleration. For example, in track and field throws, strength increase is due to an increase of the speed of contraction and in direct proportion to it, an increase of muscular tension.

Strength is divided into strength proper and speed-strength, which in turn is further divided into dynamic strength and amortizing strength. Strength proper is used in slow and static (isometric) contractions. Dynamic strength is used in fast movements, and amortizing strength is used in fast eccentric contractions such as landings. One more type of strength is explosive strength. It is the ability to apply maximum strength in the shortest time (as much force as possible in the shortest time).

The above classification of types of strength is based on following facts:

1. The strength values shown in slow movements do not differ significantly from values shown in isometric tensions.

2. The strength values shown in eccentric tensions are the greatest, sometimes twice as great as in isometric tensions.

3. In fast movements, the strength value diminishes as the speed increases.

4. There is no relation between the strength values shown in extremely fast movements (with little or no resistance) and in the maximal isometric tension (maximal isometric strength).

Explosive strength, the ability to apply a maximum force in minimum time, is essential in speed- strength sports. To evaluate the degree of development of explosive strength, the following equation is used:

$Ei = F_{max.} \div T_{max.}$

Ei— index of explosive strength

$F_{max.}$— maximal strength/force reached in a given movement.

$T_{max.}$— amount of time it took to reach maximal force in this movement.

Explosive strength is developed mainly by such explosive efforts as jumps, shot put, or jerking dumbbells or barbells, but it is easiest and safest to increase it by increasing maximal strength.

There are two more concepts in strength training: absolute muscular strength and relative muscular strength. Absolute strength is the strength that an athlete can develop in a movement regardless of his/her body weight. Relative strength equals absolute strength divided by the body weight. In sports disciplines where absolute strength is important (shot putters, heaviest weightlifters), strength training should lead to the increase of muscle mass. In disciplines where either the whole body has to be moved (gymnastics, pole vault, jumps), or its weight has to remain within certain limits (weightlifters, boxers and wrestlers of lower weight categories), the relative strength is of greatest importance. With the same level of training, heavier athletes have greater absolute strength and lower relative strength than their lighter counterparts. This lowering of relative strength is explained by the fact that the weight of the athlete's body is proportional to the body volume (cube of its linear dimensions), but the strength is proportional to the physiological cross section of the athlete's body (square of its linear dimensions). So, as the size of the athlete grows, the weight will grow faster than the muscular strength. Recently though, a different view is getting popular, namely that the increase of body weight leads to a decrease in the relative strength of chosen muscles only when this increase is not a result of strength training directed at these muscles. The following equation shows why:

$$F_r = F_{ab} \div (M_{ac} + M_i)$$

F_r— relative strength (the ratio between an athlete's absolute strength and body weight), F_{ab}— absolute strength, M_{ac}— active mass (weight) of muscles participating in the movement, M_i— idle mass (weight) of the rest of the body.

When the mass of muscles increases as a result of strength training, the absolute strength and active mass grow, but the mass of the rest of the body remains constant (the increased mass of bones and connective tissues associated with the exercised muscles is too small to count). The conclusion is that the increase of mass of the necessary for a given task muscles cannot cause decrease of the relative strength in this task. The relative strength gain of a given group of muscles is always greater than the weight gain if the weight increases as a result of the hypertrophy of that group of muscles.

To develop strength, one needs to use sufficiently great muscular tensions. The resistance needed to develop these tensions can be provided by weights, the weight of one's own body (push-ups, chin-ups), partners, springs, rubbers, or by the environment, for example, water or sand (running on loose sand), or an incline. The minimum resistance needed to provide a training effect in strength exercises is 30% of one's maximum.

While exercising one limb the other limb becomes temporarily weaker. This is because neural pathways to the working limb have preference over the non-working limb. It becomes more difficult to activate the bilateral limb's muscles, particularly fast twitch fibers.

This is the rationale for training one limb at a time. Because neural activity is concentrated in one limb during such exercise, greater strength can be generated. Researchers believe the deficit can be as much as 25% during bilateral maximal contraction.

By training the muscles simultaneously, for example doing squats or bench presses, one does not experience any deficiency.

When you train your limbs individually, you will gain more strength in each individual limb because the neural activity is concentrated on the working limb. But, when you then attempt to perform with a maximal load using these limbs together, you will experience less than the combined individual maximal output by their muscles—because you haven't trained them together (Moritani and DeVries, American Journal of Physical Medicine, 1979).

In untrained men, strength increases rapidly until 18, reaches a maximum level of strength between 20 and 30 years of age, and then their strength declines. In untrained women this rapid increase of strength ends with menarche.

Severe, short-term starvation and dehydration, like one the wrestlers, boxers, or jockeys are subjected to in their attempts at "making weight", has been shown to reduce isometric strength (Bosco, Greenleaf, Bernauer, and Card, 1974), dynamic strength, and muscle glycogen stores (Houston, Marrin, Green, and Thompson, 1981). Starvation over a 2 1/2 to 5-day period with up to 7.8% weight loss reduces the capacity to work at submaximal intensities.

M. Ikai and A. H. Steinhaus, in the article "Some Factors Modifying the Expression of Human Strength" in Journal of Applied Physiology, 1961, have shown that the forearm strength was increased 7.4% two to ten seconds after a pistol shot, 12.2% if the subject shouted when applying the force, and 26% if greater strength was suggested under hypnosis. Hypnosis that suggested weakness caused 31.7% decline in strength.

There are three basic methods of developing strength. All three rely on eventually causing maximum muscular tensions. The objectively measured strength of tensions vary in every method but the tensions are maximal in the given circumstances:

1) moving less than maximal weight until fatigue shows;

2) moving maximal weight;

3) moving less than maximal weight with maximum speed.

Each of these main methods has several variations and all rely on the auksotonic contractions (dynamic contractions) that most closely duplicate the real competitive application of strength. Other types of muscular contractions (isometric, eccentric) are also utilized in strength training, but they need a foundation that is best provided by the auksotonic exercises.

Moving less than maximal weight until fatigue shows. This is the main method of developing strength, especially in the general preparatory period. The physiological mechanisms of work with less than maximal weights differ from work with maximum and submaximum weights. As fatigue sets in, however, the picture changes. As the tension in one motor unit drops, more and more motor units join in the work and in the last movements (repetitions), the number of working motor units is maximal. This is followed by an increase of the frequency and a change in the synchronization of nervous impulses sent to the muscle. (As the fatigue sets in, more and more motor units join in the effort and also require stronger stimulation to do the work.) The movement that could be done easily at first, now is difficult. The physiological picture becomes similar to that of a maximal load (weight). The last tries are especially important here because they involve maximal tensions.

Loads in the range of 70-75% of one's maximum, allowing up to twelve repetition, increase muscle cross section, and thus, the mass of the athlete. Loads equal or higher than 80% of one's maximum, permitting maximally 4-6 repetitions, increase strength without increasing mass.

Rest intervals between sets, in strength exercises done by moving less than maximal weight until failure, are between 60-180 seconds. Number of sets— three and more (depending on the number of repetitions), number of exercises per workout— 2-4.

Loads below 50% of one's maximum develop strength-endurance, an ability that has no correlation to either maximal strength, or to general endurance as measured by the 1500 meter run (see "Strength-endurance" on page 94).

<u>Moving maximal weight.</u> This method is characteristic of training high-class athletes in speed-strength sports. Under proper conditions, it leads to a quick formation of nervous coordination that improves strength. The greater the resistance, the more muscle (motor) units that are mobilized. It should not be the only method of developing strength, however, because strength growth is not only due to coordination, and also because maximum weights are not suitable for everyone.

In this method of training, "maximal weight" means the greatest weight that can be moved without a strong effort of will, which is 95-100% of one's maximum training weight. Special psychological preparation can increase that weight to a truly maximal value. Training with the absolute maximal weights is ineffective. It brings about emotional fatigue. This is why weights that can be moved one to two or three times, without a maximal mobilization of will, are used in training. Greater weights are used rarely, once every week, or once every two weeks.

The rest intervals between sets of 2-3 repetitions are between 3-5 minutes and can be filled with relaxed stretches and movements that loosen up the muscles (shaking). The heavier the athlete, the longer the rest. Each exercise is done in six sets, and usually six exercises or more (depending on the athlete's form and need of the sport) are done in a workout. One method, popular in the Soviet Union, is that of arranging the loads in sets, alternating each set of 2-3 reps with an assigned weight, with one set of 1-2 repetitions of weight reduced by 5-10%. In a period when athletes are especially focusing on strength (or when athletes are especially responsive to strength training), strength workouts with such weights are done 3-4 times a week, every other day and occasionally, two days in a row. Such strength exercises can be done daily if the volume of strength exercises per workout is low and the exercises have local character. Strength exercises with maximal resistance, involving the majority of muscle groups, are done 1-2 times a week— even if the volume of work per workout is low, and even in case of weightlifters. Using maximal weights in exercises involving most of the major groups of muscles requires great mental mobilization and causes emotional fatigue. If these exercises are done more often than once or twice a week, coordination can be impaired as a result of repeating the exercises without full mental mobilization. Defensive inhibition can develop as well.

The greatest strength improvements are brought about by doing exercises with gradually increasing weights, up to 80-100% of one's maximum, at either a slow, moderate, or fast pace. Loads, in percentage of maximum, vary depending on the pace of movements. Advanced athletes do at slow pace— 60-100% of maximal weight, at moderate— 60-90% of maximal weight, and at fast— 60-80% of maximal weight. Less advanced athletes may reduce the amount of weight in each set and increase the number of repetitions. Do repetitions slowly. Rest between sets of one exercise, walking or performing very light exercises, for 1.5 to 4 minutes depending on speed of recovery of the muscles and the time it takes to regain the mental ability needed to mobilize for effort. Longer rest periods (near 4 min.) are needed for beginning athletes and in the case of maximal and submaximal weights.

Slow pace: 3 sets of 3 reps with 60% of max.
1 set of 3 reps with 80% of max.
1 set of 2 reps with 90% of max.
1 set of 2 reps with 95% of max.
2 sets of 1 rep with 100% of max.
2 sets of 2 reps with 90% of max.

Moderate pace: 3 sets of 3 reps with 60% of max.
1 set of 3 reps with 70% of max.
1 set of 3 reps with 80% of max.
2 sets of 2 reps with 85% of max.
2 sets of 2 reps with 90% of max.
1 set of 3 reps with 70% of max.

Fast pace: 3 sets of 3 reps with 60% of max.
1 set of 3 reps with 70% of max.
1 set of 3 reps with 75% of max.
2 sets of 2 reps with 80% of max.
2 sets of 3 reps with 75% of max.
1 set of 2 reps with 70% of max.

Usually 6-8 exercises, such as the various forms of jerk and clean, press, snatch, and squat, are done in this method.

According to the article "Bulgarian Leg Training Secrets", the Bulgarian weightlifters use pulse rate to let them know if the total load in a set is optimal and when to begin a new set of lifts. Moderate to heavy sets should increase the pulse rate to 162-180 beats per minute, and the rest should end after the pulse drops to 102-108 beats per minute.

Moving less than maximal weight with maximum speed. This method is used mainly with children. Either light weights or the resistance of one's body are used. A great plus of this method is that dynamic strength exercises can include the technical exercises of one's sport.

Exercises against elastic resistance. The resistance provided by springs and rubber cords is none or very small at the beginning of each movement and increases at the end of each movement. To achieve approximately even resistance throughout the whole movement, use a hard rubber cord or long spring. If the effort has to be concentrated at the end of the movement, use a short but soft rubber cord. The amount of resistance provided by springs or rubber cords can be estimated by attaching a dynamometer to them and noting the reading at the end of movement.

Isometric exercises are not recommended for athletes less than 16 years old (who are not past puberty). Soviet researchers recommend doing up to six various isometric exercises, each in 1-3 sets of several tensions, with 1-3 minutes of rest after 2-3 sets of each exercise. This is to be done four times a week, ten to fifteen minutes per day, using tensions lasting five to six seconds. The amount of tension should increase gradually and reach a maximum by the third and fourth second. If you are just beginning the isometric training, you should start with mild tensions, lasting two to three seconds. Increase the time and the intensity of tension as you progress. Athletes that are currently well prepared by strength training, may do 2-3 sets of each exercise, each set followed by about 5 seconds of rest. The attempt to develop strength by **isometric exercises only** may lead to a stagnation of strength in only six to eight weeks. Changing the positions in which muscles are tensed, every 4-6 weeks, may prevent that stagnation.

Usually the isometrics are done after all the dynamic exercises because of their adverse effect on coordination and their intensity, which is lower than that of the dynamic exercises that precede them. In rest periods between isometrics, breathing exercises, shaking muscles, and relaxed stretches are recommended. To control the amount of tension, athletes use special training stands with dynamometers or weights. In isometric exercises athlete can display up to 115% of maximal strength in dynamic (concentric) exercises.

The total volume of isometric exercises should not exceed 10% of the total volume of strength exercises.

The combination of isometric and dynamic tensions in one exercise is used to develop greater strength at the so called sticking points of all kinds of lifts. In such exercises, weight is lifted with intermediate stops, lasting 1-3 seconds, which force greater tension at moments of resuming the movement rather than lifting the weight continuously. The weights used in one exercise may be arranged as follows:

3 sets of 2 reps with 40% of max.
1 set of 2 reps with 50% of max.
1 set of 2 reps with 60% of max.
1 set of 2 reps with 70-80% of max.
1 set of 2 reps with 60% of max.

Rest between sets 2-5 minutes. 6-10 of such exercises can be done in a workout.

W. Shröder, states that using static exercises causes a 15.1% increase of static strength, and an 11.5% increase of dynamic strength. Using dynamic exercises caused an 18.1% increase of dynamic strength, but only a 9.2% increase of static strength.

Strength exercises in developing speed.

Speed depends on strength. In strength exercises designed to develop the speed of movements, the amount of resistance should be such as to let the athlete move with the speed similar to the speed in competitive actions. The greater the amount of resistance an athlete overcomes in competitive actions, the greater the resistance used in speed exercises, for example, weightlifters use weights of 70-80% of their maximum.

Myedvyedyev describes a study of three groups of weightlifters. The first group did 70% pure strength exercises and 30% speed-strength exercises; the second group did 60% pure strength and 40% speed-strength; the third group did 40% pure strength and 60% speed-strength. In the first month, weights equal to 70-80% of maximal were used, in the second month, 80- 90%, and at the end of the third month 90-100%. The conclusions were that:

1) Training directed at developing pure strength (70% of exercises) improves results in the clean and jerk, and training directed at developing speed-strength (pure strength— 40% of exercises) improves results in the snatch.

2) To improve the combined results in both lifts, workouts directed at developing pure strength, speed- strength, and speed must be used in training. Good results were also achieved by doing only pure strength training.

Strength exercises in developing jumping ability.

Jumping ability is a form of strength and depends on such factors as: static strength, explosive strength, mobility of the nervous system, body proportions, and takeoff position. Weightlifters, shot-putters, discus throwers, and jumpers have the greatest jumping ability. The higher the athletic class in these sports, the greater the jumping ability.

The height of a jump depends on the vertical speed of the center of gravity at the takeoff. To increase it, one can either make muscles stronger or, increase the distance over which the center of gravity travels, so there is more time for acceleration. Unfortunately, the human anatomy limits the effectiveness of this second method, because lowering the center of gravity requires bending the knees, and bending them below 140 degrees reduces the efficiency of leg muscles.

Jumps preceded by a short step or jump, landing and jumping again increase the height of a jump from standing still, but not the other way around.

Special strength exercises that improve jumping ability (various jumps) must be done fast, and with great amplitude of movements, in sets of 10-20 if their intensity (relative height) is low, in sets of 5 if intensity is moderate, and single jumps if intensity is maximal. Rest between sets is 3-5 minutes.

If the athlete has to jump several times, like for example, when blocking in volleyball or under the basket in basketball, he/she needs to develop a special form of endurance for this. It is developed by jumping several times in a row to a ball suspended 5-10 centimeters lower than the best result of that athlete's jump test for height (the distance between the highest reach while standing and at the highest point of the jump). The number of repetitions and sets depends on the level of training. After four weeks, the height of the ball is increased.

In a macrocycle, jumping exercises must be preceded by strength exercises that increase the size of muscles (general preparatory period), strength exercises with great loads and speed exercises (special preparatory period), and explosive strength and plyometric exercises (special preparatory period and first half of the competitive period). To maintain a high level of jumping ability in the competitive period, at least one workout per microcycle has to include jumps.

To improve jumping ability and/or explosiveness or speed in movements against great resistance, strength exercises are used in which one applies a sudden contraction at the moment when muscles amortize falling weight, for example, jumping down off the elevation and rebounding at the instant of touching the ground or letting the weight attached to a pulley fall down and then suddenly lifting it up. Plyometric exercises are done in the special preparatory stage of the preparatory period because they must be preceded by normal, moderately dynamic, general, and special strength exercises for the appropriate muscle groups. These so called plyometric exercises are done once or twice in a week, 3-4 sets per workout, 5-8 repetitions per set. As a rule of thumb, the resistance in a plyometric exercise should not exceed 40% of the maximal resistance in normal strength exercise of similar spatial structure, for example, before attempting jumps down (depth jumps) and rebounds, one should be able to squat with an additional load of 150-200% of body weight. Depending on the intensity, plyometrics should be discontinued one to two weeks before a major competition. The more intensive the exercises, the longer the period of refraining from them.

Strength-endurance.

The greater the resistance that the athlete has to overcome, the more his/her strength- endurance depends on pure strength. Increasing pure strength in such case increases strength-endurance. Increasing the number of repetitions, for example to 15, and/or reducing the amount of rest between sets, are other ways of increasing strength-endurance in speed- strength sports.

In endurance sports, where the amount of resistance is small, but the duration of work is great, either strength exercises, lasting as long as the competitive action, with small resistance that does not distort the technique, are done, or circuit training with resistance between 20 and 40% of the maximum in each exercise is done up to 30 times. A whole circuit may consist of 8-10 exercises.

Strength training vs. technical training.

Technique or coordination are not adversely affected by the development of strength. Properly chosen, for each stage of training and period of the macrocycle, strength exercises improve skills. If strength training is done using only simple, bodybuilding-type of strength exercises, that have nothing to do with the internal and external structure of movement in the techniques, then the special coordination and learning of techniques is going to be impaired. To assist in improving the technical skills of an athlete, lots of various strength exercises, among them those of spatial and temporal structure similar to the techniques of the sport, ought to be used.

Preparation for strength training.

For children, as well as for adults, it is necessary to first have any posture defects corrected before starting a strengthening program. If they are not corrected, the posture defects will be preserved or even aggravated by strength exercises. Defects of posture are accompanied or caused by certain groups of muscles being too short or tight, which causes their attachments to get too close, and by some other groups of muscles being stretched too much, which allows their attachments to get too far from each other. For muscles that are too short, exercises that start from a fully stretched position and end in a less than full contraction should be done. For muscles that are too long, exercises should start from shortened position and end in full contraction. It is particularly difficult to correct posture defects in children that are not working out every day under professional supervision. The corrective exercises are so boring for them that they do not do them on their own. To make sure that the exercises are done, a sport, or a game interesting for a given pupil, that forces the maintenance of correct posture, is recommended. For example, archery may be used in the case of hyperkifosis.

The strength of contraction depends on nervous activation, energy supplies in the muscle, cross section of the muscle, and on its ability to recover after work. All these factors are interdependent, but they do not develop at the same pace in the course of strength training. This is why it is not such a good idea to jump in and use the maximal loads at any given stage of training.

In strength exercises of the eccentric, explosive, and isometric type, as well as in normal, concentric exercises done with near maximum loads, muscle fibers contract and the connective tissue attached to them is stretched. When the connective tissue of a muscle is stretched with too much force, it can become damaged. Depending on the amount of stress and also on the strength of the connective tissue in a given muscle, this damage can, at a microscopic level, announce itself as muscle soreness or it can amount to a complete muscle tear (muscle strain). To make this connective tissue stronger you should do strength (strength-endurance) exercises with light resistance and a high number of repetitions. You should do at least two sets, with a minimum of 30 repetitions per set, of exercises for the muscles that are most likely to be overstressed in your sport. Good results are also brought about by doing long single sets of 100 to 200 repetitions. In both cases the weight has to make the last few repetitions "burn".

The famous Soviet weightlifter Vasily Alexeyev[62] used to warm up for his workout by throwing a 100 kilogram barbell over his head one hundred times. Then, after practicing the snatch for two and a half hours, he spent one hour in a swimming pool lifting his legs one at a time, hundreds of times— to strengthen his abdomen, and then leaped nearly one thousand times.

You should do high repetitions exercises at the end of your strength workouts, after the regular heavy weights/low repetitions exercises, and before any isometric exercises. After these high repetitions exercises, you should do relaxed stretches for the same muscles.

Those of you who plan their training using yearly or half yearly cycles (macrocycles), culminating in a major competition or a string of competitions, should do low weights/high repetitions strength (strength-endurance) exercises throughout the entire year. The majority of these exercises should be done in the first two-three months of the cycle. The purpose of this is to prepare the structure of the muscles and bones for the heavy loads that are associated with specific strength and technical training. Later, without being totally discarded, these exercises should occupy less time in your workout. It is dangerous to stop doing high repetitions strength exercises for more than a month while competing, or while doing intensive technical training for sports requiring explosive power. Your power grows because of improved coordination and increased muscle size; the results of the technical and heavy weights/low repetitions strength training. Without these high repetitions, the strength of the connective tissue in your muscles will fall behind and will increase your potential for injury.

When planning your strength (weightlifting) workouts, first establish the strength of all your major muscle groups. These are: flexors, extensors, adductors, abductors, and rotators of all the major body parts. To establish strength of given muscle group, simply find the maximal weight that it can lift or otherwise move. When beginning your strength training in a macrocycle, first develop the muscles that are going to provide a foundation (stabilizers) for the muscles that are the prime movers in your sports discipline. If you run (sprint) or kick, then you must strengthen your lower back first, because it stabilizes the vertebra to which the "runners muscles" (iliopsoas) attach. Actually though, the lower back is stressed in most sports.

In endurance sports, athletes have enough strength when the typical load that must be moved (typical strength of contraction) is less than 40% of the athletes maximum strength (maximum muscle contraction). In speed-strength sports, the typical load (typical strength of contraction) should be less than 20% of the athlete's maximum strength (maximum muscle contraction). For instance, if a bicycle road racer discovers that the typical contraction of his/her hamstring muscles when cycling is 40 lb., his/her hamstring strength should be at least 100 lb. For a sprinter with a typical hamstring contraction of 40 lb., hamstring strength should be at least 200 lb.

A study done by L. N. Burkett, shows that a great difference of strength between opposing muscle groups, as well as a strength imbalance of ten per cent between these same muscle groups (on both sides of the body), are the main causes of injuries.

On the basis of his research, D. M. Rudy[57] concluded that differences of elasticity, isotonic strength, and isometric strength between muscles of the dominant and non-dominant leg do not correlate with injuries. The lower muscle endurance of the non-dominant leg, however, is correlated with injuries.

Improving the strength and endurance of weaker muscles is the best method for injury prevention.

Weight training for young athletes.

The bones and the ligaments of children can be overstressed and damaged by weights that are too great. To find out what maximal weights are safe for children, Sulmitsev[37] did a study in which the amount of the decrease of arch of the foot was measured during lifting weights. The conclusion of this study was:

—Eleven and twelve year-olds can safely use weights of up to 30% of their body weight.

—Thirteen and fourteen year-olds can use weights up to 50% of their body weight.

—Fifteen and sixteen year-olds can use weights up to 100% of their body weight.

Strength exercises with maximal weights and of great intensity should not be done before the process of growth of long bones is completed, which happens around age of 17 years.

Use of steroids in strength training.
Steroids are an illegal means of increasing strength, mass, and of speeding up the recovery process. They are made illegal by the authorities that feel they cannot let adult individuals take a chance at getting cancer of the liver, cancer of testicles, and other ailments—as if someone

else, other than the athlete, was responsible for the medical bills or insurance premiums. To avoid detection and the very dangerous side effects, the use of steroids must be strictly supervised by competent, experienced sports medicine specialists (preferably from East Germany or USSR). In properly run training programs the steroids are introduced after many years of training, only when the athlete's technique is impeccable and when the normal, even most scientific, training methods cannot sufficiently increase the strength of the athlete to give him/her enough edge over the competition (Steroids are introduced when all other methods of improving performance are exhausted in the course of many years of training). The structural strength of muscles, tendons, ligaments, and bones must be sufficient to withstand the increased force of contraction of muscles treated with steroids.

General strength training.

General strength exercises developing basic kinds of strength (dynamic, static, strength-endurance) in all muscle groups have the task of accumulating morphological changes that result in a greater structural strength of all muscles, tendons, ligaments, and bones, as well as to provide a foundation for special strength training. These exercises have to prevent and correct strength imbalances between muscle groups that can result from special strength training, and provide structural strength for those elements of the motor apparatus that are going to be stressed by special exercises so that they do not get damaged by the most intensive special and competitive exercises. General strength exercises can involve all muscle groups at once or can be local.

Special strength training.

Special strength training has to develop the exact kind of strength of the muscle groups that determines technical proficiency in a given sport. Special strength exercises reproduce the dynamic characteristics of the sports technique and, to various degree, the spatial characteristics of it, but with preferably greater resistance. It can be done by starting the movement from an easier position or performing only a part of technique, for example, in weightlifting, jerking the barbell up from a rack. The amount of resistance in special exercises has to be such as to insure an accurate duplication of the internal structure of the technique (intermuscular and intramuscular coordination). If the resistance is too great, the movement may resemble the external spatial structure of the technique, but it will require different coordination than the one that is best in the technique, for example, the internal structure of movements in throwing a 1.5 kg ball using technique of javelin without the pre-run, is the same as in throwing a 0.8 kg javelin. In throwing a 4 kg ball in the same fashion, the external structure resembles the javelin throw, but the internal structure registered by EMG (Electromyograph) is different. The throw with a 1.5 kg ball can be used as a special strength exercise, but the throw of a heavier, up to 4 kg (depending on athletic class), ball may be used only as a directed strength exercise. In high jumping, loads (vests with weights) amounting to no more than 5% of the body weight are used in training forms of competitive exercises. If the time, rhythm, or spatial form of technique changes with a given amount of resistance, then the resistance is too great.

Strength exercises in a workout.

It is best to do strength exercises when the nervous system is not tired. The formation and perfection of relations, within neuromuscular system, that ensure build-up of strength is improved. If strength exercises are done when one is still fatigued from previous work, the excitation of the central nervous system is lower. The conditional reflex activity is less effective and strength builds up more slowly.

Strength exercises are most effective if they are done at the beginning of the main part of the workout. Since strength exercises cause fatigue, it is not always possible to place them there. In workouts that have to include work on speed, technique, or tactics, one has to move strength exercises to the end of the main part.

Generally, after the warm-up all the exercises are arranged in the order of the descending intensity of effort. Strength exercises should not be grouped primarily by the body part or the structure (form) of exercise, but by their intensity, i.e., dynamics. The more dynamic or more intensive exercises are to be done first. Exercises that have a local effect on isolated muscle groups and slow strength-endurance exercises are done at the end of the workout.

The optimal number of strength exercises per workout is 4-6. A higher number of exercises (up to 8) is done when one needs to break the monotony of the training and it requires a reduction of the number of sets and repetitions.

Strength exercises in a microcycle.

Strength exercises have to be distributed with due regard for the interaction of loads. At the basis of an increase in training lies the adaptation of the body to training loads. Adaptation is quicker if the load remains standard for some time. Because of this, one should choose a certain program of strength exercises and repeat them for a fairly long period, changing only the weight and the number of repetitions. However, the use of the same program will make it habitual and result in few adapting changes (shifts). Essential changes in strength can be achieved only if the volume of work is increased. This is not always possible or desirable. Also, monotonous execution of the same exercises is psychologically (mentally) wearing. Therefore, it is recommended that the same program of exercises be used in several related sessions, and then the program should be changed. How often this change should be made depends on several factors, such as: achieved results, period of the macrocycle, and biological development. The program of exercises should not be changed if it is still effective. It should be changed only when there is a need for a new stimuli in strength training. Usually it is done once every two to six weeks.

In the microcycle, strength exercises are done on different days of the cycle depending on the sports discipline, place of the microcycle in a six monthly or a yearly training cycle, and the stage of development of the athletes. For instance, in speed-strength sports, a strength workout is done on the first day of the cycle, right after the day of rest. In sports, or at stages of training, where techniques are the main concern, the strength workout is done after the technical workout. Usually, recovery after an intensive strength workout takes 48 hours.

The frequency of strength workouts in a week depends on a number of factors, mostly on the athletes class and stage of preparedness (training). Workout sessions three times a week are most effective for beginners. One, two, or five sessions a week are less effective (for the beginners). Top-class athletes may do more workouts. These recommendations concern strength exercises for major groups of muscles. These groups of muscles restore their work capacity relatively slowly. Small groups of muscles restore this capacity more quickly, therefore, localized strength exercises can be done more frequently.

Strength exercises in a macrocycle.

In the first stage (general preparatory stage) of the preparatory period, the task of strength training is to regain and surpass the level of strength from the past season (macrocycle). In the second stage (special preparatory stage), the task is to increase the level of chosen types of strength. In the competitive period, the task is to maintain the level of strength achieved in the preparatory period. The speed at which this strength is lost, as a result of ceasing the strength training, depends on the length of time it took to build this strength. Research done by Handelsman and Smirnov has shown that after ceasing the strength training for 15-30 days, strength went down to 79-92% of the values shown while in training. Strength built quickly is lost quickly. If the preparatory period is long and the competitive period is short, the level of strength will not be greatly lowered in this competitive period. But if the competitive period lasts a couple of months, the lack of strength exercises in that time can lead to a great loss of strength and worse sports results. To avoid this, strength exercises should be done, although in smaller quantity, in the competitive period. Also in the transitory period, some strength exercises need to be done to prevent too great a loss of strength.

Strength training in a macrocycle on example of weightlifters:

1) General preparatory period.

This period has high volume of work, with 55%-85% of current maximal weight in snatch or in clean and jerk with a high number (10-12) of sets per exercise and a high, as for weightlifting, number of repetitions (6) per set. In this period, weightlifters do many exercises developing strength and strength-endurance such as high snatch, clean from the ground and from support at knee height, and dead lifts. Squats in racks, pull for snatch and clean, and jerk from support at chest level are done with loads of 100%-130% of maximal competitive weight.

Example of sets and repetitions of a snatch from knee level to a squat:

3 sets of 6 repetitions at 55% of current maximal weight in snatch
2 sets of 6 repetitions at 60% of current maximal weight in snatch
2 sets of 4 repetitions at 70% of current maximal weight in snatch
2 sets of 3 repetitions at 75% of current maximal weight in snatch
2 sets of 3 repetitions at 80% of current maximal weight in snatch
1 set of 2 repetitions at 85% of current maximal weight in snatch

2) Special preparatory period.

The quantity of work gives way to quality, weightlifters perform lots of exercises with the full technique of snatch and clean and jerk. Other exercises used in this period; clean to squat position, squats, squats with barbell held across chest, and jerk from support at chest level.

This period uses a lower number of sets (8-10), with the number of repetitions to 3 per set, with 65-95% of current maximal weight in snatch or in clean and jerk. In the last two or three weeks of pre-start preparation, weightlifters use 100% of current maximal weight in snatch or in clean and jerk and sets of 1 repetition.

Example of sets and repetitions of a snatch from knee level to a squat:

3 sets of 3 repetitions at 65% of current maximal weight in snatch
2 sets of 3 repetitions at 70% of current maximal weight in snatch
2 sets of 2 repetitions at 80% of current maximal weight in snatch
1 set of 2 repetitions at 90% of current maximal weight in snatch
1 set of 1 repetition at 95% of current maximal weight in snatch

3) Competitive period.

In this period, weightlifters do mostly full techniques of snatch and clean and jerk. The number of sets is reduced to 6-8, with 3 repetitions per set with 70%-75% of current maximal weight in snatch or in clean and jerk, 2 repetitions per set of 80-85%, 1 repetition per set of 90%-100% of current maximal weight in snatch or in clean and jerk.

Example of sets and repetitions of a technical snatch to a squat:

2 sets of 3 repetitions at 70% of current maximal weight in snatch
2 sets of 3 repetitions at 75% of current maximal weight in snatch
1 set of 2 repetitions at 80% of current maximal weight in snatch
1 set of 2 repetitions at 85% of current maximal weight in snatch
1 set of 2 repetitions at 90% of current maximal weight in snatch
1 set of 1 repetition at 95-100% of current maximal weight in snatch

T. Hettinger and E. A. Mueller, in experiments on 21 subjects doing isometric training, discovered a seasonal variation in strength gains. The gain observed in September and October was tenfold higher than that observed in January and February. The researchers attributed this to the availability of fresh fruits and vegetables.

When planning the goals in strength development, any present shortcomings (strength imbalance, asymmetry, abnormal weakness) have to be considered first, followed by a consideration of the requirements of the technique at a given competitive level.

Developing speed

Speed is the ability to do a movement in the shortest time. One's total speed depends on its three components:
1) The ability to react quickly with a movement, for example, to the start signal.
2) The ability to do a single quick movement.
3) The ability to do movements with great frequency.

Various sports need various types or forms of speed. Sports can be divided into five groups, depending on the most typical form of speed that is required in a given sport.

1) Sports demanding maximal manifestations of all three components of speed in nonstandard situations (individual contact sports, games);

2) Sports demanding maximal manifestations of all three components of speed in standard situations (sprints);

3) Sports demanding maximal manifestations of speed of movement against external resistance in standard situations (weightlifting, track and field throws and jumps);

4) Sports demanding maximal manifestations of speed and frequency of movements with difficult coordination in standard situations (gymnastics, diving, figure skating);

5) Sports demanding maintaining a high frequency of movement over a long period of time (long-distance running), in which speed is based on endurance.

The maximum speed, which a person can show, depends on one's reaction time, dynamic strength, flexibility, technique, and mainly in sports of the fifth group— endurance. The best age for displaying a maximum level of speed is between 25-26 years. With rational training it can be prolonged past 30. In such cases, the speed exercises have to be done more frequently. Speed is movement specific. The same individual may be fast in some movements and slow in others. There is no correlation between speed of movement in movements that have different coordination. In athletes, a transfer of speed training occurs only in movements that have similar coordination. People in poor shape experience a transfer of speed in all exercises. Maximal frequency of movements depends on the efficiency of the central nervous system in regulating the speed of stimulating and inhibiting muscle groups performing the movements.

Principles of speed exercises.

Speed exercises must meet three main conditions:

1) The technique of the exercise, in its perfect form, must allow for maximal speed (this is why most gymnastic exercises or walking will not do).

2) The exercise (technique) must be sufficiently mastered so the athlete does not have to pay attention to the form of movement. The athletes effort and will-power should be directed at achieving maximum speed only.

3) The duration of exercise must be such that the speed does not drop at the end due to fatigue.

4) Initially, in developing speed, exercises are done slowly then quickly. Speed is developed first in simple, then in complex movements.

5) Every exercise is repeated four to six times. The best time in a workout is the beginning of the main part (right after the warm-up), so the athlete is not tired.

6) Rest breaks are to be filled with relaxed, loose movements, for example, jogging, loose leg and arm swings, walking.

7) The exercises have to be changed before the athlete gets bored with them.

Repetitive training is the main means of developing speed. Speed exercises require maximum power and last from 6 seconds to 22 seconds for high-class athletes. The duration of rest breaks is determined by changes in the excitability of the central nervous system and the restoration of vegetative functions (elimination of oxygen shortage/debt) so breathing is normal again. The excitation of the central nervous system is heightened immediately after the speed exercise and then gradually lowers. The rest breaks should not be so long as to let this excitation lower too much. The next repetition of the exercise should coincide with the heightened excitation of the central nervous system and thus, help achieve maximum speed. However, speed exercises result in oxygen debt. To eliminate it, sometimes even ten minutes of rest is needed. The total restoration of all the physiological indicators (carbonic acid content in the blood, lung ventilation, etc.) may take even more time. Therefore, training with short rest breaks leads to fatigue and a quick drop in speed.

Rest breaks must be short enough so as not to let excitation of the central nervous system drop too much, yet long enough for the vegetative system to get sufficient rest. It is possible to find such an optimal rest period because the restoration of work capacity is not uniform. In the first third of the rest period, about 65% of the whole restoration of work capacity takes place. In the second third, 30%, and in the third part only 5%. If restoration after, for example a 200-meter run, takes 12 minutes, eight minutes is enough to restore work capacity to about 95%. This lets the next attempt be made with almost no drop in speed.

The performance of speed exercises, and particularly those that test the reaction time, depends on the sex (females have longer reaction time), height of the individual (taller person—longer reaction time), position of the body, and body temperature. When the body temperature is high, the perception of time slows down and reaction time gets shorter. When the weight of the body is equally distributed between both feet and the position is comfortable, the reaction time gets shorter. Being set "on signal", rather than thinking about the technique, speeds up reaction. Reaction time, precision, and speed of movements are affected by emotional states. A relaxed and "quietly happy" attitude is associated with outstanding performances. In individual contact sports, or in situations that resemble them, the calm and detached (but not passive!) attitude lets you perceive the flaws of the opponent and realize your superiority (thus boosting your confidence). You then pick a target (you will look at the target and as if get to know it), get curious as to how it will be altered by your action, and then, when you decide that you would really like to see it done, you will do it. The time will slow down, the opponent will move very slow. You will feel the details of your movement, and the impact you make, happening in slow motion. The whole sequence, from getting to know the opponent, to the completion of the attack, may fit within a couple of seconds or, even as little as it takes for someone to grip you. If you decide that you are satisfied with the result, the time will return to normal. In optimal mental and physical states, more details of the actions (opponents and ours) are perceived (it seems that the time has slowed down) than in the less favorable circumstances.

The speed barrier and ways of overcoming it.

Numerous repetitions of speed exercises form a dynamic stereotype in the central nervous system. The stereotype includes space, time, and frequency characteristics of the movement. This means that one learns to move at a certain speed, and not any faster, and that the speed barrier is formed.

Here lies the contradiction of developing speed. On the one hand, to increase speed, the movement must be repeated many times, but on the other hand, the more repetitions, the stronger the speed barrier grows. Increasing the amount of work does not help; on the contrary, it consolidates the speed barrier.

There are two ways of overcoming the speed barrier. One is to encourage the athlete to exceed his/her highest speed result, remember this new sensation, and then try to repeat this sensation in following workouts. For this purpose, one runs down an inclined track (2-3 degrees), runs following the leader, runs with accelerations, throws lighter discuses, throws lighter hammers or shots in turn with ordinary ones, throws hammers with shorter wire, rows with shorter oars, etc. The speed under these lightened conditions must be such that the athlete is likely to show it under normal conditions. The speed of running down the track inclined at 2-3 degrees may be 17% greater than while running in normal conditions on the flat track. When running on the flat/horizontal track starting from the descending track, the speed can be 13% greater than normal.

The other way of breaking the speed barrier is based on the fact that the speed of forgetting characteristics of the dynamic stereotype is different for each characteristic. Spatial characteristics (form of movement) are remembered longer than temporal characteristics (speed and timing of movements). If the exercises are not performed for a certain time, memory of the time links (characteristic for the speed barrier) may disappear. The form of movement will be still intact. If in this period of rest from speed exercises, the athlete improves strength, flexibility, and the form of movement using other exercises, the speed may increase.

Methods of developing speed.

There are two main methods of improving speed:

a) The integral (synthetic) development of speed in a particular movement, for example, using feedback devices in boxing and track and field.

b) The selective (analytic) improvement of the factors determining maximum speed of movements, for example, reducing reaction time, increasing flexibility, perfecting technique, or improving strength.

Usually these two methods are used together and other methods are based on these two.

1) The competitive method utilizes frequent starts in competitions to improve speed and it is based on two facts;

a) that the duration of exercises during competition is brief so it does not lead to a lowering of speed because of fatigue,

b) that it is easier to mobilize for displaying maximal speed in competition, than it is in a workout.

2) The game method utilizes various ball games and other games to improve speed in conditions of greater emotional mobilization than in strictly regulated exercises. Because the conditions of the game are constantly changing, the "speed barrier" is not easily formed.

3) The strictly regulated exercise method consists of repeating standard exercises that can belong to either the analytic or the synthetic method of developing speed. In exercises belonging to either one of these two methods, the speed of movement can be improved by reducing the external resistance, or helping the athlete by pulling in running or suspending the body above the treadmill, swimming with the current, reducing air resistance by special shields in cycling, and running or cycling down the slope.

Preceding an exercise with the same or similar exercise performed with additional resistance, may temporarily increase the speed in the normal form (without extra resistance) of the exercise because the increased excitation of the nervous centers, caused by movement with extra resistance, is still present when the movement is done without extra resistance. This effect depends on the amount of extra resistance (not too much and not too little), number of repetitions, and the order of alternating heavy and light repetitions. For example, shot putters use heavier and conventional shots, as well as lighter shots (the difference between conventional and other shots must be, in each case, greater than 250 grams). For every one attempt with heavy shot they put two or three conventional shots. For each attempt with a lighter shot, one attempt with a conventional shot is made. Doing conventional and both heavy and light forms of the exercise within the same workout, and particularly in sequences heavy— conventional— light, may be less effective than using only one variation (heavy— conventional or conventional— light).

In cyclic sports, light and sound pacers are used to improve the frequency of movements, for example light bulbs installed alongside a track or a swimming pool are turned on in sequence and at set time intervals. Special electronic devices registering the speed of movements and converting the data into sound signals are used to inform the athlete (runner, shot-putter) about the speed of his/her movements, and to mobilize for greater effort in both cyclic and acyclic sports.

Adding extra movements to the technique may increase the speed of its main phases, for example adding an extra turn in the hammer throw, or requiring the gymnast to touch an object suspended above the apparatus to improve speed of the push off.

Reducing the distance of exercises is used in cyclic sports to improve the speed of movements. Reducing either time or space, or both of these parameters of exercise, in acyclic sports (games, individual contact sports) improves the speed of movements and the reaction time.

Strength exercises in speed training.

Increasing maximal strength improves the speed of movements with great resistance and does not affect the speed of movements with light resistance. To be effective, strength exercises must have the amplitude, external structure (spatial and temporal form), and internal structure similar to the perfected technique. Strength exercises designed to improve speed must be fast or explosive, depending on the desired results in perfected techniques.

Developing speed of reaction.

Reaction time is less specific than speed of movement so it can be developed by exercises that do not resemble actual sports actions. If the athlete has to react by performing any technique of the sport, that technique should be automatic so the athlete can pay full attention to stimuli without having to think about the technique. To develop the speed of simple reactions to one type of stimuli, the following methods are used:

1) The method of repetitive reacting: Athletes react to a sudden, repetitively, but not rhythmically, occurring stimuli (start on a signal, defend against a known type of punch, change direction of movement), or react on only one type of signal from several types of signals. This method brings improvements quickly with beginners. After prolonged use, the speed of reaction stabilizes and is difficult to improve.

2) The analytic method. In this method, the speed of reaction is trained in lightened conditions and the speed of the first movements of the exercise is practiced separately. For example, sprinters, on a signal, do starts from a high position and separately, without the signal, do complete starts from the normal low position.

3) The sensory method: It is based on the close relation between the speed of reaction and the ability to differentiate short periods of time (0.1−0.01 second). This method develops the ability to sense even the shortest periods of time, which in turn improves the speed of reaction. Training under this method is divided into three stages:

First stage—on a signal, an athlete performs a movement with maximal speed. After each trial, he/she is informed about the time of performance.

Second stage—task is performed with the maximal speed. The athlete must determine the amount of time it took. This estimate is compared with the actual time. Constantly comparing the subjective estimates with the actual, precisely measured time, improves the accuracy of sense of time.

Third stage—athlete performs the task with various, assigned speeds. This further perfects the sense of time and teaches control of the speed of reaction. As a result of many years of training, the reaction time may be reduced by 0.1-0.15 second. Humans react slower to visual signals than to sound signals.

Signal	Time of simple reaction
Visual	150-200 milliseconds (100 milliseconds for high class athletes)
Auditory	120-160 milliseconds (50-100 milliseconds for high class athletes)
Tactile	110-160 milliseconds

In complex reactions, such as the reaction to a moving object or a reaction with choice, the training is more complex. In reacting to a moving object, the ability to see the fast moving object clearly, is essential. This ability can be trained using exercises that demand reaction to moving objects. Difficulty increases with greater speed and shorter distance from the object. Initially, some workouts have to be dedicated to developing precision of the reaction and not its speed. Typical exercises in this method are, ball games with tennis balls and ball games on smaller than regular size areas. Learning to keep the object in the field of vision constantly, cuts down on that part of the reaction time that is used for finding it and helps to develop anticipation.

Developing the speed of reaction in situations where from many possible reactions, only one, that suits the situation best, has to be chosen, is based on a gradual increase of the number of variables. For example, first a response to one type of attack is learned, then a response to two types of attack, and so on. The athlete has to learn to react to preparation for the action, not only to the final moves. For this purpose, in workouts, a reaction to first exaggerated, and then gradually more natural, movements is taught. In this way the athlete learns, more or less consciously, what are the advance, sometimes very subtle, signals for various types of attack.

Reaction time depends on the age (children and elderly have the longest reaction time, individuals between 30-50 years old have the shortest reaction time), height (short people have a shorter reaction time than tall people), sex (men have a shorter reaction time than women). Fatigue, hunger, lack of sleep, and low temperature increase reaction time.

Speed exercises in a workout.

Since these exercises require relative freshness, the best time to do them is immediately after the warm-up. The rest breaks have to be long enough so the athlete can perform the next attempt with the currently maximal, or very close to, the maximal speed. Increasing the number of repetitions cumulates fatigue and increases the rest interval between them so the density of the workout gets too low. A well trained athlete must rest 5-8 minutes between sprints of up to 100 meters if the number of repetitions is not excessive. Because these rest intervals are so long, beside passive rest, light exercises similar to or imitating the main exercise are done, while the athlete is recovering, to maintain the special neuromuscular coordination for the main exercise.

Speed exercises in a microcycle.

The main condition for developing speed is an optimal state of excitability of the central nervous system and a lack of fatigue. This is why speed exercises should be done on the first day of the microcycle after the rest day, or on the second day, following the light technical workout. In the periods when development of speed is a priority, speed exercises should be done as often as possible, but in small doses. Usually, recovery after an intensive speed workout takes 24-48 hours.

Speed exercises in a macrocycle.

Speed exercises in the preparatory period are done only if their character or the form of the athlete permits it. Speed exercises that require a foundation of strength or endurance to be effective and safe, must be preceded by an adequate amount of strength and endurance training in the beginning of the preparatory period.

In the general preparatory period, general type of speed exercises, such as sprints or ball games with rules altered so the speed is stressed, are used. The effect of these general speed exercises will be easily transferred to only those competitive exercises that have similar form to them. Sprints will improve the speed of approach in jumps, but not the speed of boxing punches or the speed of evolutions on gymnastic apparatus. In the special preparatory period speed exercises (special speed exercises) resemble either parts of, or whole competitive exercises altered in such a way as to stimulate the development of speed.

Developing endurance

Endurance is the ability to work continuously without lowering the quality of the work. In other words, endurance is the ability to counter fatigue.

There are four types of fatigue: mental (boredom), sensory (a result of intense activity of the analyzers), emotional (a consequence of the intense emotions observed after performance at important sports competitions, after executing movements demanding overcoming fear, etc.), and physical (caused by muscle work).

Components of all types of fatigue are present in any activity. The physical, and to some degree the emotional, type of fatigue are the most important, with regards to sports.

Components of endurance:

Psychological components:
— motivation
— pain tolerance.

Physiological components:

1. Local endurance (of one or more groups of muscles),
— strength of a given muscle group,
— energy stores (ATP and glycogen) in a given group of muscles,
— density of capillaries in the muscle group,

2. General endurance (of the whole organism).
— strength of all muscles,
— energy stores (ATP and glycogen).
— functioning of the respiratory system,
— stroke volume of heart,
— ability of the blood to transport oxygen,
— capillarization of the muscles,
— buffer capacity of blood,
— ability to tolerate high acidity.

3. Efficiency of thermo- regulation of the organism.

4. Efficiency of the nervous system in ensuring the economy of movement through good coordination.

5. Efficiency of muscles determined by the amount of energy used up to perform assigned work.

The maximal amount of oxygen a person can use up in a minute (maximum oxygen uptake per minute) determines aerobic capability. It depends on stroke volume of the heart, on the volume of blood it can pump per minute (cardiac output), maximal heart rate, blood flow velocity, vital capacity of lungs, and ability of the tissues to absorb oxygen. The maximal oxygen uptake of excellently trained endurance athletes is 5,0-7,0 l/min., highly trained 4,0-5,0 l/min., mediocre/moderately trained 3,0-4,0 l/min. Oxygen uptake in ml/kg/min. reaches 70-75 ml/kg/min. for elite female cross-country skiers and more than 80 ml/kg/min. for elite male cross-country skiers.

Anaerobic capability is expressed by the maximal oxygen debt resulting from performed work. In well trained athletes, it may reach 20 l.

Aerobic or anaerobic capability is not the same as aerobic or anaerobic endurance. It only determines the potential of the organism, a potential that with proper skill and will-power may be realized. Jack Wilmore, in his book "Athletic Training and Physical Fitness", states that an individual's maximal oxygen uptake will increase with physical training for only twelve to eighteen months, then plateaus, even with increased training. The performance can still be improved, after maximal oxygen uptake has reached its peak, by developing the ability to exercise at a higher percentage of maximal oxygen uptake for a longer time. Athletes usually are not able to work at the pace that requires maximal oxygen uptake for more than two minutes. If the time of work is longer, the athletes work at the lower level of oxygen uptake. For example, average marathon runners can run for more than two hours at a pace requiring up to 80% of their maximal oxygen uptake. Some athletes are able to work for a prolonged time while their oxygen uptake approaches 90% of maximum.

Principles of developing endurance.

Endurance is developed only when an athlete is made sufficiently fatigued. The athlete's body adapts to this fatigue and his/her endurance increases.

When developing endurance, it is important to take into account not only degree of fatigue, but also its character. In this connection the main task of the training session when developing endurance is to obtain response shifts in the body of the desired character and necessary magnitude.

When performing many exercises, in particular cyclic exercises, the load is relatively fully characterized by: exercise intensity, exercise duration, rest interval duration, character of rest, and number of repetitions. Depending on the combination of these components, not only the magnitude of body response, but also the character of response, will differ.

The intensity of exercise determines the demand for oxygen. Low intensity, permitting demand for oxygen to be below the aerobic capability of the athlete, is called subcritical intensity. When the demand for oxygen equals the aerobic capability, the intensity of exercise is called critical. The greater the aerobic capability of the athlete, the higher is this intensity. Work at intensities greater than critical (supercritical) incurs oxygen debt and is done at the cost of anaerobic sources of energy.

The duration of the exercise determines the energy sources. If the work lasts less than 3-5 minutes, the energy will come from anaerobic reactions.

The rest interval also determines the energy sources. If in exercises of subcritical and critical intensity the rest intervals are shortened, the effort stresses more aerobic systems.

With a supercritical intensity of exercises and rest intervals that are too short for repaying the oxygen debt, the debt will add up with each repetition of the exercise and the work will be more anaerobic as the rest intervals get shorter.

The character of rest determines the speed of recovery. In exercises of critical intensity, filling up the rest intervals with light activity (jogging, trotting) maintains a higher pace of respiratory processes and thus, prevents a sudden increase of the body functions at the beginning of the next repetition.

Light movements after heavy muscular effort also help to relieve mental tension and improve blood flow in the muscles.

Faster recovery means a greater possible volume of work (in a workout and in training) and thus attaining greater form.

The number of repetitions of the exercise determines its intensity in anaerobic efforts. Increasing the number of repetitions forces a decrease in the intensity of work. More repetitions in aerobic efforts forces prolonged maintenance of the high level of activity of cardiovascular and respiratory systems.

When developing endurance of several kinds, it is necessary to first increase the aerobic capacities of the body. Three tasks have to be resolved: increasing the maximum level of oxygen consumption, developing the ability to maintain as a high level of oxygen uptake as possible for a long time, increasing the speed of the mobilization of the respiratory processes to the maximum.

Exercises demanding participation of large muscle groups (cross- country skiing, running) are used for achieving maximum efficiency of the cardiovascular and respiratory systems, and for the maintenance of a high level of oxygen consumption. Aerobic endurance workouts should be held in a natural environment and in places rich in oxygen. Exercises should be done with near-critical intensity.

The level of critical intensity (speed) depends on the magnitude of maximum oxygen consumption and on the economy of movement; it varies in different people. For beginners, the speed of running while developing aerobic endurance must be 1000 meters per 6-7 minutes. For top athletes, this speed is 1000 meters per 4-4.5 minutes. The minimum heart rate required for developing aerobic endurance can vary from athlete to athlete. It can be figured out by adding the value of the individual's resting heart rate to 60% of the difference between his/her maximal and resting rates.

$$HR_{min} = HR_{rest} + 60\%(HR_{max} - HR_{rest})$$

Exercises with an intensity far lower than critical, for example walking, must not be used in training too often. In recent years, even competitive walkers made running a considerable part of their training. It has a more vigorous effect on the cardiovascular and respiratory systems.

The continuous training is used most widely at the initial stages of the development of aerobic endurance (capability), since coordination of the functioning of the systems ensuring oxygen consumption increases spontaneously in the process of the work itself. The process is more effective if the effect of the training exercises is prolonged. The fact that the functional "ceilings" of certain organs and systems (pains in the region of the liver and spleen signal it) increase more during low-intensity, prolonged work, is of great importance. However, it is difficult for the organism to maintain maximum magnitudes of oxygen consumption when the work is uninterrupted. Usually, the work duration at a level close to maximal oxygen consumption (uptake) should not exceed 10-30 minutes. Only certain top-class athletes can maintain such an intensity of work for one hour. Oxygen consumption during a 15 kilometer cross-country ski race by top-class skiers is 85-95 per cent of the maximum when the duration of work is 55-60 minutes. Then, discoordination sets in (in the cardiovascular and respiratory systems), oxygen consumption drops, and the training effect of the work diminishes.

Anaerobic work with short repetitions interspaced with brief rest intervals (interval training) also develops the aerobic endurance (capabilities).

The main physical exercises which build aerobic endurance (running, swimming, cycling) also increase anaerobic capabilities. It is important to remember that anaerobic endurance is unstable: when special training stops, its level quickly drops. Developing aerobic endurance is the basis for developing anaerobic endurance. If the anaerobic endurance (capability) is well developed, but the aerobic not, then the accumulated products of anaerobic disintegration of the energy sources will be removed slowly, because the speed of eliminating the oxygen debt depends on the power of the respiratory system. If anaerobic work is repeated with short rest periods that are too short for full restoration, the athlete will quickly get completely tired (the abundance of the accumulated products of anaerobic work will "choke" the athlete). To develop anaerobic endurance it is necessary to first build aerobic endurance. Aerobic endurance training causes adaptations in the system of respiration, in the system of transportation of oxygen, and in the cells that use it. These adaptations at the cell level increase the ability to oxygenate the lactic acid and thus, lower its concentration. In this way, increasing aerobic capabilities improves anaerobic capabilities, not only by postponing use of glycolysis until a higher intensity of effort is reached, but also by speeding the flow of lactic acid through the organs that use it or remove it.

Aerobic capability naturally increases until the age of 20 in men, and 16 in women. Then it stabilizes and declines after 30. Since anaerobic endurance is built on the basis of aerobic endurance, it is important to properly develop the organisms of the young athletes so they will not be limited in the level of anaerobic endurance by low aerobic capability.

Particular features of developing endurance. Endurance can be developed by working out with a different intensity than the intensity of one's event. Fatigue during workouts with maximum loads, is determined by the speed of exhaustion of the anaerobic energy sources and the inhibition of nervous centers, a result of this intensive activity. Raising the level of anaerobic capabilities and the work capability of the nervous centers through work of maximum intensity improves endurance.

In developing endurance in cyclic sports (running, swimming, cycling, rowing) of submaximal, high, and moderate power, the main method is the covering of laps shorter than the competitive distance. Short laps are chosen in order to make the athlete get used to running at higher speeds than those used for the regular distance. The athlete covers these shorter laps several times during the workout to get great enough effect on the body.

Work of submaximal, high, and moderate intensity poses special requirements on the human body, different in each of these zones. Greater intensity allows for shorter distance and requires a greater role of anaerobic processes. With the decrease in intensity, the distance grows and so does the role of aerobic processes.

In each of the mentioned zones there are these three main training tasks:

1) Increasing anaerobic capabilities (mainly, their glycolitic component).

2) Increasing aerobic capabilities (perfecting the work of cardiovascular and respiratory systems).

3) Expanding physiological and psychological limits of stability in relation to the changes caused by intensive work.

In many cases the improved local endurance of the particular muscle groups doing the main work, is important.

The modern methods of developing endurance, used with high-class athletes, require a great volume of work both in each workout, as well as in the annual cycle.

Work of variable intensities is also used in developing endurance. In such work, the speed of shifting physiological functions over to a new level is improved as well as the ability to simultaneously readjust all the organs and systems. For this purpose, spurts of different intensity are used while covering the distance or performing any other tasks. Gradually their intensity grows, while the duration varies from 3-5 seconds to 1-1.5 minutes. Of great importance here is the ability to force oneself to continue work with the necessary intensity despite fatigue.

Developing endurance in encounter sports (wrestling, boxing) and sports games (ball games, hockey) is conditioned by the fact that, in these sports, the intensity and the form of movement constantly change. The entire game or bout may be a number of work periods interspaced with rest periods. For example, in tennis, the time of work makes up only about 30% of the actual game time. The athlete's endurance in such a sport will depend not only on how quickly fatigue sets in, but also on how fast recovery occurs. Both the anaerobic and aerobic capabilities play a considerable role in these sports. The moments of intense activity are performed at the cost of anaerobic processes, and the speed of recovery in "slower" periods depends on the power of aerobic processes.

In games and encounter sports, it is difficult to achieve a selective effect on the organism's individual functions. It is also difficult to regulate loads precisely. Various cyclical exercises (skiing, running, swimming, etc.) are used to develop mainly aerobic endurance in these sports.

To achieve a high level of special endurance, the use of competitive exercises (playing the actual sport) is necessary.

When playing the sport to develop endurance, athletes can choose one of the following approaches:

1) maintain the same work intensity and duration as in competition, for example, in soccer, play two 45 minutes periods. This method will produce good results only at the initial stages of training.

2) increase the duration of the game and correspondingly reduce the intensity as compared to that of competition, for example, in wrestling work on the mat for 30-60 minutes. This method is useful for perfecting aerobic capabilities in the specific conditions of the game or encounter, helping to achieve an economy of movements, relaxation, and the development of a strong will.

3) Increase the intensity and reduce the duration of the bouts as compared with the competitive ones. To increase their effect, short work periods are repeated several times.

The economy of movements is of great importance for an athlete's endurance in games and encounter sports. It calls for a good technique and the ability to relax one's muscles.

Special methods of developing endurance.

Artificially causing hypoxia, by reducing the amount of oxygen by exercising while holding breath or at high altitudes; or causing hypocapnia (lowering partial pressure of CO_2 in blood) by hyperventilation, are used to boost endurance. Controlled holding of breath is used, for example, in swimming. The swimmer inhales only once every 3-4 strokes. The artificial oxygen debt builds up, causing considerable changes in the body in spite of low volume and intensity of work.

Training for 3-5 weeks in the mountains (1000-2500 meters above sea level) is especially beneficial for athletes living and competing at lower elevations. Depending on the athletic class, mountain sports training for children and adults is conducted at elevations from 800 to 2500 meters. The partial pressure of oxygen is lower in the mountains than at sea level, which causes hypoxia that triggers increased production of the erythropoietin hormone by the kidney and stimulates red blood cell production in red bone marrow. This causes an increase of hemoglobin content in the bloodstream and causes the body to adapt to hypoxia. Endurance training in these conditions is especially effective. By the end of six months, the red cell count may reach 10 million per cubic millimeter, twice as much as the normal value. The first 5-12 days after arrival is the period of acute acclimatization which may mean a reduced ability to work, accompanied by an unusually elevated mood, excitability, overestimation of one's potential, sleep disorders, headaches, increased fatiguability, breathlessness after work loads that were handled easily at low altitudes, nose bleeding, pains in the area of liver, and an aggravation of chronic illnesses and injuries. In mountains (at the above elevations), the ability to perform intensive work is reduced, for example, the economy of running with speed close to maximal is much lower than at sea level. In the first microcycle of training in mountains, the volume of work has to be reduced by 10-20% and intensity has to be reduced to 50% or even 30% of what was done recently at a low altitude. At the end of the second or third week, the loads reach normal values.

The maximal ability to work occurs between the third and eighth day after returning to lower elevations. Then, between the eighth and twelfth day after returning, athletic form lowers drastically. This loss of form is only temporary. The form improves again and allows athletes to reach a high level of results between the fifteenth and thirtieth day after returning. The form may remain at these increased levels for up to three months. There are exceptions to the above tendencies in reactions to this type of training so, prior to using it before an important competition, it must be tried several times earlier, just as any radical change in training. The reactions of an organism during re-acclimatization are individual and more acute if athlete descends not only to sea level, but to seaside (sea climate). Acute re-acclimatization may be accompanied by a loss of coordination in familiar techniques, lowering of speed, headaches, sleep disorders, lack of will, and slowed down recovery after intensive workouts. In case of acute re- acclimatization, the intensity of work in the first weekly microcycle is reduced.

Training in mountains is used, in the transitory period as a means of active rest, in the preparatory period to increase the ability to handle training loads, and in the competitive period to improve competitive form.

On June 1, 1989 Gordon M. Binder, CEO of Amgen Inc. from Thousand Oaks, CA, said that his company would make the drug Epogen that stimulates the production of red cells. This drug may make high altitude training in the preparatory and competitive periods unnecessary.

Psychological "tuning-up" may improve the results and even slow down the appearance of unfavorable changes in the body during endurance efforts. To show endurance, one needs the ability to overcome feelings of heavy fatigue, and to continue working.

General endurance.

The ability to perform moderate efforts, involving a majority of muscles, for a long time, is called general endurance. Such efforts increase the aerobic potential of the athlete, which is independent from the form of movement. Special endurance is the ability to perform a definite activity for a long time.

It is not true that general endurance should be developed exclusively by long distance running or other locomotory actions, regardless of one's discipline of sport. General endurance training has to prepare the athlete for a faster acquisition of special endurance. When working on general endurance, we must use all the means that allow the organism to better adapt to special exercises.

General endurance is defined as the ability to perform exercises of low intensity and long duration while utilizing most of the muscles of the body. It is wrong to develop general endurance for sports that do not consist mainly of running or cycling by such exercises as running or cycling only. The function of general endurance is to prepare a foundation for special endurance train-ing so, in developing general endurance, it is necessary to use exercises involving the muscle groups, and to use a structure of movements that will be useful in developing special endurance. Downhill skiers use cross-country skiing and skaters use bicycling as general endurance exercises. Rowers do cross-country skiing and cross-country skiers do rowing as general endurance exercises. In acyclic sports, such as games or individual contact sports, general endurance exercises model the variable character of work. Boxers, for example, run with accelerations. General endurance exercises may develop the muscle groups and/or the energy supply system that is seemingly useless in specialized and competitive exercises. For example, general endurance exercises for sprinters (long distance running) and weightlifters (swimming, cross-country ski) develop aerobic endurance. The efforts of sprinters and weightlifters are anaerobic but the high aerobic capability makes the athlete healthier and speeds up the recovery after these efforts and thus, allows for an increase in the volume and intensity of specialized work. General endurance exercises involve most muscle groups or the largest muscle groups, and have the task of developing aerobic capabilities. They help in the overall development of the organism, and in the enlargement of the movement "thesaurus" of the athlete.

When developing general endurance, several exercises are combined for a greater diversification of the training effect, various training methods may be used, loads are increased gradually at the rate lower than the rate of adaptation to them. The results achieved in the general endurance exercises do not have to be maximal, but only sufficient to meet requirements of the training in selected sport.

Special endurance.

Special endurance is the exact type of endurance that is necessary for performing special and competitive exercises with the intensity and volume necessary for success. It may be expressed by increased time of performing the activity with assigned intensity (running, cycling, skiing), by increased intensity of effort with the same load (throws, jumps, gymnastics) or within the same time (running, individual contact sports, games), and by increased stability of technique (individual contact sports, gymnastics, games). Special endurance exercises have a structure of movement and its duration decided by the specific requirements of the sport. They involve mainly the muscle groups that have a decisive role in the competitive activity. Special endurance exercises directly affect whatever restricts special endurance, but the full development of special endurance is impossible without also doing competitive exercises. As the results and form of the athlete grow, so does the amount of competitive exercises used as the means of improving special endurance. Competitive endurance exercises which have the same content as the actual competitive exercise, but are performed to develop endurance and not for sports results, in such sports as running, swimming, cycling, individual contact sports, and some of the team ball games, can be used throughout the whole year.

The following factors determine the dynamics of developing special endurance: the number of workouts, the total volume of special endurance training, methods used, participation in competitions, the number of starts in a main event and related events, and the duration of training cycles.

Special endurance in various sports is based on varying proportions of the basic components of endurance. Sports can be divided into groups depending on the dominant components of endurance.

In marathon running, long-distance cross-country skiing, 100 kilometers cycling, and walking, aerobic capabilities of the organism, mental stability, and the rational distribution of energy decide about success.

In middle-distance running, 200-400 meters swimming, and a 1000 meters of rowing, anaerobic capabilities of the organism are stressed equally or more than aerobic capabilities. Endurance in such events depends to some degree on strength and speed, but having greater pure speed or pure strength than your competitors does not guarantee having greater special endurance or better results. Besides the physical abilities, the ability to overcome prolonged and rapidly increasing acute fatigue while maintaining high speed and precision of movements, is important here.

In sprints (track and field, cycling, swimming), mainly the anaerobic capabilities are stressed during the event and the vegetative system is stressed during recovery. The sports results in meets where there are many starts depends on the speed of recovery, which depends on the condition of the vegetative system. A great concentration of will is needed to reach maximum speed quickly and then to maintain an optimal speed and frequency of movements.

In weightlifting, special endurance means the ability to repeatedly mobilize for increasingly greater efforts during prolonged and emotionally draining contests; it is based mainly on pure strength.

In games and individual contact sports, frequent spurts of effort demand good anaerobic capability. The long duration of each encounter also demands a great development of aerobic capability, mental stability, as well as the ability to overcome acute fatigue and pain while performing complicated tactical and technical actions in response to the unknown actions of the opponent in a hostile environment.

In combined events such as the decathlon, the modern pentathlon, or the classic combination (skiing), having special endurance for each event separately is not sufficient. The performance in each event of the combined events, when they are performed in actual competition, is influenced by the demands the preceding events made on the athlete.

There are two main methods of making the transition from special exercises to competitive exercises in developing special endurance; by workouts consisting of many repetitions of the exercise (of the same content but shorter than the competitive exercise), and by workouts consisting of a few repetitions (of efforts longer than the competitive exercise).

In the first method, the 400 meter runner runs at 90% of maximal (for 400 meter distance) speed 10 times 150 meters with 1 minute rest breaks or runs 4 times 300 meters with near maximal speed; the 800 meter runner run 400 meters 4-10 times with 90-102% of average planned competitive speed, with 2-5 minutes rest; 1500 meter runners run 800 meters 3-8 times at 96-100% of average competitive speed, with 3-6 minutes of rest; 5000 meter runner runs 1000 meters 5 times with speed exceeding the average competitive speed, with 4-5 minutes of rest; gymnasts perform 4-6 sets of 10- 12 elements with 4-5 minutes of rest between sets (high class gymnasts do several more sets). In training middle and long-distance runners, rowers, etc., laps of 600, 800, 1000, 2000 meters and longer, depending on specialization, are better than laps of 100-400 meters. In this method, the load is increased by reducing the duration of rest breaks, or by increasing the time of work periods, the number of work periods, or the intensity of work in these periods.

In the second method, the sprinters (100-200 meters) run distances 150-200% of the length of competitive distances, with near competitive speed, 3-4 times, with 8-15 minutes of rest between runs; 800 meter runners run 1000-1500 meters as many times as it is possible with near competitive speed; 5000 meter runners run 6-8 kilometers with 93-100% of the average competitive speed (the more uniform speed, the easier the work); gymnasts do combinations with a greater number of elements than in the competitive combination.

In the above method, the volume of work is initially greater than in the competitive exercise, then the intensity is gradually increased up to the intensity in competition.

Developing special endurance by more closely recreating of the demands of competition is done by performing the actual competitive exercises several times during a workout with rest periods allowing the next repetition to be maximally intensive. For example, 400 meter runners run 400 meters 2-3 times with maximum speed, with 7 minutes of rest between runs. Frequent repetition of the competitive exercise with maximum speed or strength will lead to the formation of a motor stereotype, for example, the speed barrier, which prevents the improvement of speed. To overcome this problem, as well as to deal with events that can be done only once during a workout, efforts during a workout may be arranged in one of the following ways:

a) Covering the distance or performing the event with speed greater than currently possible at the whole distance, and making short 5-15 second rest breaks that allow the heart rate to drop by up to 15 beats per minute. The total time, with rest breaks, of covering the distance cannot exceed the planned competitive time. The distance is divided gradually into shorter units. The number of units increases with the target distance, for example, distances of up to 400 meters in swimming are divided into 3-4 units, with the first unit equal to half of the distance; distances of 800-1500 meters are divided into 4-5 units, with the first unit equal to one third of the distance and the rest breaks are gradually shorter.

b) Performing the whole event, replacing new, insufficiently learned techniques with other techniques. In gymnastics, developing special endurance by competitive exercises when the most difficult elements of the program are not mastered yet, is made possible by replacing these elements with the elements that have been mastered and that put demands on the organism that are similar to the new ones.

c) Covering the competitive distance while increasing, from workout to workout, the portion of the distance covered with greater speed than the current average competitive speed. The athlete runs the distance, and gradually increases the number of laps covered with greater speed.

d) In games and individual contact sports, special endurance can be improved by performing competitive exercises as if under the worst circumstances— with increased intensity and for the longest possible duration, for example, unexpectedly ordering extra bouts in wrestling or boxing.

Although special endurance is best revealed by competitive exercises or those very similar to them, it is possible to estimate this endurance by special tests that partially recreate the conditions of competitive exercises.

Examples of a special endurance tests for various sports:

Swimming 100-200 meters—6 times 50 m. at 90% of maximal speed at 50 m., with 10 seconds of rest between laps. Changes of speed in laps and heart rate are used to evaluate special endurance.

Running 5000 meters—10 times 400 m. at 110% of competitive speed, with 1 minute rest between laps. Changes of speed in laps and heart rate are used to evaluate special endurance.

Wrestling (greco-roman)—three sets of throwing dummy (first set—40 seconds supples/drop back throw, second set—40 seconds of four various throws in sequence, third set—20 seconds of a favorite throw). Number of throws, correctness of technique, and heart rate are used to evaluate special endurance.

Volleyball—circuit consisting of techniques done either for the maximal number of repetitions per constant time, or a constant number of repetitions in the shortest time. Correctness of the techniques, time or number of repetitions, and changes of heart rate, are used to evaluate special endurance.

Figure skating—two repetitions of the competitive combination with the most difficult elements replaced by easier ones. The correctness of technique and changes of heart rate are used to evaluate special endurance.

Types of endurance training.

The types of endurance training are classified according to the amount of exercises used, their sequence, the intensity and duration of work, and the rest intervals between exercises. When planning and conducting training, one should regulate the amount of work and rest according to the needs of the athletes. Classification makes it easier to describe differences in the effects of various arrangements of exercises. There are the following types of training:
—continuous
—variable
—repetitive
—interval
—circuit

1. Continuous training is characterized by constant, low to moderate intensity work and relatively (to other types of training) long workout. It is recommended for middle and long distances runners, bicyclists, rowers, and cross-country skiers (cyclic sports). Other athletes can also use it, especially at the initial stages of their athletic career and in every macrocycle in the general preparatory period. This type of training improves the organism's aerobic potential, efficiency of thermo- regulation, tolerance for high body temperature, while developing general endurance, and increasing resistance to the symptoms of fatigue and the results of loss of fluids. It increases the economy of work, the ability to mobilize muscle groups for long efforts, and the self-control of the athlete during long exhausting efforts. In continuous training, the adaptive mechanisms of the athlete's organism are mobilized only once in each workout. Following this mobilization, the adaptation remains at the same level, with the exception of the final spurt. Efforts of long duration cause great expenditures of energy, forcing the organism to use, and later to rebuild, all its reserves. Short efforts do not use up the deep reserves of the organism. Long, continuous work with a heart rate of 150/min. constitutes aerobic effort and does not reach the anaerobic threshold. It can be performed for a long time without signs of great fatigue. Continuous work with a heart rate of 165/min. constitutes mixed aerobic and anaerobic effort. Continuous work with a heart rate of 180/min. causes maximal intensification of the aerobic processes and an increase in anaerobic processes.

The main part of a typical workout in continuous training consists of performing one form of movement with such low intensity so as not to fatigue too quickly. Only at the end of the exercise, can limbs feel somewhat heavier and breathing become much faster. The intensity (pace of movements) remains the same throughout the exercise (run, swim, etc.). Such workouts are done for up to six weeks (long mesocycle). Each consecutive workout is longer because the distance, or number of movements performed, increases. After approximately six weeks a change is made. The intensity is gradually increased from workout to workout (but remains constant within the same workout), and simultaneously the duration of work is gradually reduced.

2. Variable training has various duration times for performing each exercise, while the duration of the whole workout remains constant. The intensity of exercises varies and it is lowered when partial recovery is needed. This training brings best results if the intensity of exercises in a workout is initially low, then gradually increases to less than maximal values, and then gradually lowers. The intensity of work is changed according to the reactions of the athlete. This type of training is used in the preparatory period.

3. Repetitive training consists of repeating certain types of exercise in a workout. It has a constant intensity of exercise, rest periods that ensure full recovery, and a variable number of repetitions of the exercise. Every repetition of the exercise means repeated adaptation to work. This training forces multiple mobilization from rest, to full activity. It improves the organism's adaptability to work. The duration of rest periods is regulated according to individual reactions to work. When the ability to handle the training load increases, first the number of repetitions increases and then the intensity or the difficulty of the exercise. This type of training is recommended for the beginning of the preparatory period in the macrocycle, especially for beginners. Highly trained athletes do not benefit much from this type of endurance training. Repeated work with a heart rate of 150/min., followed by rest until full recovery, did not have enough training effect for high class athletes (Volkov N. J., an article "W poszukiwaniu naukowych podstaw teorii treningu", Sport Wyczynowy number 2, 1971, Warszawa). Repeating exercises lasting 1.5-3 min. each, at 165/min., caused a big oxygen debt. In exercises lasting 3-15 min. each, a decrease in the anaerobic processes and a lowering of the oxygen uptake were observed. Repeated exercises of 1.5-3 minute duration each, at 180/min. heart rate increased anaerobic processes.

4. Interval training has a strictly regulated time for work and rest, the training load, the intensity of work in each exercise, and the number of repetitions of the exercise. Rest periods should be such as to ensure that the new stimuli is applied while the effects of the previous one are still present. In other words, when the athlete has not yet recovered from the previous exercise. The athlete should not use maximal training loads in interval training. This type of training is used for developing speed-endurance, but because of the high intensity of work, it can be used only with well prepared athletes. A high intensity of work puts great demands on the organism and in insufficiently prepared athletes, can destabilize form. Interval training consisting of short, speed-type efforts causes mostly biochemical adaptations in the muscles. The character of biochemical adaptations in muscles depends on the type of muscular effort (speed, strength, endurance). Efforts longer than three minutes stress mainly the aerobic energy systems. Even much shorter bouts of work, if followed with long rest periods, will have mostly an aerobic effect. When the rest periods are short, the effort is increasingly anaerobic, which gives a better overall training effect. Most often the heart rate at the end of the effort reaches 180/min. (more for highly trained) and at the end of the rest period, after 45-60 seconds, falls to 140-120/ min. 25-50 repetitions of a 200 meter sprint, with heart rate values as above, is considered optimal for developing overall endurance.

A typical interval workout used by middle and long-distance runners for developing aerobic capabilities consists of, 1-2 minutes work periods with pulse reaching 160-180/min. by the end of each work period, rest periods lasting 1-2 minutes or until pulse is 120-140/min. and are filled with light activity. If the heart rate at the end of work periods is over 180/min., it means that the workout has increasingly anaerobic character; the oxygen debt incurred during the work period cannot be sufficiently paid back during the rest break, and that the number of repetitions of work periods is excessive.

An interval workout designed to improve anaerobic- alactacid capabilities has work periods lasting up to 10 seconds, with an intensity of effort from 90 to 95% of maximal, and rest breaks between work periods lasting 2-3 minutes. Work periods can be arranged in sets of 3-4, separated by 7-10 minutes of rest, filled by light activity after each set. The initial number of sets per workout is also 3-4, and is increased with the growing form of the athlete.

5. Circuit training is the main means of developing general endurance and other physical abilities in acyclic sports during the general preparatory period.

Example of exercises in circuit training.

Workouts in circuit training consist of repeating various exercises that affect all the main groups of muscles, in a set sequence. The choice of exercises depends on the athlete's needs and the training period. The sequence of exercises should be such that each next exercise, for the same groups of muscles, is more effective thanks to the one before, and the exercises are alternated so each muscle group can recover before being exercised again.

If the separate exercises have low intensity, the effect on endurance is enhanced by the lack of rest between exercises and between repetitions of the circuit.

The exercises and rest breaks may be arranged in several ways. The athlete may have to perform exercises repeating them 50-75% of the maximal number of repetitions while trying to reduce the time of making three rounds from 20 minutes, down to 15 minutes, or, for example, in boxing down to the duration of the bout. Another way is to have the time of the workout equal the target time right from the beginning and increase the amount of work done in this time. The initial number of repetitions of each exercise is 25-30% of the maximal number of repetitions and it is increased as the training level increases. Eventually the number of rounds is increased too. This way of doing circuit training is used for developing endurance in boxing, volleyball, tennis, and track and field.

When the goal is to develop strength-endurance, weights in a range of 50-70% of maximum are used in circuit training. There are two variants of circuit training with weights. In the first variant, each exercise is done for 30 seconds and followed by 60 seconds of rest. The number of repetitions of each exercise is increased, while its time is constant. The number of rounds starts at one or two and is increased to three over a period of 3-4 weeks. The rest intervals between rounds last 3-5 minutes.

In the second variant, the weight is 60-70% of maximum and the number of repetitions is 6-10, done during 15 seconds. As the level of training improves, this time is reduced to 10 seconds. Rest after each exercise is 90 seconds, number of rounds is 2-3, and the rest between rounds lasts 3-5 minutes. After 3-4 weeks, the weight is increased again to 60-70% of the current maximum.

To make circuit training more effective for developing endurance in a given sport, the arrangement of the work and rest periods should be close to that in the competition, for example, to the time of rounds, and rest breaks between them, in boxing.

Circuit training can be used in all periods of the macrocycle by changing its exercises.

There is a form of endurance workout that is used to develop general endurance, as well as a means of active rest. There are two forms of this workout: a) small running play and b) big running play.

Small running play consists of exercises arranged in the following order:

First part:
1. Jogging.
2. Slow jogging or trotting interspaced with jumps and running using various steps.
3. Light running for 500-1000 meters.
4. Rest.
5. Dynamic flexibility exercises interspaced with running.

The second part consists of doing one of the following exercises within distances of 400-500 meters:
1. Relaxed sprints for 60-120 meters,
2. Accelerations for 20-60 meters,
3. Running with high rhythm/frequency of stride 60-120 meters,
4. Run with obstacles, such as hurdles,
5. Various jumps (from leg to leg, on one leg, combined),
6. Run with sudden accelerations for 10-30 meters.

The whole set of exercises done within this 400-500 distance can be repeated after a short rest. The number of repetitions depends on the form of the athletes.

The third part consists of trotting and jogging, or light running for 500-1000 meters.

Small running play lasts about 60 minutes and, instead of some of the running, may include technical exercises of the sport.

Big running play differs from small play by adding several 150-200 meter distances, run with a set pace, interspaced with trotting. Big running play ends with trotting and jogging. It is used in the preparatory period and it lasts 80-90 minutes.

Another version of the big running play:

First part (20-30 minutes), all exercises done while running or jogging.
1. Running
2. Strength exercises
3. Flexibility exercises
4. Coordination exercises.

Second part (20 minutes).
1. Run 400-500 meters (4-6 times)
2. Accelerations for 120-200 meters (4-6 times)
3. Multi-jumps
4. Strength exercises with partner.

Third part (15-35 minutes).
1. Pace run for for 300-800 meters (5-10 times)
2. Light running until the heart rate falls down to 120-140/min.

Fourth part (20-25 minutes).
1. Light running
2. Relaxing exercises
3. Jogging/trotting
4. Marching.

Big running play in speed-strength sports:

First part.
1. Walk and march with jogging and light running.
2. Slalom between trees, bushes, etc.
3. Light jumps, running sideways and backward, and other exercises for legs done in motion.
4. Light running for 300-500 meters.
5. Rest while marching
6. Flexibility and agility exercises while standing, marching, and jogging (bends, twists, squats, lunges, arm swings, legs swings).

Second part.
1. Run 60-80 meters 4-6 times.
2. Skip 20-40 meters 6-8 times.
3. Various jumps and multi-jumps (10 jumps in a row) 6-8 times.

Third part.
Easy, natural run for 300-150 meters, 4-6 times. March between repetitions until breath calms down. These distances get shorter (closer to 150 meters) as the end of the preparatory period gets near.

Fourth part.
Jogging, marching, cooling-down and relaxing exercises.

Strongly built athletes that are hypertonic and need to learn how to relax and improve the economy of their movements, will run slower, but longer distances. Slender athletes that are naturally relaxed, will run shorter distances at a higher pace.

No single training method is sufficient to develop any given ability or skill. Training has to include the proper set of methods and types of training that will suit the situation.

Endurance exercises in a workout.

Endurance is the ability to overcome fatigue. This is why endurance exercises can, and should be done after technical, speed, or strength exercises if any such exercises are to be done in the same workout. The endurance exercises should not be continued when an athlete shows the following signs of heavy fatigue: head and arms hang down, the rib cage caves in, the frequency of breathing increases suddenly, the upper body sweats heavily, cold sweat appears on the face, face pales or gets very red, eyes become dull, voice is muffled and interrupted, and movements lose precision, rhythm, and amplitude.

Endurance exercises in a microcycle.

Endurance workouts are done at the end of the microcycle, after speed, strength, or technical workouts, and before the day of rest. Usually, recovery after an intensive endurance workout takes 48-72 hours.

Endurance exercises in a macrocycle.

The general and special endurance is developed simultaneously in all periods of the macrocycle. Only the share of the exercises for developing either general or special endurance changes as the periods change. In the general preparatory period, general endurance and strength-endurance have to be developed. This period of training prepares athletes for intensive, specialized training in the next periods of the macrocycle. For developing general endurance, extensive means, leaving long lasting effects on the organism, are used. Workouts in this period have a great volume of work. Strength-endurance is also increased in this period. Strength exercises directed at developing strength-endurance should involve those muscle groups that play the greatest role in a given sports discipline. Examples of such exercises are: running on sand, running with weights attached to shoes, swimming with added resistance (also see high repetitions/low resistance strength exercises). The internal and external structure of these exercises must be the same as the competitive exercises of one's discipline. Exercises are done with moderate speed and their gradual intensification prepares the athlete for developing special endurance in the next stages of training. In the special preparatory stage, most endurance work is directed at developing special endurance. The intensity of specialized endurance work increases, while the volume of work stabilizes at the level reached in the previous stage. In the competitive period, the task is to perfect special endurance while maintaining general endurance and strength-endurance. This is done by lowering the volume of work to 60-70% of the value reached in the preparatory period, while increasing intensity of work. Competing is one of the means of improving special endurance. The number, frequency, and character of competitions should be planned. In cyclic sports, for example 4000 meter cycling, the time interval between competitions that, without additional endurance workouts, causes improvement in special endurance, is between 2 and 7 days, with results improving most during the longest time (3 weeks), when 3 days of rest separate the competitions. In sports that do not permit such frequent competitions (boxing, marathon, combined events) workouts are either done between the starts, athletes compete in a reduced number of events, or they compete at easier distances. The volume of loads imposed by competitions should grow gradually. In the transitory period, the task is to maintain an acceptable level of general endurance. The intensity of work is lowered and other sports are used to maintain endurance.

Research done by Handelsman and Smirnov shows that ceasing endurance training for three months resulted in lowering it by 8-16%.

Developing movement coordination

Movement coordination, as a nervous regulation of muscular activity, is a basis for developing efficiency in movements and perfecting technique. It is an expression of the ability to localize processes of excitation to the proper motor centers and to prevent a spilling over of excitation to other centers, interfering one movement pattern with another movement pattern. A lack of this ability is evident, for example, when having to jump in place and simultaneously make big circles with arms, one ends up jumping and raising and lowering the arms.

Good coordination improves one's strength by engaging the muscles most adequate for a given task in the most efficient order, inhibiting their antagonists, and regulating the frequency of nerve impulses. Coordination affects the speed of movement by regulating the mobility of nervous processes.

Coordination greatly influences the speed and precision of learning techniques, which is why tests of coordination are used in the selection for technical sports.

Coordination can be divided into general and specific. The general coordination allows the athlete to quickly learn various, often complicated, movements and movement patterns. Most (but not all) exercises developing general coordination consist of movements performed for their own sake. The goal is to learn the spatial and temporal form of movements.

Specific coordination allows the athlete to perform techniques in various circumstances smoothly, precisely, and with ease. Specific coordination results from practicing a technique long after mastering its correct external (spatial and temporal) form. The fine regulation of applied strength and a perfection of timing is sought.

General coordination is supposed to facilitate the development of specific coordination because the performance of every new exercise is based on previously mastered motor habits. The more of these basic motor habits that are mastered by the athlete before specialization, the easier it will be to master the techniques of the sport.

There are seven coordination abilities: movement adequacy, balance, movement differentiation, reactivity for signals, spatial orientation, sense of rhythm, and synchronization of movements in time.

During certain periods in our life we are most sensitive to exercises developing the particular elements of motor coordination. These periods are called sensitive or critical.

The sensitive or critical periods in the development of elements of coordination are as follows:

Movement adequacy—(motor behavior/the choice of movements adequate for the task)—age 8 to 13, peaks 9 to 12;

Balance—age 9.5 to 14, peaks 11 to 13;

Movement differentiation—(the ability to correctly perceive/estimate differences in form, distance, and amount of strength in performed movements)—age 7 to 15, peaks 10.5 to 13;

Reaction to acoustical and visual stimuli (signals)—age 7 to 12, peaks 8 to 11;

Spatial orientation— age 6 to 17, peaks 12 to 17;

Rhythmic motion— age 6 to 14, peaks 9 to 12;

Synchronization of movements in time— age 7 to 13, peaks 7 to 10.

W. S. Farfiel, describes three levels of difficulty in movement coordination:

First level— performing movements requiring spatial precision; the speed of performing the movements does not matter.

Second level— performing movements requiring spatial precision, with a certain speed or in a limited time.

Third level— performing movements requiring spatial precision and speed while adjusting to constantly changing conditions.

Fundamentals of developing coordination.

Coordination is developed by teaching new and varied exercises and by performing known exercises in new conditions. When teaching new exercises, one should not strive for perfection, but for rough proficiency in the general form of the exercise.

The richer the athlete's store of motor skills, the more skills the athlete can easily learn or change.

Balance can be static (hand stands, one leg stands in gymnastics) or dynamic (skating, skiing). Balance is developed by exercises that make it difficult to maintain a stability of stance. Apart from developing a sensitivity of analyzers (visual, vestibular, kinesthetic) and an ability to adequately react to information coming from them, the athlete must know the biomechanical characteristics of the stance. For example, the stability of leg stances on the balance beam is best regulated by slight movements of the ankle joints, and not by movements of whole body.

Static balance is perfected by: prolonging the time of maintaining the stance; closing eyes while doing previously mastered exercises; reducing the area of support (narrower beam, smaller distance between hands or legs); increasing the distance from the center of gravity to the support surface; performing additional movements while maintaining balance; assuming static positions immediately after a dynamic movement of the whole body; maintaining stance against actions of the partner; raising the height of the apparatus; and doing the exercise on an unstable support.

Dynamic balance is perfected by methods similar to the ones used for perfecting static balance, except that exercises are done in motion, for example, closing eyes while running or riding along a steep curve.

Spatial orientation, or the feeling of space, is perfected by exercises that require precise control of a body position in space, as well as a quick assessment of the distances to other objects. Example of such an exercise: throw a ball about three feet (one meter) above your head but in front of yourself, turn 360 degrees and catch it. In the more difficult form of this exercise, the athlete throws two small (tennis) balls and catches them after turning. This ability is also developed by performing exercises in unusual positions, for example, athletes in pairs throw a ball to each other while lying on the floor.

Synchronization of movements in time is perfected by exercises that consist of unrelated movements, for example, one arm is making large circles in sagittal plane while the other punches to the front or side. The degree of difficulty is raised by adding more movements of other limbs, for example, performing the above exercise while marching, jogging, and running, as well as increasing the difficulty of each movement.

Specific coordination is perfected by performing techniques from unusual initial positions; with the weaker limb (right-handed throwing with left hand, boxing with right guard); with changed speed (slower or faster execution of gymnastic combinations, faster pre-run in jumps); with added movements (more turns in discus throw); with different equipment, apparatus, partners, or opponents; or in a smaller area (in a smaller ring, court, on narrower support, on track more densely packed with obstacles).

Insufficient relaxation after contraction and excessive tonus at work and rest (hypermyotonia), interfere with good coordination and thus with the form, speed, and strength of movements. There are relaxation exercises for each type of tension. Insufficient relaxation after contraction happens to an athlete that is tired, or under stress, or is not sufficiently skilled at relaxing muscles. Depending on which of the above factors plays a greater role, excessive muscular tension can be reduced by improving special endurance, mental stability, and by doing the following general relaxation exercises: tensing and subsequent relaxing of the same group of muscles, relaxing some muscle group while tensing or moving other, and performing techniques which require the relaxing of some muscles to be effective. Especially effective for relaxation are the weight exercises, where an athlete can fully relax immediately after the load is removed, for example raising from a squat with the barbell or doing pull and jerk—leaving the barbell on the rack and immediately squatting by loosening the muscles.

The more the above exercises resemble techniques of a particular sport, the greater is their effectiveness. For this reason, an athlete has to perform competitive exercises in such a way as to reduce tension, such as preceding the exercise with a mental rehearsal focusing attention on the moments where relaxation is required in the practiced technique, learning to relax facial muscles (which leads to overall relaxation), diverting attention from repetitive movements (talking while running), listening to music with proper rhythm, and practicing techniques while tired, but only to such a degree that it does not impair coordination.

Excessive tonus (hypermyotonia) can be reduced by a systematic and frequent use of loose swinging movements and a shaking of the muscles between speed or strength efforts, as well as by swimming or even relaxing in water, by massage, sauna, or warm baths.

The ability to relax muscles at will increases with rational athletic training. Both the time it takes to contract a muscle, and the time to relax it, are shorter as the class of the athlete improves. Beginners need more time to relax a muscle than to contract it, athletes of international class need less time to relax a muscle than to contract it, but both of these times are shorter than that of lower-class athletes.

Athletes' Class	Latent Contraction Time (seconds)	Latent Relaxation Time (seconds)
Beginners	0.2980	0.3820
Intermediate	0.2708	0.3730
Advanced	0.2500	0.2532
International	0.2304	0.2185

Latent contraction and relaxation times and athletes' class

Coordination exercises in a workout.

Exercises designed to improve coordination quickly fatigue the nervous system, which is why they should be done in short sets, with frequent rest breaks. Also, muscular fatigue impairs coordination so the best time for coordination exercises is in the first part of the workout.

Coordination exercises in a microcycle.

Because these exercises do not fatigue muscles and are fun to do, they can be done in every workout, for example, in a warm-up.

Coordination exercises in a macrocycle.

Coordination exercises can be done throughout the year. Every year approximately 15% of coordination exercises should be replaced by new exercises. If no new, unknown exercises are introduced into training, the athletes lose the ability to quickly learn new techniques or coordination exercises.

Developing agility

Agility means the ability to quickly learn new movements, and to quickly change motor activity depending on the changing situation. It is an expression of mobility of the central nervous system of the athlete.

Agility is measured by the difficulty of coordination of assignments, precision of performance, the time between moment of change and the beginning of the response, and the time required for achieving a necessary level of precision.

Fundamentals of developing agility.

Agility is developed, first, through the development of the ability to master movements involving problems of coordination and, second, through the development of the ability to change movements according to changing situations. Improving the precision of perception of one's movements in space and time is of great importance here.

The main method of developing agility is to learn and master various new movements (motor skills). Any exercise can be used as long as it includes new elements. As the new skill becomes more and more automatic, the exercise loses its importance for developing agility.

Exercises requiring an instant reaction to the sudden changes of situation (games, encounters, downhill skiing) are used to develop the ability to quickly change one's movements (motor activity).

Agility exercises in a workout.

Exercises developing agility cause fatigue in a short time. They require a maximum precision of muscular sensation and have little effect when fatigue sets in, so the best time for agility exercises is in the first part of the workout. When developing agility, rest intervals should be long enough to allow for a complete restoration. Exercises should be continued when there is no trace of the fatigue from previous work loads.

Agility exercises in a microcycle.

Agility exercises, or technical workout dedicated to new techniques, should be done on the first day of the microcycle when there are no traces of fatigue from previous workouts.

Agility exercises in a macrocycle.

In the annual or semi-annual training cycle, agility exercises are used mainly in the general preparatory period and in the transitory period. Otherwise, agility is developed in the course of technical training.

Developing flexibility

Some authors classify flexibility as an anatomical quality and not a physical ability, because flexibility depends to a great degree on the shape of one's joints. Since such physical abilities as strength and endurance also depend on the peculiarities of one's anatomy (strength— depends on length of bones, the distance of tendon inserts from the axes of rotations, muscle-tendon ratio, and predominant muscle fiber type; endurance— depends on the relative size of rib cage and thus the ratio of lung volume to body mass), I will not put flexibility in a different category than other physical abilities.

Flexibility is the ability to perform movements of any amplitude in a joint or a series of joints. Greater amplitude means greater flexibility. Flexibility is joint specific. Some joints of an individual can have a flexibility greater than average while some other joints can have less than average flexibility. Flexibility in a joint is a sum of joint mobility depending on the shape of joint surfaces, the length and elasticity of ligaments, and the elasticity of muscles associated with that joint. Flexibility, as well as strength and endurance, can be brought to high values by anybody and at any time in one's life (if joint surfaces permit normal mobility). If a more than natural range of motion is needed, for example more than 70 degrees of turn-out (external rotation) in a hip joint which is desired in ballet, then the flexibility exercises need to be done before the joints are fully formed and ossified (before age 10-12).

Flexibility, like coordination, also depends on emotions, because of the connection between the cerebellum and the areas of the brain responsible for emotions. Try juggling, balancing, or stretching when you are upset!

Mental rigidity (having fixations) is usually accompanied by a low level of physical flexibility.

Flexibility training is position-specific. Research done by Nicolas Breit, comparing the effects of stretching in the supine and the erect position, shows that:

a) subjects, who are trained in an erect position, tested better in this position than subjects who trained in a supine but tested in an erect position,

b) greater gains were recorded for both groups in a supine test position than in an erect test position. The subjects tested in the erect position had to overcome an extra amount of tension in the muscles they stretched because of the reflexes evoked by standing and bending over.

Flexibility training is speed-specific because there are two kinds of stretch receptors, one detecting the magnitude and speed of stretching, the other detecting magnitude only. Static stretches improve static flexibility and dynamic stretches improve dynamic flexibility. This is why it does not make sense to use static stretches as a warm-up for dynamic action. There is a considerable, but not a complete, transfer from static to dynamic flexibility.

Flexibility improves with an increased blood flow in the muscles.

The greatest and fastest gains in developing flexibility are made by resetting the nervous control of muscle tension and length.

Strength exercises utilizing the full range of motion in a joint can stimulate the muscle fibers to grow longer and elongate the connective tissue associated with the muscle.

Stretching the ligaments and joint capsules and finally reshaping joint surfaces takes years and brings about the smallest amount of improvement.

After the required reach of motion is attained, the amount of work dedicated to maintaining flexibility may be reduced. Much less work is needed to maintain flexibility than to develop it. The amount of "maintenance" stretching will have to be increased as we age, however, to counter the regress of flexibility related to aging.

Different stretching methods bring about different results (dynamic stretching improves dynamic flexibility, static improves both static and dynamic flexibility), in different amounts of time (difference between ballistic, static relaxed and isometric stretching). These differences are most likely the result of the way a given kind of exercise acts upon our nervous system. Muscles are usually long enough to allow for a full range of motion in the joints. It is the nervous control of their tension, however, that has to be reset for the muscles to show their full length. This is why ten minutes of stretching in the morning makes one's full range of motion possible later in a day without a warm-up. This is also why repeating movements that do not use a full range of motion in the joints (e.g., bicycling, certain techniques of Olympic weightlifting, pushups) can cause a shortening of the muscles surrounding the joints of the working limbs. This shortening is a result of setting the nervous control of length and tension in the muscles at the strongest values or at those repeated most often. Stronger stimuli are remembered better. Eastern European coaches will not let their gymnasts ride bicycles even though they seem to have all the flexibility they need. It is said that strenuous workouts slightly damage the fibers of connective tissue in the muscles (micro-tears). Usually they heal in a day or two. A loss of flexibility is supposedly caused by these fibers healing at a shorter length. To prevent this, static stretching after strength workouts is recommended. All this sounds very good but, the same gymnasts that are kept from bicycling, run with maximal accelerations to improve their special endurance. Such running is a strenuous, intensive strength effort for leg muscles, but in running, these muscles work through a full range of motion in the hip and knee joints, and because of that, there is no adverse effect on flexibility. If stretching after a workout was enough, then these gymnasts could ride bicycles with the same result. The situation with pushups is very similar. If you do a couple of hundred a day, on the floor, so the muscles of your chest, shoulders, and arms contract from a shortened position, no amount of static stretching will make you a baseball pitcher or a javelin thrower.

A strength increase in extreme ranges of motion (occurring after isometric stretching or after weight exercises done in a full range of motion), seems to be a result of the longitudinal growth of muscle fibers.

Exercises consisting of movements with maximum (for a particular athlete) amplitude are used to develop flexibility. These so called extension or stretching exercises are divided into active and passive exercises. In active exercises (movements), a joint is made more mobile through the contraction of the muscles passing over it. In passive exercises (movements), forces external to these muscles are used.

The first group of exercises includes simple movements (leg raises, trunk rotations), springing movements (ballistic stretches—not recommended), and swinging movements similar to the first ones (simple movements), for example, leg raises done with less control.

The second group includes splits and exercises performed with the help of muscles that are not associated with the joint which is exercised.

Besides the exercises used to develop flexibility, special static exercises, called static active flexibility exercises, are also used. They are intended to develop the ability to maintain the body in an extended and rigid posture (holding the leg up in gymnastics).

Flexibility in sports.

There are three kinds of flexibility:

— Dynamic— The ability to perform dynamic movements within a full range of motion in the joints. It is best developed by dynamic stretching. This kind of flexibility depends on the ability to combine the relaxing of the extended muscles with the contraction of the moving muscles.

Example of dynamic flexibility.

— Static passive— The ability to assume and maintain extended positions using one's weight (splits), strength not coming from stretched limbs such as lifting and holding a leg with your arm, or other external means. Passive flexibility usually exceeds active (static and dynamic) flexibility in the same joint. The greater this difference, the greater the reserve tensility (flexibility reserve) and the possibility of increasing the amplitude of active movements. This difference diminishes in training as the active flexibility improves. Doing static stretching alone does not guarantee an increase of dynamic flexibility that is proportional to the increase of static flexibility.

Static flexibility may increase when the muscles are somewhat fatigued. This is why static stretching should be done at the end of a workout.

Example of static passive flexibility.

— Static active— The ability to assume and maintain extended positions using only the tension of the agonists and synergists while the antagonists are being stretched. For example, lifting the leg and keeping it high without any support. Your static active flexibility depends on your static passive flexibility and on the static strength of muscles that stabilize your position.

Example of static active flexibility.

The principles of flexibility training are the same in all sports. Only the required level of a given kind of flexibility varies from sport to sport.

The flexibility of an athlete is sufficiently developed when the maximal reach of motion somewhat exceeds the reach required in competition. This difference, between the athlete's flexibility and the needs of the sport, is called "the flexibility reserve" or "tensility reserve". It allows the athlete to do techniques without excessive tension, and prevents injury. Achieving the maximum speed in an exercise is impossible at your extreme ranges of motion, i.e., when you have no "flexibility reserve".

In choosing stretches, you should examine your needs and the requirements of your activity. For example, if you are a hurdler, you need mostly a dynamic flexibility of hips, trunk and shoulders. To increase your range of motion, you need to do dynamic leg raises in all directions, bends and twists of the trunk, and arm swings. Your technique can be perfected by several dynamic exercises done by walking or running over the hurdles. The hurdlers stretch, a static exercise, does not fit into your workout because it strains your knee by twisting it. Simple front and side splits are better for stretching your legs. The explanation that in the hurdlers stretch, your position resembles the one assumed while passing the hurdle is pointless. Dynamic skills cannot be learned by using static exercises, and vice versa. The technique of running over the hurdles is better developed in motion.

Swimmers should have long hamstrings and chest muscles. When doing the breaststroke, if you go up and down in the water instead of moving just under the surface, it means that your chest muscles are too short. In the backstroke this shortness also causes your face to get under the surface when the arm enters the water, which is when you want to take a breath. In the crawl, short hamstrings pull your feet out of the water and make your legwork inefficient.

Wrestlers and judoka need an especially great static strength in extreme ranges of motion to get out of holds and locks. This strength is best developed by isometric stretching and lifting weights, beginning lifts from maximally extended positions.

You should be careful in choosing your stretches, however, because too much flexibility in some parts of the body can be detrimental to your sports performance. For example, in jumping, an excessively loose trunk at the moment of take-off causes a scattering of forces.

Olympic weightlifters need to shorten the muscles surrounding the hip and knee joints for the proper execution of lifts. Muscles that are too long let the weightlifter "sink" too deep on his legs while getting under the barbell. This makes it difficult to stand up and complete the lift.

Types of stretching exercises.

Flexibility can be improved by doing exercises like running, swimming, and lifting weights as long as your limbs go through the full range of motion. Not all athletes though, can always lift weights or run middle and long distances. At some stages of training, it can interfere with the development of their special form. Properly chosen stretching exercises are less time and energy consuming than these indirect methods. Developing the maximal flexibility permitted by bones and ligaments is one of the easiest tasks in athletic training. It takes little time and effort to maximally elongate muscles that limit the natural range of motion in joints.

Your choice of type of stretching exercises (or a combination of types of exercises), depends on your sport and the shape you are in. The order the types of exercises are listed in, corresponds to the sequence of performing them in a workout.

1. Dynamic stretching: Involves moving parts of your body and gradually increasing reach and/or speed of movement.

Perform your exercises (leg raises, arm swings) in sets of five to twelve repetitions. If after a few sets you feel tired— stop. Tired muscles are less elastic, which causes a decrease in the amplitude of your movements. Do only the number of repetitions that you can do without diminishing your range of motion. More repetitions will only set the nervous regulation of the muscles' length at the level of these less than best repetitions, and may cause you to lose some of your flexibility. What is repeated more times or with a greater effort will leave a deeper trace in your memory! After reaching the maximal range of motion in a joint in any direction of movement, you should not do any more repetitions of this movement in this workout. Even if you can maintain a maximal range of motion over many repetitions, you will set an unnecessarily solid memory of the range of these movements. You will then have to overcome these memories in order to make further progress.

Do not confuse dynamic stretching with ballistic stretching! In ballistic stretches, the momentum of a moving body or a limb is used to forcibly increase the range of motion. In dynamic stretching (as opposed to the ballistic stretching), there is no bouncing or jerky movements.

Besides perfecting the intermuscular coordination, dynamic stretching improves the elasticity of the muscles and ligaments, and changes the surfaces of joints in the process of long-term flexibility training.

Dynamic flexibility is usually reduced by fatigue, so do not do dynamic stretching when your muscles are tired, unless you want to develop a specific endurance and not flexibility. Stretching is most effective when carried out daily, two or more times a day. In one experiment, the results of dynamic stretching for five days, twice a day (two sessions per day), with thirty repetitions per session, were twice as great as the results of doing the same number of repetitions, also twice daily but every other day (one day of rest after a day of stretching). Eight to ten weeks is sufficient to achieve improvement, which depends on muscle elasticity. Any further increase of flexibility is insignificant, and it depends on the long-term changes of bones and ligaments. This requires, not intensive, but rather extensive training, i.e., regular loads in the course of many years.

Dynamic stretches are performed in sets, gradually increasing the amplitude of movements in a set. The number of repetitions per set is between five and twelve. The number needed to reach the maximal amplitude of movement in a joint depends on the mass of muscles moving it. A reduction of amplitude is a sign to stop. A well conditioned athlete can usually make a set of forty or more repetitions at maximal amplitude.

Dynamic stretches should be used in your early morning stretch and as a part of the general warm-up in a workout. Start your movements slowly, gradually increasing the range and the speed of movements. Do not "throw" your limbs, rather, "lead" or "lift" them, controlling the movement along the entire range.

The early morning stretching is done before breakfast and consists of a few sets of arm swings and leg raises to the front, rear, and sides (dynamic stretches). Before doing these raises and swings, warm up all the joints by flexing and twisting each of them. No isometric stretches are to be done in the morning. Isometric stretches may be too exhausting for your muscles if done twice a day.

The whole routine can take about 30 minutes for beginners and ten to fifteen minutes for advanced. Yes, after reaching the desired level of flexibility, you will need less work to maintain it. You should not get tired during the morning stretching. Tired muscles are less elastic and if you get tired, you will defeat the purpose of this exercise. The purpose of this stretching is to reset the nervous regulation of the length of your muscles for the rest of the day.

2. Static active stretching: Involves moving your body into a stretch and holding it there through the tension of the muscles-agonists in this movement. The tension of these muscles helps to relax (reciprocal inhibition) the muscles opposing them, i.e., the muscles that are stretched.

It is difficult to develop static active flexibility to the level of your dynamic or static passive flexibility. You have to learn how to relax stretched muscles and you have to build up the strength of the muscles opposing them, so that parts of your body can be held in extended positions. Although this kind of flexibility requires isometric tensions to display it, you should also use dynamic strength exercises for its development. For example; in training hold your leg extended to the side; keep raising and lowering it slowly in one continuous motion. When you can do more than six repetitions, add resistance (ankle weights, pulleys or rubber bands). After dynamic strength exercises, do a couple of static (isometric) exercises, holding the leg up for six seconds (or longer), then do static passive flexibility exercises like isometric or relaxed stretches. Your static active flexibility depends on your static passive flexibility.

3. Isometric stretching: It has been found, that if a muscle is actively contracted while in an elongated position and its ends are relatively fixed, very vigorous firing of the Golgi organ occurs, and subsequently, increases in the stretch. Eventually, when your maximal (at this stage of training) stretch is achieved, the last tension is held for up to 30 seconds or even more. This increases the strength of the muscles in this position. Isometric stretching is the fastest method of developing static passive flexibility. Because of the strong and long tensions in this type of stretching, it should be applied according to the same principles as other strength exercises. You should allow sufficient time for recovery after exercising, depending on your shape, total volume, intensity, and the sequence of efforts. It may be a good idea to use isometric stretching in strength workouts and, on days when recovering from these workouts, use either static relaxed stretching, or replace the last, long tension in the isometric stretching by just holding the relaxed muscles in the final stretch.

Isometric stretching is not recommended for children and athletes that are not past puberty. Your muscles have to be healthy and strong for you to use this method (isometric stretching). If you neglected your strength training, or were doing it incorrectly, the isometric stretches may harm your muscles. In isometric exercises, muscle fibers contract and the connective tissue attached to them is stretched. When the connective tissue of a muscle is weak, due to improper strength training, or when it is stretched with too much force, it can become damaged. Depending on the amount of stress, and also on the strength of the connective tissue in a given muscle, this damage, at a microscopic level, can announce itself as muscle soreness or it can amount to a complete muscle tear (muscle strain). To make this connective tissue stronger, you should do strength exercises with light resistance and a high number of repetitions. These exercises are to be done slowly. Make full stops at the beginning and at the end of each movement.

It is difficult to tell for how long (how many months) you need to perform the high repetitions exercises that strengthen the connective tissue of your muscles after you have found òut that the connective tissue is too weak for the isometrics. To find out, you have to periodically test the reaction of your muscles to isometric stretches. If the muscles get sore it means that the connective tissue is still too weak.

When everything is all right, you will feel nothing— no pain or soreness.

To develop exceptional strength, as well as flexibility, combine isometric stretches with dynamic strength exercises like lifting weights; using the same muscles. A few weeks after starting the isometric stretching you may hit a plateau. Regulating the tension and length of muscles will stop bringing any improvement in your stretches. Do not worry. Do your exercises concentrating on the strength gains you will achieve. These gains are expressed by the increased time you can maintain a position, the amount of weight you can support, or the ability to stand up (slide up, walk up) from your attempts at splits. After some time, when your strength improves, you will notice a great increase in your flexibility.

Isometric stretches are strenuous exercises requiring adequate rest between applications. For best results, they should be supplemented by dynamic strength exercises. In the workout, all dynamic exercises must precede the isometrics (not counting episodic inclusion of isometric tension before speed- strength actions, which sometimes acts as a stimulating factor, and in certain other cases).

There are three methods of doing isometric stretches:

First method: Stretch the muscles (not maximally) and wait several seconds until the mechanism regulating their length and tension readjusts, then increase the stretch, wait again, and stretch again. When you cannot stretch any more this way, apply short strong tensions to bring about further increases in muscle length. Hold the last tension for up to 30 seconds.

Second method: Stretch as much as you can, hold this stretched and, at the same time, tensed position until you get muscle spasms, then decrease the stretch, then increase it, tense it, and so on. The last tension should be held for up to five minutes. It makes some people scream.

Third method: Stretch the muscles almost to the maximum, then tense for three to five seconds, then relax. Through successive tensions and relaxations, stretch further and further until the stretch cannot be increased. Hold the last tension for up to 30 seconds. After a minute of rest, repeat the same stretch. Do three to five repetitions of a whole stretch per workout. Use isometric stretches three or four times per week. Gradually increase the time of the last tension to about 30 seconds.

In all these methods, you should stress the strength gains in a stretched position. When you cannot increase the stretch, concentrate on tensing harder or longer, or both. In time it will "translate" into a greater stretch. To increase the tension of a muscle at any given length— put more weight on it. In splits, not supporting yourself with your arms will help.

No matter which method of isometric stretching you choose, when doing the stretches, breathe as naturally as possible. It is not always easy with isometrics, but keep trying.

4. <u>Static passive stretching (Relaxed stretching)</u>: Involves relaxing your body into a stretch and holding it there by the weight of your body or by some other external force. Slow, relaxed static stretching is useful in relieving cramps and spasms.

Relaxed stretches are yet another means of developing static passive flexibility. Although much slower than isometric stretches, relaxed stretches have some advantages over isometrics. They do not cause fatigue and you can do them when you are tired. It is hard to develop any problem doing them. Two major drawbacks; your muscular strength in extended positions does not increase as a result of relaxed stretching and the stretches are very slow. For the same person, that in using isometrics gets into a full side split in 30 seconds without a warm-up, it may take up to ten minutes of relaxed stretching (with no warm-up), to get to this same level. Within a couple of months of doing relaxed stretches this time gets shorter. Eventually it may take you from one to two minutes to do a full split. (With a good warm-up, of course, you can do it at once.) In your workout, relaxed stretches should be done as the last thing. Do them after isometric stretches or even instead of them. If you have enough time in a day, you can also do them, whenever you feel like it, without a warm-up.

In doing these stretches, assume positions that let you relax all your muscles. Remember isometric stretches? Some of their positions are designed to tense stretched muscles; e.g., side and front split exercises; by placing your weight on them. In relaxed stretching you want as little weight on your muscles as possible. In splits, this is done by leaning the body forward and supporting it with your arms. Relax completely. Think about slowly relaxing all the muscles. Do not think about anything energetic or unpleasant.

When relaxing into a stretch, you will feel resistance at some point. Wait in that position patiently and after a while you will notice that you have slid into a new range of stretch. After reaching the greatest possible stretch (greatest at this stage of training), hold it; feeling the mild pain in stretched muscles. Get out of the stretch after a minute or two. Do not stay in a stretch until you get muscle spasms. You can repeat the stretch after a minute.

Injury prevention and flexibility.

A muscle does not have to be maximally stretched to be torn. Muscle tears are the result of a special combination, a sudden stretch and a contraction done at the same time. Great differences in strength and endurance, or fatiguability between two opposing muscle groups, as well as a strength imbalance of ten per cent between these same muscle groups on both sides of the body, are the main causes of injuries. Improving the strength and endurance of weaker muscles is the best prevention of injuries. A careful analysis of the form of movement may also hold the key to injury prevention. A good technique feels effortless. Try to eliminate the moments in your technique when the maximal tension of already stretched muscles is used to counter the fast movement of a relatively big mass, or to accelerate suddenly against great resistance, e.g. tears of supporting leg in kicking, hamstring tear in starting from the starting blocks. Great flexibility alone will not prevent injuries.

Flexibility exercises in a workout.

Dynamic flexibility exercises should be done for about 10 minutes at the beginning of the warm-up; after exercises designed to raise the body temperature and the blood flow in the muscles; and before the specialized part of warm-up, for example, technical exercises. In sports demanding displays of passive flexibility (splits), passive flexibility exercises can be done after dynamic ones. In other sports, passive exercises are to be done in a cool-down at the end of the workout.

Doing static stretches before a workout that consists of dynamic actions only is counterproductive. The goals of the warm-up are: an increased awareness, improved coordination, improved elasticity and contractibility of muscles, and a greater efficiency of the respiratory and cardiovascular systems. Static stretches, isometric or relaxed, just do not fit in here. Isometric tensions will only make you tired and decrease your coordination. Passive, relaxed stretches, on the other hand, have a calming effect and can even make you sleepy.

When the main part of the workout is over, it is then time for the cool-down and the final stretching. Usually only static stretches are used here. You can start with the more difficult static active stretches that require a relative "freshness". After you have achieved your maximum reach in these stretches, move on to either isometric or relaxed static stretches (or both); following the isometric stretches with relaxed stretches. Pick only one isometric stretch per one muscle group and repeat it two to five times, using as many tensions per repetition (attempt) as it takes to reach the limit of your mobility (at this stage of your training).

Flexibility exercises in a microcycle.

These exercises do not require lots of energy and can be done every day. Dynamic flexibility exercises are even recommended to be done twice a day, every day.

Flexibility exercises in a macrocycle.

Most of the development of flexibility has to be achieved in the preparatory period. In the competitive period flexibility is maintained rather than developed, because intensive competitive exercises stress the muscles enough.

VI. DEVELOPING PHYSICAL SKILLS

Technical training

Technical training is impossible without a sufficient level of physical abilities.

The skill training of the athlete is the method of teaching and perfecting the technique of competition and training actions. The skill, or technical training can be divided into general technical, and special technical training. The purpose of technical training is to make an athlete a master of the technique and not its slave. The athlete must be ready to change or discard any technique if research or experience shows that it is inefficient. The attachment to particular tactics, techniques (or forms of movement), or training methods is a sign of inferior athletes with inferior mental ability. The biomechanical characteristics of the ideal technique change depending on the athlete's changing abilities, so the same technique, performed by the same athlete at various stages of his/her athletic career, will differ from its previous versions.

An effective technique, in cyclic as well as in acyclic sports, is characterized by:

a) A smooth blending of all phases of movement. In acyclic techniques these phases are the preparatory phase, the main phase, and the final phase. Well mastered movement is always smooth. This smoothness depends on coordination and results from a great economy of movement. A continuity of movements and a proper succession of applying forces; not only muscular, but also gravity, inertia, and reactive forces; are necessary for techniques to be effective. If, at some point in shot putting the movement is slowed down, the effect of the previous movements is lost. It is important, before the end of action of one muscle group, for another group to switch in, so the following movements are performed at a mounting pace. This happens when each force begins to act in the place and at the moment when maximum movement speed, caused by the action of the previous force, has been reached.

b) A proper rhythm of movements in the technique. It is a measure of the correlation of the duration of the individual phases of the exercise. A proper alternation of muscular tension and relaxation in the phases of movement indicates a mastering of the technique. Rhythm integrates individual phases of movement into one coordinated action. The duration of each phase of a movement (technique) influences its efficiency.

c) Precision of movement. Movements that make up the technique must reach their goals in a strictly defined fashion, with a precisely defined speed and path of movement.

d) Predicting the results of your own actions. Thanks to proper practice, the athlete, before and during any action, can predict the sequence and outcome of movements at crucial points of the technique.

e) Anticipation. To effectively carry out techniques in the changing circumstances of games or individual contact sports, the athlete has to accurately anticipate the actions of opponents, partners, and movements of equipment (ball, puck). Accurate anticipation depends on good tactical thinking and knowledge of the situation. In a given situation, the opponent or partner has a limited choice of actions, which facilitates anticipation.

The choice of exercises used to develop or perfect any technique must take into account the needs of the individual athlete and the way this technique is going to be performed. Many technical exercises used today were developed when the technique was different than today's standard. For example, the judo shoulder throw as demonstrated by Jigoro Kano[35], the founder of Judo Kodokan, has little resemblance to the shoulder throw as performed today. In the old form, after pulling the opponent forward and rotating the back toward the opponent, the "thrower's" center of gravity was just below the opponent's center of gravity (below the waist level). Today, the shoulder throw specialists, performing this throw, squat as low as possible, or even kneel. They pull so explosively with their arms that their hips, simultaneously descending below the level of the opponent's knees, do not contact any part of the opponent's body. The exercises that were suitable for practicing the old standard form are harmful if used for the modern version. If done correctly, performing incomplete throws (uchikomi); which was, and still is, the traditional method of perfecting all throws; in the modern version of shoulder throw will damage the back of the athlete because the training partner who is pulled strongly, but not thrown over the shoulders, will fall on top of the squatting thrower. Usually, when thoughtless judo coaches have their athletes, who do this throw in its advanced form, practice it using traditional uchi-komi, the athletes instinctively cheat— faking the pull (kuzushi). It spares them from back injuries but also develops a weak, flawed technique.

Two forms (old—upper row, modern—lower row) of the judo shoulder throw (seoi-nage).

Principles of developing and perfecting technical skills.

The degree of difficulty of the new technique must be within the the athlete's ability to overcome it. This depends on the number of new skills involved, the possibility of a positive transfer of already mastered skills, and the level of physical and mental abilities required. The ability to continually learn new techniques or their variants depends on the athlete's coordination and on his/her store of physical skills. The development of the new technique must be coordinated with the development of the physical abilities supporting it. Some techniques do not make sense if done with less than a certain speed, precision, and strength, or without a certain height of jump. So in a macrocycle in which this particular technique is being developed, the required abilities must be developed first, to avoid learning an improper form of technique. In the meantime, the athlete may work on those elements of the technique that can be perfected before reaching the level of the ability necessary for learning the whole technique. Breaking up the technique into separate elements (analytic method of learning technique) can be used, without distorting these elements, mainly when the competitive exercise or technique consists of relatively independent elements joined by distinctive junctions. For example, gymnastic combinations and combinations (but not individual techniques such as punches or throws) in individual contact sports.

The first step in learning a new technique is seeing it. If an athlete learns a technique that already exists, then the demonstration (personal or using pictures and movies) is easy. When the technique has never been performed, then, depending on resources, one can use drawings, models, or generate computer images. Apart from creating the visual image, the athlete may learn the "feel" of the technique on special training devices (simulators, spotting, trampolines). Combining sensations from previous experiences, visual images, and kinesthetic sensations learned on simulators, is used by the athlete when initially putting the whole technique together mentally in ideomotor exercises.

The next step is deciding what exercises will be best. In cyclic sports, the simplicity of the elements of technique and the fact that they can't be separated, makes it necessary to use only a synthetic method of learning technique and use exercises that recreate the whole technique. If some elements of the technique need to be altered to make it better, one can make the desired changes in these elements of technique by setting special tasks to be performed while doing the technique. For example, by using light or sound pacers, one can change the frequency and length of a runner's stride.

In acyclic sports some techniques are so complex, that in order to learn them, one has to use exercises that recreate only parts of the whole technique, for example, elements of the javelin throw such as pre-run, cross over, and the actual throw; or in the hammer throw, the rotations and the release. This is called the analytic method of learning technique, and exercises for this method must be chosen carefully. Certain phases of technique cannot be separated and made into individual exercises without distorting the character of these phases of technique and thus, make putting these parts back together difficult. In the high jump, one should not practice an approach run without the take off because the speed, rhythm of movements, and radius of the approach, depend on the individual technique of take-off. In the long jump, practicing sprints may develop speed, but the speed of running is only one of the elements the approach that contributes to a good jump. Sprinting does not teach one how to develop maximal speed at the moment of take off and how to hit the board accurately. Breaking judo throws into "breaking balance" (kuzushi), "entry" (tsukuri), and "completion/finishing off" (kake), and then practicing the incomplete throws consisting of only kuzushi and tsukuri, may cause the bad habit of stopping at the end of tsukuri, losing all momentum, and then having to generate enough power to finish off the throw. Similar to this, are the results of breaking up the phases of the shot put or discus throw and practicing them separately.

In gymnastic combinations, consisting of fairly independent elements, practicing separate elements does not have this adverse effect and does not cause difficulties when putting the elements together.

To overcome the adverse effects of practicing separate elements of the technique, one can use exercises imitating the whole technique, (for example, without equipment) and keep altering the partial exercises (vary the initial and/or final position, vary the task). Exercises imitating the technique in conditions of lower difficulty should not be excessively easy because this can lead to a formation of the skill without an application in learning or performing the actual technique.

When learning whole techniques or their phases, one should set a task for each movement, establish an initial and final position of the body (or bodies) or equipment, and then find a way of accomplishing the task and/or changing the position. The athlete has to establish "control points" of the technique or of the technical exercise, so as to get both immediate goal/task for each phase of movement and the feedback needed to correct the movement. As the technique is perfected, the attention shifts from its details to its one decisive phase. The result of the technique depends on which phase the athlete concentrates on. For example, in the long jump concentration on the speed gives better distance than concentration on the force of push-off.

The more versatile and coordinated the athlete is; and if the techniques are taught in proper sequence, so the new ones differ only slightly from the ones that are mastered; the less he/she will rely on partial exercises (analytic method).

In individual contact sports and in games, perfecting techniques independently from tactical situations is methodically unsound. The coach should not tell the athlete how to perform details of the technique. He/she should only show possible solutions, so the athlete can find the form of technique that most suits his/her mental and physical characteristics.

As the athlete learns the technique he/she goes through the following stages of mastering it:

1) The first stage is characterized by a generalization of excitation in the central nervous system, which causes movements to be overly restrained, muscles tensed more than necessary, performance of additional movements, and the use of more muscle groups in the movements than needed. This stage of learning may be very short, or impossible to notice in properly trained athletes. Their general and versatile background causes very little or no generalized excitation in the nervous system because the new technique contains elements of previously mastered movements. They start learning at the second stage.

2) The second stage is characterized by increasing precision and a greater economy of movement. The level of metabolic changes caused by performing the technique lowers. The improvements are caused by a gradual concentration of the excitation in the appropriate centers of the central nervous system. At this stage, the sequence of processes of excitation and inhibition in the central nervous system begins forming. The firm habits are not yet formed. The athlete should pay attention to the details of the technique. Verbal descriptions or directions about the technique are given before attempting the technique, and while performing it, verbal corrections can be used to point out the proper movements and the unnecessary movements.

3) The third stage is characterized by an automatization of movements without a verbal qualification of these movements by the athlete. The technique becomes increasingly stable and precise. Further improvement in the economy of movement allows for a greater number of repetitions.

4) The fourth stage of mastering the technique, when this technique is established as a firm habit, is dedicated to perfecting it in varying conditions and in various combinations. This leads to a greater precision and a further perfection of the technical habit.

Too intensive a flow of impulses from working muscles causes an irradiation of stimulation in the central nervous system and interferes with the reception of phases of tensing and relaxing muscles (intermuscular and intramuscular coordination). A lack of precise feedback from the muscles during intensive exercises results in imprecise movements. For this reason, beginners should practice technical skills with a lowered intensity of the efforts.

Such basic elements of coordination as balance, a sense of rhythm, and orientation in space, decide about the quality of the technique/technical proficiency and are developed in specialized forms in the course of technical training.

Balance is perfected by exercises that make it difficult to maintain a stability of stance.

Static balance is perfected by prolonging the time of maintaining the stance; closing eyes while doing already mastered exercises; exercising on a narrower beam; narrowing the stance (smaller distance between hands or legs); raising higher above the support surface; performing additional movements while maintaining balance; assuming static positions immediately after a dynamic movement of the body; maintaining stance against actions of the partner; raising height of the apparatus; and doing exercises on an unstable support.

Dynamic balance is perfected by methods similar to the ones used for perfecting static balance, except that the exercises are done in motion; for example, shadowboxing/shadowkickboxing blindfolded, practicing defenses against leg sweeps or trips (only the defending wrestler is blindfolded), and closing eyes while running or riding along a steep curve.

To properly integrate elements of the new technique, the athlete must know its standard rhythm. Later, when the technique is already mastered, the athlete may alter the rhythm to suit individual needs. To learn the standard rhythm, athletes pay attention to rhythm while watching perfect executions of the technique, watch movies of the technique shown at normal and slower speed with a soundtrack reproducing the rhythm of movements, and try to reproduce the rhythm by counting or beating it.

Spatial orientation, or the feeling of space, is perfected by exercises that require an increasingly greater accuracy of differentiation between the spatial characteristics of movements and their outcome. In team sports, the accuracy of passing the ball, and of dosing the force behind it, is initially developed by sending the ball or puck alternately at dissimilar distances. For example, 25 and 45 meters, 30 and 50 meters ("contrasting assignments"), and then at gradually more similar distances, differing by 5 meters or less ("approaching assignments"). The accuracy of shots at the goal or throws into the basket is developed in similar way, either by changing the size of the goal or the distance from the basket. In individual contact sports, athletes develop the ability to accurately (within 1 centimeter) evaluate the distance from the opponent by sparring with partners of different height and arm's reach. In gymnastics, and in sports where standard exercises are performed on a standard apparatus, spatial orientation depends mainly on the accuracy of estimating one's position, amplitude, and direction of movements. Exercising on special stands, with spotting, putting marks on the apparatus, suspending targets to be hit in various techniques, exercising with closed eyes, and other such means of immediate feedback are used to perfect the ability to accurately reproduce movements.

The methods for improving the precision of movements must be chosen carefully so as to avoid situations where one aspect of the technique is perfected, while the other deteriorates. For example, improving spatial orientation and balance at a reduced speed, may result in learning an improper speed and rhythm of movement.

Technical skills ought to be effective, stable, plastic, flexible, varied, and reliable.

Having a stability of the skill, means that it can be consistently demonstrated or applied without any deviation from the correct form.

Stability of the skill is most quickly developed by frequent workouts consisting of multiple repetitions of the technique in standard conditions (the same partners, equipment, or apparatus), without fatigue or distractions. Only a flawless technique should be stabilized, and not any more than what the sport requires. In individual contact sports and in ball games, a technique that is too stable causes problems because of the constantly and unpredictably changing conditions of competitions. In gymnastics, however, a greater degree of stabilization is permissible.

Plasticity of the skill, is the ability to alter and improve it in the course of training. It requires good coordination and overall versatility. Premature specialization does not allow for the development of sufficient versatility. As a result the techniques may become rigid; impossible to alter and improve.

Adjustability of the skill, is the ability to adjust it ad hoc in the changing conditions or actions of the opponent. It requires technical versatility, familiarity with many techniques related to the one just used, quick reactions, and a good feel for action/equipment or opponent.

To make a technique sufficiently adjustable, athletes use exercises with strictly regulated variation and exercises with unpredictable variation. Exercises with strictly regulated variation include, an execution of the technique from a different initial position, with greater resistance, in various technical combinations, or with a different task. Exercises with unpredictable variation can be regulated to a various degree, but not so much as to exclude unknown factors (free sparring, practicing game combinations with opponents, performing technique in adverse weather).

The reliability of skills depends on their stability and adjustability, and on such athletic abilities as, special endurance, mental stability, and good coordination. In speed- strength sports, reliability of skills is considered sufficient if the athlete performs the skill with at least 95% intensity (95% of the best personal result) in 70-80% of the total attempts. In endurance sports, reliability of skills depends on special endurance. In cyclic sports, this is developed by performing the technique (or competitive exercise) over a longer distance than the competitive one or, by increasing the number of repetitions of the exercise while reducing rest intervals. This last method is also used in acyclic sports. When using these methods of improving special endurance, and thus, the reliability of technique, one should not allow the athlete to become so tired that the technique is distorted. At certain stages of developing technique, fatigue, if it is not excessive, helps to perfect coordination and economy of movement (as fatigue sets in, the energy expenditure of long distance runners may be reduced by 5-6% without any reduction in the speed of running).

To develop reliability in conditions of great mental and emotional tension, athletes are distracted by various means during some regular technical workouts and during model technical workouts. These workouts recreate the conditions of competitions, with judges that are more or less impartial, and with a hostile public.

As soon as the technique is stabilized, before the end of the preparatory period, actual competitions of minor importance are also used for developing technical reliability. The techniques, that are to be perfected by frequent participation in competitions, must be stabilized, because if they are not stable, athletes will revert to their old skills under the stress of competition. In the competitive period, at the stage of direct preparation for the major competition, top class athletes may compete every day to develop an "immunity to interference".

Immediate feedback in technical training.

The accurate and readily available information about a performed exercise, permits correction or improvement before the less than perfect form of this exercise is permanently recorded in memory. Athlete who is getting an immediate supply of quantitative information about the parameters of the movement, can compare it to fresh sensations of the movement, and immediately correct it. Quickly providing quantitative information about the parameters of the just completed movement, combined with subjective attempts at evaluation of these parameters, leads to an increase of precision of sensations. Even greater, is the importance of information received during the movement, because it allows for corrections to be made as the movement is performed and enforces correct form. The greater the awareness of the temporal and spatial characteristics of the movement, the easier is it is to control it.

Feedback is used to teach runners, speed-skaters, or cross-country skiers how to freely change the running speed, the length of strides, and/or their frequency. The athlete runs a distance with an assigned, but not maximal, pace. The time of covering the distance, and the number of steps, are measured. The length and frequency of strides are figured out, and the athlete is told these numbers. The distance is covered many times, during several workouts, and the athlete is asked to make adjustments in the running speed by changing either the length or frequency of strides, or both. After each try, the athlete compares his/her subjective evaluation of the outcome to the objective data. If the athlete makes a mistake, he/she repeats the try, attempting to correct it until adjustment is right.

Rewzon (quoted from "Trening Sportowy—Teoria i Praktyka" by Z. Naglak, 1979, after an article by S. W. Farfiel in Sport Wyczynowy 1/9, 1964), when teaching the long jump to high school pupils, did not require them to make a maximal distance, but to accurately land at various, less than maximal distances. Informing the pupils about the actual length of the jump, and the difference from the assigned distance, led to a greater skill in adjusting the length of jump. This skill influenced improvement of the maximal distance.

Rewzon also has found that simple repeating of the same task, with the same parameters, is much less effective than when the parameters vary widely. Starting with assignments of reaching parameters of a movement that are vary widely with every try, the coach then gradually assigns parameters that are increasingly similar, and continues to inform the athlete about the accuracy of each try. Eventually, this leads to an ability to very precisely differentiate the parameters. This method can also be used to teach "hitting the board" in the long jump.

A similar method can be used to develop control and improve the reaction time and speed of movement. In training of fencers (épée), an electrical circuit measuring the time elapsed between the signal to start a technique, and the contact with the target, was used to teach fencers to react with assigned speed. The subjective evaluation by the fencer, of the amount of time between the signal and the hit, was compared with the real time. Fairly quickly, the subjective evaluation and the objective data became close, and fencers were able to perform the task with 0.01 second accuracy.

Dynamometers or piezoelectric sensors showing boxers the force of a punch, teach them to put only as much effort into the punch as is needed. Punches of maximal force do not necessarily result from what a boxer perceives to be the greatest effort (greatest mobilization). Throwing punches that are sufficient enough to get the result (KO., injury, pain), spares energy because a small increase of mechanical power requires a disproportionally greater increase of effort. For example, in running, the requirement of oxygen during a run grows with the cube of speed.

In swimming, piezoelectric or pneumatic sensors attached to each limb, inform about the duration, force, and frequency of movement.

Practicing individual contact sports techniques in slow motion, with and without resistance, and at maximum speed with and without resistance, can lead to such perfection and automatization of the techniques, that the athlete can apply them when appropriate, without being aware of it during the action. After the action; for example, in a judo throw; the athlete may have a visual recall of the opponent's action that led to the performance of a technique, but no recall of the actual technique. There is nothing wrong with such a level of automatization if it does not lead to a passive, stalking kind of fighting; relying on the opponent to trigger the action. Such passive tactics are unreliable because only so many techniques can be automatized to such a degree, and nonstandard opponents or tactics may render them useless. With aggressive, "take charge" tactics, a lesser degree of automatization is sufficient, so that the athlete is still aware of the action.

General technical training.

A formation of the store of skills and the knowledge that is necessary for learning the technique of a selected sport, is the task of general technical training. The skills formed in general technical training are included in specialized skills (techniques), making the perfection of techniques easier. For example, a number of gymnastic techniques are used when learning to pole vault or to figure skate. This is called a "positive transfer of skills".

The athlete's general technical training includes learning how to do the exercises of the sport that are used to develop physical abilities. Before a certain exercise can develop physical abilities, an athlete has to learn its correct execution.

General technical training provides the athlete with "movement erudition".

Special technical training.

The forming and constant perfecting of skills, which allow the athlete to use the abilities (physical abilities) to the fullest in competitions, is the main task of special technical training. This task can be realized in stages: learning the basics of a sports technique, individualizing its forms (depending on the athlete's individual abilities), forming the motor and mental skills for its successful performance in current competitions, transforming the skills into habits, transforming or renewing the forms of technique according to the athlete's increased abilities, and creating of new techniques as the athlete attains a sufficiently high level of mastery.

As skills become habits, the superfluous movements disappear, conscious control of the technique is lowered, muscular tension is reduced, and the feedback about the action is reduced; which can lead to performing it unknowingly. In learning the technique, and then forming a skill, verbal descriptions and corrections accompanying the demonstration, are admissible. At the habit stage, verbal descriptions are out. A general remark; the quality of a coach is inversely proportional to the amount of words used in a workout. The same goes for athletes.

Technical exercises in a workout.

Learning new, or perfecting known techniques, demands total concentration. Most often, proper execution of the technique requires a high level of strength or speed, or both. For this reason, technical exercises should be done at the beginning of a workout (right after the warm-up), and in the main part of the workout. The effectiveness of the exercises developing the technique is determined by the correctness of the movements learned, and not by the fatigue. This decides the length of rest interval between exercises and the amount of technical exercises in a workout. If, at the initial stages of learning a technique, the athletes are allowed to get tired, the fatigue will alter the technique, and the incorrect technique will be learned, perhaps permanently.

Technical exercises in a microcycle.

The frequency of performing technical exercises is more important then their total volume; so short, frequent workouts are better than long, occasional ones. Technique ought to be practiced as often as possible without adversely affecting the athlete or the technique. One or two technical workouts are done in the first days of the microcycle, so the fatigue does not interfere with forming lasting and correct habits. One workout can be done at the end of the microcycle when the organism is tired, so as to learn using the technique in adverse conditions. In this workout, only well mastered techniques should be practiced.

Technical exercises in a macrocycle.

In the general preparatory period, the task is to learn new techniques or develop better versions of the old. The great volume of general exercises done at this stage of the macrocycle, limits the amount of time and energy available for technical workouts. To make up for the limited time available for the technical exercises, those technical exercises that are well mastered (in previous macrocycles), and can fulfill the functions of the general exercises, may be used in the general development of certain abilities and to simultaneously preserve technical skills. Usually, these exercises have to be altered in some way (put 1-2 kg wrist weights on and do basketball exercises), to make them either strength, endurance, or some other type of general exercises. In the special preparatory period, athletes perfect details of the technique and achieve automatization of technical habits. Technical exercises in the preparatory period are performed with submaximal intensity, at a so called "controlled speed", which allows the athlete to control the movements. In speed-strength sports, during the stabilization of the skills, technical exercises (actually competitive exercises), without extra resistance, are done with an intensity of up to 90% of the maximal individual result. When the skills are stable, which happens at the end of the preparatory period, the intensity of competitive exercises, without extra resistance, is first increased to the 90-93% range, and then to maximum. The initial restricting of the intensity when performing these competitive exercises, is to prevent forming a habit or a technical barrier (stabilizing the skill at the level permitted by the less than sufficient development of speed and strength) at a stage of training when the physical abilities do not reach their ultimate development in a current macrocycle. When the maximal level of abilities is reached, then the techniques are practiced with maximal intensity. In sports that do not require the ultimate development of speed or strength, the skills that are to be stabilized, can be practiced with maximal intensity as soon as possible. In the competitive period, technique reaches a high level of automatization. Training means are used to ensure lasting technical habits under the conditions of competition. In the transitory period, little technical work is done because the task of this period is to "untrain" all the systems of the athlete's organism after long and intensive specialized work. The athlete has to unlearn those elements of technical habits that must be discarded in order to further improve technique in the next macrocycle.

Technical training in a macrocycle using the example of weightlifting, and track and field throwers:

The technical training of beginning weightlifters is done during the general preparatory period (which can last for up to six months). It consists of exercises with 40%-50% of current maximal weight in snatch, and clean and jerk, with 6-8 repetitions per set.

Advanced weightlifters perfect technique in the special preparatory and in the competitive period. If necessary, technical corrections are made while warming up for each technical exercise.

The technical training of track and field throwers is done once a week in the general preparatory period, twice a week in the special preparatory period, and three times a week, plus competition, in the competitive period.

Tactical training

Sports technique is directly linked with tactics as a form of combining all the actions to attain the goal. Technique and tactics can only be conditionally divided. During competition, a technique cannot be separated from the tactics of it. They both depend on each other. The choice of tactics depends on mastered techniques, and proper tactics permit an efficient application of techniques. The athletes tactical training includes; mastering the theoretical basis of tactics, learning data about opponents, mastering practical tactics and their combinations and variations, and developing tactical thinking. Practical tactical training should be part of all technical training. For theoretical aspects of tactical training, lessons and seminars are used.

Like any other aspect of athletic training, tactical training is divided into general and special training.

General tactical training.

General tactical training has to instill broad tactical thinking. Learning tactics of related sports is one of the means used in this type of training.

Special tactical training.

Special tactical training aims to achieve mastery of the tactics of the selected sport. This is helped by the "transfer" of the tactical skills and knowledge, acquired as a result of learning related sports.

Tactical exercises in a workout.

Tactics should be taught together with the techniques they are based on. In many cases, practicing tactics has to wait until the athletes are sufficiently proficient in the techniques that are to be utilized in these tactics. Nevertheless, the technical and tactical training should be as simultaneous as possible. Because learning new, or perfecting known tactics has the same requirements as technical exercises, the tactics should be done at the beginning of the workout (right after the warm-up), and in the main part of the workout. Occasionally though, tactics should be tried at the end of the workout, to see if these tactics can be carried out by tired athletes.

Tactical exercises in a microcycle.

Tactical work is done on the same days as techniques. It is usually done at the beginning of the microcycle.

Tactical exercises in a macrocycle.

Tactical preparation is planned, in a six months or twelve month cycle, in such a way that athletes start from the individual elements of the tactics, and proceed to eventually combine them all. Preparatory (general, directed, special) and competitive exercises, that at first model partially, and then, possibly fully, competitive tactics, are the main method of teaching tactics. Tactical training merges with technical training, the development of physical abilities, and psychological preparation. It leads and unites the whole training process, because the combined effect of all the aspects of athletic training eventually is fused into a single competitive tactical action. The outcome of this action (competition), depends on the total (physical, skill, and psychological) preparation of the athlete.

In the general and special preparatory periods, tactical training, theoretical and practical, has the following tasks:

a) Theoretical

— Revealing the strong and weak points of the tactics used in the previous macrocycle.

— Improving the theoretical knowledge of one's sports discipline.

— Becoming familiar with tactics of similar sports disciplines.

— Studying new tactics (variants)

b) Practical

— Perfecting learned tactics.

— Approval and inclusion of new tactics (variants).

— Improving physical and technical preparation, as well as the mental characteristics necessary for mastering new tactics.

New tactics are practiced in facilitated or simplified forms until the athletes perform them without difficulty. The athletes then practice in normal, and later in artificially complicated, forms. The degree of difficulty may be increased in one of the following ways:

a) opponent or opponents is not restricted by certain rules, but the practicing athlete or team must obey them all;

b) space or time, or both (time allotted before attempt in gymnastics, weightlifting, track and field; size of mat or ring or time of bout in individual contact sports; field or period in ball games), of the performance is limited;

c) additional tasks are to be realized at a previously stipulated signal (in judo, switching to chokes or locks while practicing holds, changing distance or type of punches in boxing);

d) limiting the number of attempts (in judo or wrestling first throw wins, in fencing first hit,);

e) realizing tactical tasks when athlete is at a physical disadvantage (tired, weaker than opponent) or at a psychological disadvantage (unexpected changes in organization of the test, distractions).

In the competitive period the tasks are as follows:

a) Theoretical

— Getting to know the tactics of the opponents. Knowledge of the opponent is necessary for finding the best means of defeating him/her. Knowing about the injuries, old and new, helps to determine on which techniques the opponent cannot rely, and what actions he/she is vulnerable to.

— Getting to know the local conditions of the places where competitions are to be held.

— Getting to know the rules and peculiarities of judging and refereeing in the coming competitions.

— Learning about the newest tactics of one's own, and of similar sports disciplines.

b) Practical

— Perfecting previously learned tactics.

— Approval and practice of chosen tactics.

— Eliminating tactical mistakes/flaws.

— Establishment and approval of new tactical plans based on the current needs.

In this period, athletes put out maximum effort, and spend the most time on tactical preparation. In addition, most attention has to be dedicated to methods of perfecting tactics, and switching from one tactic to another. The athletes practice against partners or teams that use the typical tactics of their opponents, and also in conditions as similar as possible to the conditions of the forthcoming competitions. Preparatory competitions are used to perfect various tactics.

In the transitory period tactical training consists of:

— A theoretical analysis of tactics and the quality of tactical preparation from the previous season.

— An explanation and analysis of causes of successful and unsuccessful starts in the season.

— A generalization of experience of the past season.

— A study of new tactics.

VII. PSYCHOLOGICAL TRAINING

General psychological training

Strong will is necessary in sports and in all kinds of human activity. Its components are such qualities as purposefulness, discipline, initiative, self-control, persistence, courage, resoluteness, and staunchness. Sports training requires efforts of will in various situations: in overcoming physical fatigue, showing up on time for workouts, doing exactly what the plan calls for and not less or more, concentrating one's attention on one, or several objects for a long time, and overcoming the embarrassment and fear of the unknown.

Purposefulness turns workouts into serious, consciously regulated actions, not a thoughtless mechanical performance of exercises. Developing purposefulness requires informing athletes about the goal of each action they take. It means making them knowledgeable in the theory of physical culture and sport, and making sure they know what their immediate and long-term training goals are. Athletes must know what the task of each workout is and how it relates to the long-term plan. Each workout, upon completion, must be briefly evaluated with the athletes.

Discipline is always connected with self-control, which is the ability to subordinate one's behavior to the requirements of the task. Initially, developing discipline requires a subordination to the will of the coach, rather than one's own. Discipline is developed by an observance of a set schedule of activities, a schedule which must be reasonable, and in which expediency is understood by the athlete. All the requirements of the schedule must be fulfilled by the athlete. In addition, athletes must obey the rules of conduct, which tell what (and how) to do, and what not to do. Even a partial failure will undermine the athlete's self-esteem.

Initiative and self-sufficiency are the ability to set goals and organize actions without constant supervision. They are developed by putting the athlete in situations which require quick evaluation. He/she has to plan the reaction, carry it out, and take responsibility for it. The situations must constantly change so the athlete cannot repeat the same response automatically. Usually team ball games are used as a means of developing initiative.

Resoluteness is the ability to overcome great difficulty or danger. It is associated with courage and initiative. The exercises that develop resoluteness must contain new and unexpected elements so as not to become habitual, they must be difficult, but not beyond the capability of the athlete, they must be progressively more difficult and must be repeated systematically, and each time these exercises are used, the goal must be achieved. A series of unsuccessful attempts develops indecisiveness.

Staunchness consists of courage in the face of danger or difficulty, self-control (not loosing one's head in a difficult situation and not panicking), the ability to overcome fatigue, and the persistence to achieve the set goal (the will to win).

Different sports have different requirements of the "will" qualities. Certain qualities become "central" or "essential" and others become "supporting". In long distance running, it is persistence that is essential. In ski jumping, it is courage and resoluteness. In gymnastics, self-control (discipline) is essential. Supporting qualities of will also vary depending on sports discipline.

The development of the will qualities needed and shown in athletic actions is conducted simultaneously with the development of physical abilities and skills (The qualities of will are developed simultaneously with, and on the basis of, physical abilities and skills.). The physical and mental aspects of athletic training are inseparable.

Will is developed by overcoming difficulties. The difficulties have to be overcome systematically, not occasionally, and the increased degree of difficulty should not make them impossible to overcome. An athlete must be taught to carry out the training or competitive task. It must be a habit to always finish the assignment and to be responsible (dependable). An athlete must be convinced that there are no easy shortcuts to athletic success, and as this success becomes closer, the effort must be increased.

Carrying out the task to the end is especially difficult in competition. Objective and subjective circumstances may stand in the way of completing the competitive task, and a coach has to use good judgment in defining the task or in insisting on completing it. Not finishing the competitive tasks teaches a lack of commitment that results in a habit of stopping to struggle as soon as the level of difficulty increases (critical situation develops). This is how psychological barriers are formed. One of the methods of overcoming psychological barriers, is to successfully complete competitive exercise under the same conditions (in the same place, on the same apparatus) as in the previous unsuccessful performance.

The athlete's ambition may be greater than his/her level of abilities and skills. The difference between ambitions and abilities makes the athlete afraid to loose self-image should the outcome be below these ambitions, and causes the athlete to avoid competitions. This lack of confidence has to be dealt with, not only when the athlete has developed this feeling, but also when he/she is overly self-assured. When the athlete is overly self-assured, he/she can take unnecessary risks, and in the case of failure, get injured or greatly disillusioned, even to the point of a nervous breakdown.

Regular participation in competitions and the use of competitive exercises in workouts (try-outs, rivalry in exercises) is needed to permanently shape the will of the athlete. A single competition means little in the process of developing the will qualities.

The assignments must be carefully rationed in accordance with the athletes current level of abilities to develop true confidence and self-knowledge.

There are several ways of arranging the competitive tasks in a workout so they are sufficiently demanding, but not impossible to complete:

— athletes compete to decide who will do the most repetitions of an exercise,

— organizing contests in tasks that require mostly psychological mobilization; for example, who will learn a new movement or a combination of movements faster,

— competition where tasks of the normal competitive exercises are altered; for example, using heavier equipment, throwing for accuracy rather than distance,

— lowering the level of a performance, but requiring several repetitions of that level of performance.

Apart from the competitive forms of exercises in workouts, normal competitions, of lesser importance than the main, target competition, are used in will training. The degree of difficulty in preparatory competitions should be higher than in the main competition. This creates a reserve of strength of will.

Even though the psychological loads in athletic training are correspondingly increased with the physical loads, additional difficult situations have to be created, especially when the athlete adapted well to the current loads, to ensure a proper development of the chosen will qualities. Depending on the quality that has to be developed, various changes are made in the physical exercises.

To develop persistence and self-control, the coach may unexpectedly order the athlete to run an additional lap at the end of an exhausting workout, with a higher than normal speed, and to finish first; to play an additional period at the end of a practice game and win it; or to do additional repetitions of exercises with weights, in the form of competition.

Confidence, as well as plasticity and reliability of skills, are developed by working out in a difficult environment, or with unaccustomed apparatus or equipment; for example, exercising outdoors in bad weather, or on difficult terrain, doing exercises with extra weights.

In technical sports, accuracy can be developed in addition to the above qualities by making the goal posts narrower, performing high jumps and pole vault between narrower posts, or throwing discus or hammer from a smaller circle.

Courage can be developed by increasing the degree of risk in exercises: boxing in a smaller ring, balancing on a higher beam, diving from a higher platform, decreasing the radius of curves on the cycling track or in the skating rink.

Staunchness and self-control are developed by introducing distractions while athletes exercise, for example, resetting the pacer to signal a different rhythm than the one athletes have to maintain, making a loud noise before penalty shots.

The will to win is developed by altering the rules to make winning in training more difficult, or by handicapping. This can be done by: requiring a longer period of holding the opponents shoulders on the mat in wrestling, increasing the number of points that give victory, fighting alone against several opponents, shortening rounds or bouts, sparring or competing with an opponent of higher class, limiting the number of players in one team, while the other one has the regular number of players, reducing the number of attempts in jumps.

Usually the methods of developing will qualities in particular sports rely on exercises from these sports. Occasionally though, exercises from different sports, that are of no use in that particular sport, are used. Making a gymnast or a weightlifter do a cross-country run does little for their technical or physical training, but since they have no special preparation for this type of effort, and they know it will not directly pay off, the athletes have to make a greater effort of will.

Will training is not something that only the coach directs and athletes perform. Athletes have an active role in setting their goals. This requires self-knowledge on their part, and the knowledge and skills provided by the coach. The athlete must successfully fight negative habits, reject short term pleasures that interfere with long-term goals, persuade oneself to undertake difficult tasks, regulate psychosomatic functions by such means as autogenic training, and constantly monitor oneself. This constant monitoring of oneself, by keeping a detailed training diary, is an effective means of self-education and self-motivation, and provides an athlete and coach with information necessary to plan training.

Special psychological training

Several factors affect the emotional stability of the athlete. All of these factors have to be affected by all adequate means to desirably influence athlete's psychological state. Good communication with coach, involvement in planning the training, friendly atmosphere in a club, and no complications in other interpersonal relationships, are general environmental factors, but they have a direct bearing on the effectiveness of special psychological training.

Special psychological training affects the mental states directly related to an upcoming performance in competition or in a especially difficult workout. It involves immediate motivation for completing the task at hand, control of the psychological pre-start conditions, a regulation of emotions in the course of performance, and a regulation of psychological states after the performance. The official result of competition tells us who won and how. Besides this result, expressed, for example, in points, there is an effect of the competition which means psychological consequence of achieved result. This effect has to do with the way the result was achieved, and the relation between the result, potential, and ambition. Victory may be achieved by means that do not improve the confidence of the athlete; for example by disqualification of the opponent; or one can lose by dishonest judging and actually be a winner.

The immediate motives are based on the permanent, constant motives of participating in sports. They are dependent on the circumstances the task is to be carried out in, the importance of the task, and the athlete's level of preparation and emotional state. The coach, knowing the abilities and interests of each athlete, must use situational factors to intensify the permanent motivation. Athletes who motivate themselves, use such means as positive monologue, mental rehearsal, mental manipulation of emotions (mental reproduction of the images triggering or limiting emotions), and ideomotor exercises for modeling the whole competitions (from arrival to end), or simply the competitive actions.

According to Professor Oleg Dashkevich, D.Sc. (Psychology) from the Central Institute of Physical Education in Moscow, motivation (both immediate and permanent) to earn prestige or material rewards brings inferior results in comparison to motivation to participate in the sport for its own sake. To athletes with such motivation, the result matters less than the process of achieving it. Such an attitude allows them to correctly apprise their potential, analyze victories and failures, and to fully mobilize themselves (the above from an article "Harnessing Emotions" by Cherepanova in *Sport in the USSR* number 5, 1989).

In spite of the above, Olympic athletes of Soviet Union are rewarded financially for their performance. According to articles published in Soviet newspapers (*Argumenti i Facti*, and in *Moscow News* reported in *Orange County Register* of September 22, 1988), Soviet athletes have assigned plan targets for each athlete. A fulfillment of the plan is rewarded by financial prizes, and failing is punished by reducing the prize. In 1988, the reward for a gold medal was 12000 rubles, 6000 for silver medal, and 4000 for bronze. If the plan called for an athlete to win a gold medal, but the athlete won only a bronze, the amount paid was only 2000 rubles, half of the prize for a bronze medal. Apparently, the Soviets believe that moderate financial rewards optimally mobilize well motivated athletes.

The force of immediate motivation must be optimal for the task. Too much motivation (a desire to win at all cost), over-excites, which lowers the ability to achieve good results in competition. The optimal level of motivation is in reverse proportion to the degree of difficulty and complication of the task. The difference in the level of motivation needed for actions requiring a limited variety of simple techniques, and for actions requiring a great variety of complicated techniques, is most visible in situations when one move can decide about a victory or loss. In such situations, an athlete of low technical skill, who has a few simple techniques and is very excited, can win against an opponent of great technical sophistication.

Some athletes can personally sabotage their success as a defense against the unwanted by-products of success. Athletes that succeed are exploited politically or commercially. Athletes are forced to represent a country (not necessarily their own), a political party (to which they may be indifferent or contemptuous of), or a company. Some athletes can't stand the company of comedians, politicians, and dealers who use the athletes to dignify them, or their goals. The athletes excel as a result of hard work, courage, and the risk of their own health and life. They don't like sleaze. People are prone to sabotage their success if they fear that it will put them in situations, or in company that they detest.

The two most common psychological pre-start conditions are the start fever and the start apathy. In the case of start fever, the goal is to diminish the degree of excitement, but not so much as to lose enthusiasm. In the case of start apathy the goal is to cheer up and instill confidence. The pre-competition warm-up used for regulating the pre-start apathy includes, short, highly dynamic exercises, imitations of final efforts, and highly dynamic games. To calm down overly excited athletes (pre-start fever), exercises emphasizing smoothness, accuracy, concentration, and special breathing exercises are used. Games may also be used to release emotions.

Pre-start states are affected by rationally conducted training, with a proper alternation of tasks, a correct proportion of loads and rest, and an adequate number and quality of preparatory and control competitions. The level of psychological stress has to be within the athlete's ability, but not too low. To increase the level of stress, the coach may postpone a planned try-out for a day, or make assignments more difficult. To relieve the stress, workouts or try-outs can be conducted in a nice, outdoor setting, or indoors, using well chosen background music, and/or using artificial aeroionization. The more excitable the athlete, the later should he or she imagine the start.

The psychological pre-start state ought to occur immediately before start. The time between the end of a warm-up and the start, is the best time for mental readiness to appear. The greater the power output required, the greater the psychological tension ought to be, because more muscle fibers contract with strong psychological mobilization than without it.

Psycho-regulatory/psychosomatic training, including autogenic training, autosuggestion formulas designed to improve sports performance, and ideomotor exercises, is used in an athlete's special psychological training, and even in the course of competition. This type of training is particularly useful when other methods of dealing with pre-start conditions are not sufficiently effective. It includes methods of suggestion and autosuggestion leading to relaxation, as well as mobilization for effort.

The psycho-regulatory/psychosomatic training, as a method of regulation of mind and body, acts on the muscles, internal organs, and the nervous system through a modification of muscular tension and mental concentration.

The psychosomatic training is planned as follows:

1) Introduction
— general information
— attempts to relax muscles
— attempts to learn relaxing breathing

2) Autogenic training proper

a) first stage
— relaxing muscles, using suggestions and autosuggestions that induce a sensation of heaviness
— exercises relaxing blood vessels, using suggestions and autosuggestions inducing sensation of warmth

b) second stage
— regulation of heart function and breath control by using suggestions and autosuggestions
— regulation of function of the solar plexus, and regulation of blood circulation in the head using suggestions and autosuggestions
— autosuggestion formulas for improvement of performance.

3) Auxiliary sports exercises
— local control of muscular tension
— relaxing eyes and speech organs
— partial relaxation

4) Modeled training

The sessions can be conducted with a group, or individually, depending on the preferences of the individual athletes. This method cannot be forced upon the athlete.

Ad 1. Information about the training has to be given during the first session, in a clear, simple manner, with a discussion allowing the participants to find out their tasks, and decide whether they want to participate in it.

The attempts (tries) to relax the muscles have the purpose of revealing tensions resulting from bad posture and improper use of muscles. Practical exercises let the participants realize how to relax the muscles, counteract the active movements and passive mobilization (unnecessarily high tonus), as well as recognize the muscular effort which accompanies each movement, including breathing.

Sequence of actions in learning to relax muscles:

a) Starting on your forehead, and moving down to your toes, tense each muscle group one by one, and keep it tensed for 5-7 seconds.

b) Relax that muscle group, and for 20-30 seconds, concentrate on the pleasant sensation in this muscle group as it relaxes.

c) Repeat the sequence for each subsequent muscle group.

Do this 3-4 times a week, for 15-20 minutes at a time. As a result, when you feel tense, you will be able to recall these sensations and relax.

Ad 2. The purpose of autogenic training is to improve the functioning of the body and mind through relaxation and concentration. During exercises of autogenic training, one achieves a state of auto-hypnosis, different from hypnosis in that there is no dependency on another person. The exercises of autogenic training ought to be conducted in a silent place, somewhat dark, not too hot, so as to limit the external stimulation of the organism. The first task is to learn to assume a position that facilitates relaxation of the muscles and blood vessels, and the slowing down of all functions of the organism. The most frequently used position is seated in an armchair, with head resting on the head rest, hands on the armrests. The angle in the elbow is 120-130 degrees. Eyes are closed, legs resting on the floor, feet parallel. The whole body should be relaxed. Another position used, is lying down on the back. Head has to be bit elevated, it helps to relax the muscles of the neck. Eyes closed. Arms parallel along the body (but do not touch it), hands turned palms up, fingers straight and relaxed. Legs outstretched and relaxed.

Exercises begin by concentrating on the sensations coming from arms and legs, and then learning to cause a sensation of heaviness in the arms, legs, and the rest of the body. After assuming one of the above described positions, the participant repeats "the right hand is heavy" for 5-6 times, then says "I am calm". The next 5-6 times, the participant repeats "the left hand is heavy" and again "I am calm". Then the same routine is repeated for the legs. It is important to repeat these statements (formulas) passively, without wanting to make the limbs heavy. After a few such exercises, the participant starts feeling heaviness in the arms and legs. As one progresses in the exercises, these sensations appear more quickly, are more pronounced, have a wider range, and resemble the sensations felt just before falling asleep. The formulas of autosuggestion repeated in the course of learning to relax the muscles (inducing sensation of heaviness), may be "said" in thoughts and may be accompanied by visual mental images.

As soon as the participant has learned to quickly invoke the sensation of heaviness in the whole body, it is time to learn how to produce the sensation of warmth. When the body feels heavy, the participant repeats "the right arm is warm" six times, then once, says "I am calm", then does the same with the left arm. After the arms, the routine is repeated for the legs. Later, the formulas of autosuggestion change. Instead of focusing on each limb and on one sensation at a time, one formula is used— "my body is heavy and warm".

The "heaviness" exercises cause a relaxation of the muscles. The "warmth" exercises cause a relaxation of the blood vessels. After these exercises are mastered, it is time to learn how to slow down the heart rate and breathing.

The heart slowing exercises start with "discovering" the work of the heart. The participant places a hand on the chest above the heart, and tries to sense its beats. It is important to feel the heart beat and not the pulse. When the participant has learned to sense the heart beat, he/she uses autosuggestion formulas for slowing down its beats. Recommended formulas are "the heart beats quietly and strongly" or "the heart beats quietly". The breath slowing exercises start by first inducing the feeling of heaviness and warmth, and then repeating, "the heart beats quietly", "the breath raises and lowers like a ship on the quiet sea", "I breathe lightly and quietly" or "my breath is quiet". One should not forcibly regulate the rhythm of breathing. The participant, seated or prone, is passive while repeating the formulas, letting the organism do its part.

The remaining stages of the autogenic training (regulation of function of the solar plexus, regulation of blood circulation in the head) have less importance in sports.

The psychosomatic "turning off" in the course of the exercises, is a state of auto-hypnotic concentration, causing a sensation of euphoria and relaxation as a result of cutting off the external stimuli and silencing the psychological internal conflicts. This state is accompanied by a muscular and vascular relaxation, similar to that in the sleep, as well as the possibility of influencing the regulation of blood circulation, breathing, and digestion. A mastering of the vegetative reactions in various states of muscular tension is essential, as is the silencing of internal conflicts. Getting rid of anxiety and fear is important for the athletes before competition.

Journal of Personality and Social Psychology[23], in August 1989, published an article by a team of psychologists at Clark University in Worcester, Massachusetts, that showed that simply having people put their facial muscles in a configuration typical for a given emotion, produced that emotion.

In 1984, Dr. Paul Ekman[23] and other psychologists at the University of California Medical School in San Francisco, published an article in the journal *Science*, showing that mimicking different emotional expressions causes physiological changes, such as changes in heart and breath rate, that are characteristic for a given emotion.

The whole program of psychosomatic training ought to be conducted in connection with normal athletic training in the course of 8-9 sessions, within 2-3 months.

Ad 3. After completion of the psychosomatic training, athletes perform exercises that stabilize and perfect the effects of the autogenic training, and augment them with special sports exercises. In this third stage of the psychosomatic training, the ability to regulate at will the muscular tension and vegetative functions is used for biologic regeneration after efforts; mostly for gaining better athletic form before competition. Controlled relaxing of the muscles helps in all-round athletic training. Systematic autogenic training with (specific for athletic performance) autosuggestion formulas, increases the activity of muscles during performance. The formulas have to deal with particular techniques or athlete's behavior in specific situations in contest and not be of the "I will win" type. Combining physical athletic training with the autogenic training and autosuggestion, designed for the improvement of performance or self-image, ensures success. Athletic training without autogenic exercises/training, leads to psychosomatic disorders such as often observed in even high class athletes at the time of competition.

Relaxing the tongue, and the muscles surrounding the eyes and the face, facilitates relaxing the whole body and stops analytical, critical, and often self-defeating thoughts. Full relaxation of the muscles surrounding the eyes helps when performing exercises demanding good coordination. Seeing bright colors and changing graphic patterns, instead one uniform color after closing the eyes is caused by nervous tension.

Partial relaxation means relaxing particular groups of muscles, or slowing down certain functions of the organism without involving the whole body. This type of relaxation may be used in the final stage of the psychosomatic training for the ideomotor activation. Ideomotor exercises are initially purely mental, not involving muscles, and consist of creating a mental image of the tactical and technical actions necessary in the contest. These mental images are then rehearsed with alternate full relaxations, and short maximal tensions of the muscle groups that ideally should be used in these actions. Ideomotor exercises are especially recommended for track and field athletes and wrestlers. Ideomotor exercises were compared to physical exercises by A. C. Puni.

The physical exercises improved precision of movement by 58%, increased speed of lifting the barbell 17.5%, speed of running in place 11.9%, strength 4.9%.

The ideomotor exercises improved precision of movement by 34%, increased speed of lifting the barbell 6.4%, speed of running in place 16.8%, strength 3.3%.

Ad 4. Modeled training prepares the athlete for the great emotional stress of participating in competitions. A mental rehearsal of all the activities that are associated with competition, increases the sense of familiarity with the competition and thus, reduces fear and anxiety. It serves to protect the athlete from nervous breakdown.

Psychosomatic training may be used as a way of preventing mental fatigue and neurovegetative disorders. Mental fatigue results from a lack of mental adjustment in the athlete to the training and environment. The technique of psychosomatic training facilitates recovery after efforts between the starts in time of one competition, as well as in periods between competitions. The elimination of useless movements and excessive muscular tension through relaxation and ideomotor exercises, increases work efficiency. The skill of shutting off external stimuli (often triggering and intensifying the pre-start anxiety) makes it possible to achieve the state of psychosomatic balance and mental toughness.

Autosuggestion, employing formulas for improvement of performance, is a technique of forming the personality by acting on the subconscious mental and physiological processes. Through words and images, we influence our mental and psychosomatic potential, emotions, attitudes, and self-image. This is done by repeating formulas describing our desired behavior, and invoking images of this behavior while in a state of relaxation. The conditions for practicing autosuggestion are the same as for relaxation exercises. One has to find 15-30 minutes alone, undisturbed, and unconcerned about anything. After reaching a state of relaxation, we say, in low voice, the descriptions of our desired behavior or emotions, and very realistically imagine this behavior. The athlete must be relaxed, and at the same time concentrated on thoughts and images which have to be stored in the subconscious. Faith in the effectiveness of the autosuggestion is essential for getting desired results.

Professor Oleg Dashkevich[10], D.Sc. (Psychology) from the Central Institute of Physical Education says that assurance and doubt appear in every athlete immediately before performance. According to research, the optimal proportion of assurance to doubt is 67% to 33%. If the proportion is 50% to 50%, then the athlete cannot fully mobilize for the performance and performs below his/her potential. Athletes that doubt themselves cannot stand critique, avoid taking reasonable risks, and think mainly about avoiding shame.

Excessive assurance can lead to taking unnecessary risks or to a nervous breakdown if the assurance is not matched by potential.

The encephalograms of the athlete's cerebral cortex, taken after performance, indicate that the processes occurring after a victory facilitate effective memorization of the actions that lead to the moment of triumph. The more unexpected the victory was, the greater was this cerebral activity, and the greater the brightness of the pictures in the memory.

The processes occurring after the defeat were different and chaotic, which explains the difficulty in analyzing the defeat. Only people with good psychological training and stability can fully cope with it.

A concentration of attention on the task in a workout or in competition, if strong enough, prevents distractions from affecting performance. It mobilizes senses, increases awareness, and improves the recall of memories. Conducting some workouts in conditions that distract athletes (noise), performing techniques with maximal loads in various conditions, working out in the presence of public and judges, rehearsing the competition, and explaining the importance of the competition, improves the ability to concentrate.

Immediate psychological preparation for the start is divided into two stages: gathering information about the conditions of the contest, and into concentration proper. Gathering information on the spot, starts with the arrival at the place of competition, and ends with the assuming of the starting position. The athlete checks out the apparatus, equipment, and makes trial attempts. Mental rehearsals and last minute corrections are done at that time.

In the stage of concentration proper, the athlete removes from consciousness all that is not related to the task, and isolates self from stimuli external to the task. The most important, and the only thing on the mind of an athlete is the sports result or record. The duration of concentration has limits within which it is beneficial. These limits vary, depending on the individual athlete, sports discipline, and on the importance of the contest. The greater the height or weight in events such as jumps, pole-vault, or lifts, the longer the concentration is.

In weightlifting, the concentration proper is divided into three phases:

a) initial (getting to the platform),

b) preparatory (before the actual lift),

c) intensive (during the lift).

Success in weightlifting is decided by the phase of intensive concentration. The best results are achieved by those that think about the maximal effort they can perform. Those that think about "nothing" or even worse—about possible failure, lose. The more intensive the mental effort is while imagining the movement, the greater the power output while performing it physically. The effectiveness of mental concentration depends on the intellectual potential of the athlete.

According to an article by A. Batashev, a winner of a gold medal at the Olympic Games in Seoul in small-bore pistol, Nino Salukvadze's daily shooting workout lasts four to five hours. Sometimes she spends 10 minutes on one shot. First she shoots "mentally", carefully going through technique and imagining the bullet piercing the bull's-eye. She reminds herself when to raise the arm, when to lower it, when to take a breath and when to hold it, when to tense, and when to relax the proper muscles. Two or three seconds before she pulls the trigger, she tries to think about nothing, so nothing interferes with the image of the perfect shot that she has just mentally rehearsed. At this time only the sights of her pistol remain in the world that surrounds her.

Psychological (will-power) training in a macrocycle.

General psychological training is done in the course of the entire preparatory period. In addition, at the end of the general preparatory stage, and at the beginning of the special preparatory stage, special psychological training is done. In the competitive period, only the special psychological training is done. In the transitory period, only the general psychological training is done.

VIII. PLANNING AND CONTROL OF TRAINING PROCESS

The main goal of athletic training is achieving desired results by employing the means that are most economical, and at the same time, enhancing the development of an athlete. Determining what the ultimate goal and intermediate goals are, is essential for planning training. Properly defining the goal/goals makes the choice of adequate training methods possible. The only source of relevant information about the goals of training is competition (Demands of competition determine the methods of training). The level of skills and abilities that competition demands for success, is compared to the current level that the athlete displays. A training plan can then be made, taking into account the principles of training. The training plan should be effective, simple, and controllable, and should permit changes in its structure easily, in case of little changes in its goals.

The quality of competition depends on the current level of skills and abilities of athletes, and on the external conditions (environment, climate, public, organization, rules, class of opponent) in which the competition is conducted. External conditions influence the degree to which the abilities and skills are utilized. Knowing the importance of particular skills, abilities, and external conditions in a particular sport is necessary for designing the model of an ideal athlete in this sport, also called the model of a master. In this way, a knowledge of the demands of competition permits planning of the training process.

The model of a master in any sports discipline includes the age when the best results are most likely to be achieved, the number of years of training needed to reach the mastery, body size (height, weight, and in some sports arm reach or body proportions), the required score in a perception/IQ test (Raven's[55] test); the required value of an index of technical efficiency, and the results of tests of abilities relevant for a given sports discipline. For example, in the case of a model of a master pole-vaulter; results of a 20 meter (65 ft.) dash with and without pole, from a flying start; the time of a 300 meter sprint; the maximal amount of weight (in % of body weight) lifted in a squat and in a bench press; the distance of an overhead forward throw of a shot (16 lb.); a long jump with and without a pre-run; a height jump without swinging the arms; the ability to do a somersault forward and backward; and a certain minimum percentage of proper responses in a visual reaction test with choice (Piorkowski's test).

The model of a master sprinter includes results of the following tests: a 30 meter dash (100 ft.) from high start and from march; a triple-jump and a penta-jump without a pre-run, done using one leg only (whole technique on left leg then on right leg); a triple-jump and penta-jump using both legs in the technique; a deca-jump using both legs, without a pre-run; a long jump without a pre-run; a height jump with arm swing; the flexibility of the trunk measured by sit and reach test; the flexibility of the hip joint measured by the angle between thighs in a side split; the strength of leg extensors (quadriceps), hip flexors (iliopsoas), hip extensors (hamstrings), and foot flexors (calves), measured for each leg separately; the strength of trunk extensors (lower back); reaction time; time of one, and of ten fast flexions of the lower leg; and the time of ten flexions of the thigh.

The following tests are included in the model of a master shot putter: shot put without a slide or turns; the distance of throwing a standard shot backward overhead; throwing shot forward from below waist; a long jump without pre-run; a triple-jump without pre-run; a height jump; and maximal weights lifted in squat, bench press, pull (on chest), and snatch.

Long-term planning

Long-term plans of athletic training are determined by the optimal ages for developing the abilities needed in a particular sport, and by the age at which the best results are achieved. The long-term training process is divided into preparatory training, initial specialization, intensive training in the selected sport, perfection of the sport skills (stage of the maximum results), the stage of retention of results, and the stage of maintaining the overall training level. The shift from one stage to another is conditioned by the biological changes of the athlete's organism; the initial growth of the body and the increase of its functions, stabilization at maturity, followed by a decline. The duration of each stage depends on the requirements of the sport and the needs and talents of the athlete. Each stage, with the exception of the preparatory training and initial specialization stages, is subdivided into macrocycles (one year or six months cycles). In the first two stages of the long-term athletic training, success in competitions has little importance. The task is to lay a sound foundation for future specialized training, and neither the intensity, nor the volume, of work should be such as to make it necessary to divide the year into periods. At higher stages of training, from the stage of intensive training on, the goal of training is maximum results. This requires a great intensity of work, and because it cannot be safely maintained for long time, forces a division of the macrocycle into periods with a changing ratio of intensity, to volume of work. In the training of children, an increase of loads results, for the most part, from the growth of the organism merely assisted by adequate for given stage of ontogenetic development means of physical education (methods and exercises) and not from intensive training that makes periodization necessary.

W. P. Filin divides sports into technical (gymnastics, figure skating), where endurance is not stressed and mastery is reached at 18-20 years (men), speed-strength (sprints, throws, jumps, games), where after a short effort, there is long rest and mastery is reached at 21-23 years (men), and sports where endurance or strength is stressed to the maximum (middle and long-distance runs, wrestling, weightlifting), where mastery (or full readiness) is reached at 23-25 years. In the first group, specialization starts at 11-12 years (boys), in second at 14-15 years, in third at 16-17 years.

D. Harre recommends the first stage of training (preparatory training) in technical sports at 5-7 years, second stage (initial specialization) at 10-15 years. In speed-strength sports, first stage at 8-10 years, second stage at 13-15 years. In endurance sports, first stage at 10-12 years, and second stage at 14-18 years.

Age of first starts:
Swimming: 9 (USSR), 6 (GDR),
Figure skating: 9 (USSR), 6 (GDR),
Gymnastics: 11 (USSR), 9 (GDR),
Track and field: 11 (USSR), 9 (GDR),
Soccer: 13 (USSR), 10 (GDR),
Boxing: 15 (USSR), 10 (GDR),
Wrestling: 15 (USSR), 10 (GDR),
Weightlifting: 15 (USSR), 14 (GDR).

Age of selection for sports training:
Acrobatics: 7-8
Archery: 11-13
Badminton: 7-8
Basketball: 7-8
Biathlon: 10-11
Boxing: 13-14
Cycling: 12-13
Diving: 6-7
Equestrian sports: 11-12
Fencing: 7-8
Gymnastics: 6-7
Hockey (ice and field): 10-11
Ice skating (figure): 5-6
Ice skating (speed): 10-11
Rowing (canoes and kayaks): 11-13
Rowing (sculls): 10-11
Sailing: 9-11
Skiing (cross- country): 9-11
Skiing (downhill): 6-7
Skiing (jumping): 10-11
Soccer: 10-12
Swimming: 3-7
Team Handball: 10-12
Tennis: 6-8
Track and field: 10-12
Volleyball: 11-12
Water polo: 11-12
Weightlifting: 10-13
Wrestling: 10-12

Age of initial specialization and first starts:
Acrobatics:11
Archery: 14
Basketball: 10-12;
Biathlon: 14
Boxing: 15-16
Cycling: 16-17
Diving: 8-10
Equestrian sports: 12
Fencing: 10-12
Gymnastics: women 10-11, men 12-14
Hockey (ice): 12
Hockey (field): 14
Ice skating (figure): 8-10, pairs: 14
Ice skating (speed): 14
Luge: 14
Modern pentathlon: 14

Rowing (canoes and kayaks): 14
Rowing (sculls): 16-18
Rugby: 16
Sailing: 10-17 (depending on class: optimist: 10, cadet: 12, OK/420: 14, fin and 470: 17)
Skiing (cross-country): 14
Skiing (downhill): 10-11
Skiing (jumping): 12
Soccer: 11-13
Swimming: 10-12
Team Handball: 14
Tennis: 12- 14
Track and field: 13-14
Volleyball: 14-15
Water polo: 16
Weightlifting: 14-16
Wrestling: 15-16

Age of reaching and maintaining the maximum results:
Archery: 25-30
Basketball: women 19-25; men 23-26
Biathlon: 25-30
Boxing: 21-25
Cycling: 21-24
Diving: women 20-25; men 22-26
Equestrian sports: 25-30
Fencing: women 24-28; men 25-30
Gymnastics: women 14-16, men 18-24
Hockey (ice and field): 25-28
Ice skating (figure): women 16- 24; men 17-25
Ice skating (speed): women 19-24; men 20-25
Rowing: women 22-26; men 23-27
Sailing: 25-30
Skiing (cross- country): women 21-25; men 23-30
Skiing (downhill): women 18-25; men 19-25
Skiing (jumping): 20-26
Soccer: 23-26
Swimming: women 16-19; men 18-19
Team Handball: 22-28
Tennis: 22-25
Track and field
— combined events: women 23-25; men 25- 26
— hammer throw: 26-30
— javelin and discus: women 21-24; men 24-27
— jumps: women 19-22; men 22-24
— long-distance running: 26- 30
— marathon: 27-30
— middle-distance running: women 22-25; men 25-27

– pole vault: 24-28
– sprints: women 20-22; men 22-24
– triple jump: 24-28
– walking: 27-30
Volleyball: 20-25
Water polo: 25-30
Weightlifting: 25-30
Wrestling: 24-28

The preparatory training stage begins when children enter school and ends with initial specialization. The length of the preparatory training depends on the sport. In sports with the so- called normal pace of development, this stage lasts until about 13, and is dedicated to developing those abilities that cannot be as easily developed later in life. The exercises initially used at this stage do not necessarily belong to any sport. In sports, for example gymnastics, that require an early application of certain types of exercises so as not to miss the so-called sensitive ages where flexibility and certain qualities of coordination are developed, children, besides normal p.e. lessons, must attend real workouts as early as age six. The children that were not selected for any of the early starting sports can get their general physical preparation at school, although if possible (when and where excellent coaches are available), sports clubs will enroll children attracted to a given sport, so as to ensure that the training at this stage is conducted properly. Depending on the sport and the talent of the future athlete, this stage of training may last from two to five years. The purpose of this stage is to lay a sound foundation for future sports training, to make the children healthy, to give them a well-rounded general physical preparation, and to set up a rich foundation of varied motor skills and knowledge (physical or motor erudition). Basic techniques of various sports may be used, with preference given to natural movements like running, jumping, climbing, and various games. Developing speed, agility, coordination, and general aerobic endurance are the main tasks of training. The most important goal is developing coordination and teaching the techniques of many exercises that will be used at later stages of training, because children learn new movements easy. The development of strength or endurance has less importance. In a workout or p.e. lesson, short periods of exercises consisting of fast movements are followed with rest breaks sufficient for a nearly complete recovery. The character of work of individual muscle groups is changed in the next exercise. Exercises are often conducted in the form of games and competitions. Children are not to be overly fatigued. Exercises of the sport that originally attracted the children to training, constitute 30-40% of the total volume of all exercises in the first 2-3 years of training. In technical sports, for example, gymnastics, the volume of specialized exercises is greater. In specialized exercises, the weight and size of equipment and apparatus is reduced, distances are shorter, rules simpler, and training is more play than work.

Children will try many sports and they may decide to specialize in a different one than their original choice.

Stage of initial specialization. This stage lasts usually from two to four years. In technical sports, it starts when children are nine or ten, but it starts later in speed-strength sports, and even later in endurance sports. Training at this stage prepares a physiological, morphological, and psychological foundation for the selected sport. Training is still very diversified, but a greater emphasis is placed on mastering both the fundamental techniques of the selected sport, and the techniques of other sports used for general physical development and versatility. General exercises at this stage are selected to suit the needs of the sport to a greater degree than the previous stage. Within the selected sport, narrow specialization is avoided. For example, swimmers learn all strokes and distances, and track and field athletes learn all techniques of all track and field events (throws, jumps, relays, sprints, and longer runs). Greater stress (than at the previous stage) is put on developing strength, mainly through exercises that develop it along with agility. Elements of special endurance are also developed. This approach allows for revealing gradually the suitability for a particular sport or event. Workouts include special exercises of the selected sport, and exercises from other sports developing general physical fitness. The main task is still the development of general fitness. The volume of exercises increases at this stage more than the intensity. Increases in intensity of exercises must be made carefully, so as not to harm the growing body. Growing in itself is a strenuous effort. Putting too much emphasis on specialized exercises leads to an early plateau of the specialized skills when they will be practiced at later stages of training. The early specialization deprives athletes (at this stage, still children) of well-rounded, versatile, general physical development. At the stages of training (intensive sports training, stage of maximum results) when the main goal is perfecting technique and tactics, as well as the physical abilities that support them, early specialization will pay off by lowering the potential level of development. Both the quality and the amount of skills and abilities developed at these later stages of training will be limited.

At the stage of initial specialization, children are already allowed to compete. Depending on the sport, it takes from one to four years from the beginning of the stage of initial specialization, to the first start. The frequency of competition is limited by the high emotionality and sensitivity of the children's nervous system.

Macrocycles at this stage of training consist of long preparatory periods and short competitive periods. Yearly plans coincide with the school year (with its subdivision into terms and its holidays).

At the beginning of sports specialization, results improve at a greater rate than the increase of volume of special training loads. This is probably caused by the increased reactivity of the young, developing body. At the first stage of adaptation to special exercises, there is a broad positive transfer of skills and abilities previously acquired.

The stage of intensive training. This stage is for perfecting the techniques and tactics of the selected sport, and for developing those psychological and physical abilities that are necessary for reaching individually maximal results in the sport. This stage and the following one, together, last from eight to twelve years. The intensity and volume of the training loads (work) increase at a greater rate than thus far, and athletes systematically compete. The special preparatory and competitive periods occupy more time in the macrocycle than at the previous stage. Training is increasingly individualized. Total training time and number of workouts in a week usually reach their maximum at this stage. Athletes with outstanding potential submit all their time and energy to all means of training. The four year cycle of preparation for the Olympic Games may begin at this stage.

The stage of sports perfection (maximum results). The goal in this stage is to set personal records. Training is increasingly specialized. The volume and intensity of the training loads (work) increase, and eventually reach their maximum. This stage coincides with the age most conducive for the highest results in a particular sport. In gymnastics, figure skating, and swimming, it is between 14 and 20 years. In weightlifting, throwing, and long-distance running, it is between 21 and 30 years. In other sports this age is between 18 and 26 years. The organization of training at this stage, in addition to biological considerations, has to take into account the timing of major competitions (Olympic Games, World Championships).

The stage of retention of sports results. As the athlete's body ages, its functional and adaptive abilities stabilize and eventually decline, thus limiting the sports results. Some athletes; for example, weightlifters, hammer throwers, and marathon runners; retain their ability, or even make progress, after 30-35 years. Currently, the decline in sports results usually occurs after 8-10 years of highly specialized training. The elimination of flaws in methods of planning and conducting the long-term training may extend this period. In this stage, the volume of training loads (work) is initially stabilized, although the volume of selected types of exercises may be periodically increased. The perfection of tactics, techniques, and competition skills are the tasks of this stage. The macrocycles have prolonged competitive period.

The stage of maintaining overall training level. This stage is entered between 36-40 years of age. Maintaining health, abilities, and skills is the purpose of sports training, which now has recreational character.

Training plans for each of the above stages of long-term training must reflect the individual talents and deficiencies of the athlete, the biological age, the sports results, and the changing general tasks of training in the particular stage. It is necessary to know what the minimum and maximum training loads are for athletes of various class at a given stage of training, what the rate of increasing the loads for athletes of various class is, and how the loads vary during a given macrocycle.

To make effective training plans, it is necessary to know what the connections are:

a) between the behavior in competition and the means (exercises, methods, and loads) of the training preceding it;

b) between each type of preparation (general, directed, special);

c) between work, fatigue, and recovery;

d) between types of cycles (workouts, microcycles, mesocycles, periods);

e) between types of cycles, their training content, and the resulting level of athletic form.

Annual training plans

When making plans for a macrocycle, the following factors have to be considered:

1. Major tasks facing the athletes in the coming year.

2. Trends of development in a given sport and achievements of theory and practice of that sport.

3. Schedule of starts.

4. Measurable goals and training tasks for ensuring the effectiveness of preparation for competition and of competitive actions.

5. Initial level of skills and abilities needed in competition.

6. Amount of work that will be dedicated to developing each skill and ability.

7. The proportions between general, directed, and special preparation.

8. General concept of what training loads have to be used, and how they will be arranged (what structure will the macrocycle have, and how long will its periods be).

9. What, how, and when to test, so as to get information useful in correcting the training process.

First of all, a rough estimate must be made of a realistic number of workouts in a day, in a microcycle, as well as the number of microcycles in a year. A struggle for better results means more training work, especially in the preparatory period. Today's athletes workout 260-290 days a year, with 60-70 days of rest. On the average, international class athletes spent 1000 hours per year on sports training.

Plans for a period are made by:

1) Determining the number of mesocycles and desired distribution of training loads in the period.

2) Deciding on the structure of the microcycles (number of workout days, training load of a single workout).

3) Methods and types of training to be used in developing skills and abilities.

Microcycle are planned taking into account:

1) Data concerning volume of work.

2) Data concerning intensity of work.

3) Correction of training tasks and means used in a microcycle; depending on the reactions of the athlete and on the demands of the sport.

The length of cycles, and the amplitude of changes of training loads in them, must depend on changes in the athlete's form. To determine when each type of load has to be increased or decreased, it is necessary to constantly monitor all systems of the athlete's organism.

Control of the training process

Control of the training process means measuring changes in physical abilities, technical skills, tactics, and mental preparedness, and then adjusting the means of training to obtain planned results. If conducted properly, control of the training process allows conclusions to be drawn about used training methods, thus helping with planning the training. A systematic, planned training process requires constant feedback provided by frequent and systematic testing.

Athletic form is an optimal blend of physical and psychological abilities, and technical and tactical skills. It can be measured by respective kinds of tests, but the best, although not always the most practical, indicator of good form is a consistency of results in competitions. These results must be achieved with sufficient frequency and be objectively measured.

In many sports, it is impossible to measure the level of skills and abilities by using the competitive exercises because either the load in them is too great (long-distance running), or it is unknown (individual contact sports, games). In such cases, measuring the abilities and skills in their directed, or even in general, form must provide information about the level of competitive form. These tests must reflect demands of the particular sport, for example, the tests of long-distance runner must include aerobic efforts (first zone of intensity of efforts); tests of a sprinter must include anaerobic-alactacid efforts (fourth zone); test of boxers must include anaerobic-lactacid efforts (third zone).

The results of test have to be compared with the behavior of the athlete in control competitions. This is the only way to verify the usefulness of the tests.

According to Marek Zaton (article in Sport Wyczynowy number 12, 1987), tests conducted in workouts are superior to laboratory tests. Laboratory tests are less sensitive to changes of loads, exercises, or structure of training. Instead of a periodic control of the training process, he proposed continuous studies, because only such studies allow for an early correction of undesirable changes.

An article in Tieoriya i Praktika Fizicheskoy Kultury number 11, 1984, titled "Some results of analysis of the system of complex control in sports and perspectives of its development/ Niekatoryie itogi razrabotki sistiemy kompleksnego kontrola w sportie wys-shych dostizheniy i perspectivy yeye razwitiya", by I. P. Ratov, discusses principles of efficient control and mistakes made by researchers in attempts to measure the training process.

Principles of control of sports training:

— Control should be complex (deal with all relevant abilities and skills) and systematic.

— Criteria, parameters, tests, and methods of control should be informative, objective, and reliable.

— Parameters and methods of control should be uniform within groups of related sports disciplines and within types of control (didactic, biomechanic, biomedical, psychological).

— Technical measuring devices should be subjected to calibration and attestation.

— Number of parameters and methods of control should not be excessive, beyond researcher's ability to analyze.

— Procedures used in control should be comfortable for the subject.

— Choice of criteria, tests, and methods of control should be related to the goals and needs of particular stages of the training process.

It is difficult to observe these principles. According to I. P. Ratov, control of the training process takes one fourth of the training time. The Institute of Science and Research in Moscow informs that in control of sports training, 300 instrumental methods are used to measure over 3000 parameters!

Another serious fault of procedure of control is the non-synchronic registration of parameters of different types of control (didactic, biomechanic, biomedical and psychological). Various data are registered at various times, in various conditions, making it difficult to find their mutual relationship.

According to an article "O niedostatkach i nowym podejsciu do kontroli treningu/On insufficiencies of and a new approach to control of sports training" in Sport Wyczynowy number 12, 1987, serious mistakes are being made in using statistical apparatus (methods). Mean statistical values, that are commonly used by researchers, describe an average level of athletic performance which can be reached in an indefinite number of ways (because these average performances depend on various combinations of contributing factors related to the training process). In this situation, a single peak performance of an athlete is more reliable than many average performances as determined by a multitude of cases. **Records cannot be accidental!** A set of parameters registered at the moment of a single peak performance is much more valuable, because it reveals the true abilities of the athlete.

Gathering the data on the training loads for the purpose of steering the training process also makes little sense. First, there is a lack of a unequivocally meaningful relationship between indicators of the loads, and the dynamics of the sports results achieved in important competitions. Second, there is lack of uniform physical measure units for measuring the training loads. The notion of the training load as it is currently understood is misleading for coaches and athletes. Neither the choice of this term (training load), nor the meaning ascribed to it, have sufficient scientific justification. The purpose of the athletic training is not to perform any quantity (volume) of exercises but, taking into account quantitative and qualitative characteristics of the exercises, to achieve a result in the form of a lasting change. This is not determined by a mechanical sum of the training loads. Besides, there is enough evidence showing that efficiency of the training process depends on an **optimal composition** of the loads.

Use of a much lower volume of training loads (work) than average, has lead many athletes to record results. To find the exact proportions of the loads, it is necessary to model the load and test its influence on the athlete on special measuring devices. To find out the influence of psychological stress/loads, and to evaluate the attitude of the athlete, it is necessary to analyze precisely the motor activity (motor manifestations) of the athlete. Motor activity is the most sensitive indicator for evaluation of the choice of means of training; physical as well as psychological. As far as biochemical indicators are concerned, even if they are measured systematically and precisely, if done without the simultaneous, objective registration of the motor characteristics, they cannot form a basis for rational decisions concerning training. Biochemical data must be supported by data concerning the degree of technical rationality of athletic exercises. Only then is it possible to learn, and objectively evaluate, the physiological power that the athlete puts into the performance of an assigned motor task.

Technical control most often is concentrated in the period of starts when it is too late for any corrections. More to the point, would be to design methods of evaluation of technique that accompany peak performance, and on this basis, devise methods of reaching and/or maintaining this high level of technical proficiency. This would require to shift the weight of controlling operations on the tests (motor assignments), performed in special training/control devices which would allow to lead the athlete to the level of motor activity corresponding to the planned values of record results.

Control should be accompanied by instant correction of the performed exercise. Unification of training and measuring devices within related groups of sports, would permit a simultaneous measurement and comparison with parameters of various subsystems of complex biomedical, biochemical, and psychological control. As a result, an integral evaluation of the athletic form revealing the "weak links" that limit the possibility of reaching record results, could be done quickly. Efficient control can be ensured by tests in which the athlete discovers his/her whole potential. It is important to develop a scientifically sound scale for each sport, providing precise criteria of quality in performing the exercises, parameters of corrective actions, and other control indicators. Having such a scale for measuring technique, comprising quantitative indicators and a criteria of efficiency in performing exercises, and an objective, instrumental methods of measuring and evaluating, would permit revealing and evaluating results of the application of various combinations of training means. This follows the dynamics of the adaptative changes of the organism, not on the basis of indirect biochemical or psychological indicators, but on the basis of biomechanical and didactic data related to "resultativity" of a given exercise, performed in extreme conditions.

Testing of the technique should provide data for comparison with the ideal (for a particular athlete) technique. The task of control can be broken in this case into three components: 1) designing the ideal technique, 2) description of its indicators, 3) evaluation of the condition and technical level of the athlete.

According to I. P. Ratow, there is no abstract, ideal technique. What exists and functions is, the technique related to the level of development of motor and psychological abilities of the athlete, his/her theoretical preparation, and the particular conditions at the time of performance.

Marek Zaton, in his article "Some aspects of control of the changes of work ability in sports training", published in Sport Wyczynowy number 12, 1987, states that it is easier to measure the state of a process than its dynamic flow. The frequency of the observations must be related to the pace of changes of the measured phenomenon. In nature, the uneven pace of changes of processes is the rule. The cyclic character of training reflects the amplitude and direction of changes that it causes in the athlete's body. The organism's responses to training have a cyclic character and occur continuously in spite of the "effort—rest—effort" (on-off) type of schedule of training. The amplitude and the character of the organism's responses are variable, depending on several external stimuli and on the organism's susceptibility to these stimuli.

Applying even the most subtle methods of research permits the gathering of only a limited amount of data about these changes.

The so-called multiaspect evaluations of an organism's reaction to a given stimuli is done in various laboratories by psychologists (motivation, aspiration, IQ, neurotogenic effects of exercise, etc.), physiologists (evaluation of local and general changes), biochemists and histologists (activity of enzymes and structural changes in cells), biomechanics (strength, technique, coordination), and other specialists. It involves various research methods and concerns various properties of the organism, which is why the coach relying mostly on intuition, picks from this data what seems to be the least contradictory. Then, still acting intuitively, the coach tries to plan or correct the training process.

It seems that sports training requires a completely different approach. The team of specialists should study and interpret the behavior of the organism in a typical training situation and not in the artificial settings of various laboratories.

In many research laboratories, effectiveness of the training process in various sports is evaluated by universal tests. This is based on statistical differences in results between athletes of various sports. Then, as a results of such studies, models of master athletes for the respective sports disciplines are created. These models are the foundation of systems of training. Such an approach to studying athletes may serve to teach about changes in particular functions of an organism over a long period of time, but it does not give a basis for decisions concerning training plans for the near future. Also, it is worth remembering that many athletes (of the same discipline), if tested by universal methods, can match the master model for their discipline, but their specific performance does not come close to that of the masters.

Measuring reactions of the organism while punching a heavy boxing bag are more valuable for evaluating the competitive form of boxers than typical ergometric tests. The maximum oxygen uptake (VO_2max.), maximal lung ventilation, and heart rate reached during ergometric tests were consistently lower than those reached while punching the bag or fighting. The results reached during fighting were greater than during punching the bag. The values of maximum oxygen uptake, maximal lung ventilation, and heart rate measured during specialized effort changed, depending on the methods and loads used in training, while the values of the same indicators reached during the ergometric tests in the same time were stable, even if the special form (as measured by these values reached in specialized tests) of the boxer went down.

The correlation between the heart rate during effort and during recovery, and the time of simple reaction, were used to evaluate the individual adaptation, depending on the external structure of exercises in the same zones of intensity. It turned out that each subject adapted differently to efforts of the same intensity. One subject was overfatigued after each application of aerobic effort when the general exercises were used, but after the same aerobic effort done using specialized exercises, he was not overfatigued. This means that in choosing exercises, not only the zone of intensity, but also the form of exercise (because of its psychological consequences), has to be taken into account.

There are great differences in the relation between heart rate and oxygen uptake (VO_2) in various exercises. For example, during a run with speed 12 km/hour, one boxer had a heart rate of 150/min. and an oxygen uptake (VO_2) about 65% of his maximum, but during exercises with the speed bag having the same heart rate, his oxygen uptake was only 42% of his maximum. In this situation, researchers decided not to use the relation between oxygen uptake and heart rate to evaluate the intensity of work, but used only heart rate.

Research that does not take into account the cyclic character of training is rarely reliable. It is impossible to evaluate an organism independently from the training stage, amount of rest, and the sequence of the kinds of workouts preceding the measurement. The same work performed on different days of the microcycle can cause diametrically different reactions in the same athlete.

In an experiment, a high ranking swimmer had his pulse and maximal oxygen uptake (VO_2max.) measured while swimming in a harness (ergometer Costilla). He was consistently achieving his maximal pulling power of 17 kG. This was done after a warm-up, and before the main part of workout in the course of several workouts. His maximum heart rate and maximal oxygen uptake, as measured by this test, varied widely throughout the microcycle.

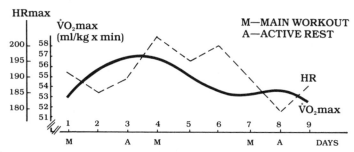

Changes of HRmax and VO2max in subsequent workouts of swimmer's training. Reprinted with permission from Marek Zaton: "Niektore aspecty kontroli zmian zdolnosci wysilkowej w treningu sportowym." In Sport Wyczynowy 12:8, 1987. Copyright © 1987, Sport Wyczynowy.

On those same days, the swimmer was tested in the laboratory on equipment that is routinely used to evaluate the aerobic fitness (organism functioning) of athletes of all sports disciplines (ergometer Monark, gas analyzer, etc.). His universal laboratory tests did not show any changes in measured maximum heart rate and maximal oxygen uptake. The results of these laboratory tests were constant even when substantial changes were made in the structure of training, exercises, and loads. The researchers decided that the universal laboratory tests are of little use in evaluating the effectiveness of training of highly ranked athletes. This conclusion is confirmed by a comparison of routine, universal laboratory tests with specific road tests done on a group of bicyclists throughout all stages of their yearly training cycle.

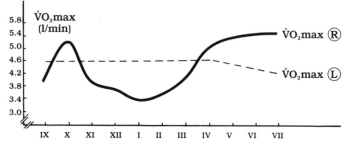

Laboratory and road tests of cyclists during macrocycle. Reprinted with permission from Marek Zaton: "Niektore aspecty kontroli zmian zdolnosci wysilkowej w treningu sportowym." In Sport Wyczynowy 12:8, 1987. Copyright © 1987, Sport Wyczynowy.

Universal laboratory tests were showing uniformly high maximal oxygen uptake in athletes that achieved high athletic rank and had ended their ontogenetic development phase (growing). The measurements of maximal oxygen uptake done in specific road tests were showing something else, namely, that the specific test results were related to the training effect, and could be used to evaluate this effect.

It is important to choose properly what to measure, and by which method of measuring, so that the method can be used in specific actions of the athlete without interrupting them. This is necessary for the control to be effective. The cyclic character of training has to be taken into account. For example, for specific tests, the main workout of the microcycle can be chosen, and the reactions of the organism for all phases of the workout and for repetition of this type of workout can be measured.

In particular phases of the training cycle, the changing proportions of the various training means may cause changes in the cell metabolism of the muscle groups that are stressed by these means. This also causes changes in the number of active capillaries, the oscillation of coordination in stimulating particular muscles, and hormonal and enzymatic changes. Research of these phenomena is most effective in conditions of the workout.

Workouts are conducted in environments (water, long distances, contact with opponent) that limit the type of factors that can be measured. The choice of these factors may be based initially on the researcher's hypothesis, assuming that these factors are essential for the kind of effort that is researched. Later on, the usefulness of these factors is verified.

Training plans are made mainly on the basis of previous experience. Most of the time, it is assumed that applying a known, proven, structural, and quantitative (load) variant, should bring a desired effect. Evaluation of the behavior of the athlete is done by comparing it to the past or to other athletes. But it happens often that at the time of the main competition, the athletic form worsens or does not improve as planned. In this situation, a very precise analysis of the training process may point out the probable faults. Only systematically repeated measurements of a set of factors or of one factor, for example, in the course of the main workout in the microcycle, may directly point out the fault (cause of failure). If in the future, the factors behave similarly, it will indicate the need to correct structure, loads, exercises, or rest intervals. For example: in consecutive control matches preceding the World Championship in 1978, a boxer, whose start in the World Championship was very disappointing, experienced a lowering of the maximal heart rate and a stabilization of the lactic acid concentration. In the course of his preparations for the Olympic Games of 1980, when the same factors were systematically controlled, researchers concluded that the behavior of these factors was caused by spending too much training time on workouts utilizing the continuous training method. In addition, the behavior of factors was accompanied by a marked increase of the recovery time of these factors and of the indicators of gas exchange. Not exceeding the necessary volume of continuous work, intensifying workouts and introducing more rest breaks, resulted in a change of the behavior of the measured factors, and in good athletic form (demonstrated by an increase of the maximal frequency of punches). As a rule, the maximal heart rate and the concentration of the lactic acid in the blood of the boxers that were in good shape went up during consecutive fights. Initially, researchers thought that was a symptom of limited parasympathetic control resulting from the extreme emotional stress of the fight, but it turned out that this means increased competitive form. Usually, an increase of the maximal heart rate reached during short periods of the fight to more than 200 beats/min., is followed in a few days by improvement in the competitive form; expressing itself in good mobility in the ring, good sense of distance, good footwork, and good tolerance of changes of the pace of action. The increase of the maximal heart rate is usually accompanied by a more efficient recovery, as measured by the speed of return to resting values of heart rate. It shows that through the analysis of the changes of the measured indicators in consecutive main workouts, particularly in the mesocycle immediately followed by competition, it is possible to control the efficiency of the training process.

The researchers also established that studying the recovery after workout may serve as a means of evaluating the delayed training effect. Efficiency of recovery is related to losses of weight, evening and morning resting heart rate, and reaction time for visual stimuli. Consequently, the analysis of the reactions of the cardiovascular system may be used for evaluating the current athletic form.

A lowering of the I_{ER} (Index of Efficiency of Recovery), higher than normal weight loss, increase of the resting heart rate by 10-20 beats per minute, and a significant increase of the reaction time after the special endurance workout, are signs for that the load should be lowered by decreasing the number of repetitions or intensity of work in the next workout. If the I_{ER} is increasing, it means that the loads in subsequent microcycles have to be increased.

In the previously mentioned study of the group of road cyclists, it was shown that the maximal oxygen uptake and the speed change in such a similar way, that it is possible to omit measuring the maximal oxygen uptake and evaluate effort capability using only changes of speed (threshold speed). This means speed in given zones of effort intensity as measured by the concentration of lactic acid in blood.

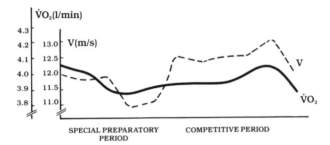

Changes of cyclist's speed and VO₂max. during macrocycle. Reprinted with permission from Marek Zaton: "Niektore aspecty kontroli zmian zdolnosci wysilkowej w treningu sportowym." In Sport Wyczynowy 12:8, 1987. Copyright © 1987, Sport Wyczynowy

. A study was done on a group of swimmers for whom achieving high values of the maximal oxygen uptake was important. The experience of coaches and the literature on the subject suggested doing a high volume (time) of aerobic work. However, in all high class swimmers, such training caused a stabilization or even a lowered oxygen uptake in ergometric tests and while swimming in a tether. A intensification of work in the mesocycle immediately preceding the period of starts, initially caused a great oscillation of maximal oxygen uptake, and then a constant growth, but only if measured by a specific test. It was concluded that the aerobic work led to an improvement of economy of effort (utilization of energy) and that combined work (anaerobic + aerobic), and anaerobic work led to an improvement of aerobic (VO₂ max) and anaerobic potential.

The degree of realization of goals of each workout, microcycle, mesocycle, or period ought to be subject to the evaluation of the training process. The desired values of the desired changes in the organism of the athlete must be compared with the actual effects of training. The goal of testing is to compare the training tasks with achieved effects in a workout, microcycle, mesocycle, or period.

<u>What to measure</u>– the training load and the current state of the athlete, in particular his/her work capabilities in the competitive

activity, and in three kinds of preparation for it, i.e. general, directed, and special preparation. An evaluation of the realization of the goals of special preparation is done through preparatory forms of the competitive exercise, and must have complex character.

When to measure— the schedule of measurements should be subjected to the cyclic character of the training process at the level of one exercise, workout, microcycle, mesocycle, or period.

How to measure— this depends on the kind of competitive activity, competitive strategy, and on the possibility of evaluation of particular features of the athlete. The measurement may be complex or partial. The complex methods of measurement measure several abilities and skills by one test. Partial methods of measurement permit an evaluation of the level of one ability, taking into account its role and its form in conditions of the competition, for example, test of complex reaction in boxing.

The most sensitive and most immediately responsive process to training means, is the process of current adaptation for performed work, which is called "the immediate training effect" or in other words, what causes "operational state". Observation of this process may give information about the effectiveness of the adaptive changes counteracting acute fatigue. It also permits an analysis of the direction of influence in the means of training (informs about the type of changes caused by given means of training). Comparing the reactions of the athlete during the competitive actions, to the results of measurements done during workouts, lets one evaluate the similarity of the adaptive changes. The observation of the immediate training effect also informs about the effectiveness of the rest breaks and let one choose the best type of rest.

Observations of the changes occurring after a few hours or a few days, called the "delayed training effect", are essential for determining the course of the process of supercompensation because these observations provide data about the increase or decrease of adaptations for particular loads applied in the microcycle. This lets one evaluate the effectiveness of training and informs about the direction of adaptive changes in microcycles.

"Cumulative training effect" is the result of summing up the immediate and delayed training effects, and is more stable than immediate or delayed effects. Its evaluation lets one determine the influence of the training process in mesocycles and periods of the macrocycle, and reveals the combined result of the training means, methods, and loads applied in that time. This evaluation lets one verify the tasks of the next period and set the level of adaptive changes that must be reached for fulfilling the demands of the next training period.

A detailed diagnosis of the long-lasting, current, and operational (during and after a single exercise) states of adaptation of the organism is possible only if these states are traced to their exact causes. Thus, one can conclude that the physiological laboratory tests done in long time intervals, cannot give information sufficiently detailed for practical application. This is because these tests do not reveal the relationship between the adaptative changes to the training means (exercises, methods, and loads) that caused them. Laboratory tests of adaptation to efforts are also too universal for evaluating the specific effects of specialized training. The physiological characteristics of function of the organism during competitive exercises is the only basis for determining the effectiveness of training.

Information obtained from all the above quoted studies proved that systematic observation of such simple indicators as heart rate, changes of weight, and time of simple reaction, can be used for evaluating adaptation for training loads.

Control of planned loads in a workout

The evaluation of the degree of recovery of the athlete's organism is necessary for planning everyday workouts. Athletes must systematically monitor and record the functions of their bodies. Records have to be made every day and compared with observations (opinions) of the trainer and the team doctor. The doctor analyzes the self-evaluation records and observations of the trainer for the purpose of making proper decisions regarding the choice of training methods and loads.

Every day, the athlete measures pulse rate, temperature, frequency of breathing, strength of grip, weight, describes any pains or other complains, kind and amount of foods, time of meals, ability for work, and state of mind.

Pulse rate has to be measured several times a day; in the morning before raising out of bed, before the beginning of the main workout in this day, in course of the workout (it may be measured several times to see if the target rate has been reached and to see when to end the rest breaks), immediately after the main part of the workout and once again, five minutes after that, and finally, just before going to sleep.

The Bulgarian weightlifters use the pulse rate to let them know if the total load in a set is optimal and when to begin a new set of lifts. Moderate to heavy sets should increase the pulse rate to 162-180 beats per minute, and the rest should end after the pulse drops to 102-108 beats per minute.

Variations of the pulse rate measured in the morning, in comparison to the previous morning and evening values, are used to determine what type of efforts ought to be used in that day's workout.

Long lasting studies of athletes have revealed that each workout causes changes that are related to an increased tension of either the sympathetic nervous system, or the parasympathetic nervous system. Increased tension of the sympathetic system results from using mostly intensive efforts in a workout. Increased tension of the parasympathetic system results from extensive training methods, and the employment of a high volume of work in a workout. To gauge the effect of the workout on these two systems, the indicator of efficiency of restitution (I_{ER}) may be used in conjunction with the evening and morning pulse rate comparisons.

$$I_{ER} = 100\% \, \frac{HR2 - HR3}{HR2 - HR1}$$

HR1 — heart rate before the workout

HR2 — heart rate immediately after the main part of the workout.

HR3 — heart rate five minutes after the end of main part of the workout (in the fifth minute of a cool-down).

Knowledge of the degree of restitution after the workout permits corrections in the intensity and volume of workouts of individual athletes:

1) I_{ER} between 50-60%, evening pulse rate (heart rate) and morning pulse rate up 5-7 beats per minute — means the loads are optimal, not leading to overworking.

2) I_{ER} between 50-60%, evening and morning heart rate down 3-5 beats per minute — means total load is optimal, but there is an incorrect proportion between the time of effort and its intensity (the time is too long).

3) I_{ER} between 50-60%, evening and morning heart rate up 10-15 beats per minute — means total load is optimal, intensity is too high.

4) I$_{ER}$ above 60%, evening and morning heart rate without changes—means ability to adapt to the load was not fully used (load too low), load needs to be increased.

5) I$_{ER}$ above 60%, resting heart rate with a tendency to go down—means it is possible to increase intensity (use more intensive loads).

6) I$_{ER}$ above 60%, resting heart rate up 5-10 beats per minute—means it is possible to increase the time of work (use longer lasting efforts).

7) I$_{ER}$ less than 50%, resting pulse rate without changes—means total load exceeded the ability to compensate (these symptoms are always accompanied by a loss of weight and a longer reaction time).

8) I$_{ER}$ less than 50%, resting heart rate up—means overworking, caused by loads that are too intensive.

9) I$_{ER}$ less than 50%, resting heart rate down—means overworking, caused by efforts that last too long.

Evening heart rate is taken around 2200 hours (10 p.m.), 10 minutes after going to bed. The morning heart rate is taken 4-5 minutes after waking up, while still in bed.

The above recommendations are to be applied to the main workouts of the microcycle, but the measurements and calculations have to be done every day, after every workout, to spot any irregularities.

40-60 minutes after the end of a workout, the heart rate is normally 10-20% faster than its value at rest.

Gradually lowering values of heart rate after the workout, particularly after an endurance workout, means that the recovery proceeds normally. If such a gradual lowering of the heart rate is interrupted by a sudden jump to lower values, it may be a sign of overtraining.

A frequency of breath, measured in the morning, that is greater than normal for an individual, may indicate a problem in the cardiovascular and respiratory systems.

A workout day with light or moderate loads, has a greater oscillation of functional indicators as compared with the day of rest. Immediately after an effort, occurs rapid recovery of arterial pressure, breath frequency, heart rate, and then the rate of recovery slows down. The initial (pre-exercise) level of the above indicators is reached after several hours, sometimes even in the morning of the next day.

A workout day with a heavy load has greater increases of functional indicators. If the heart rate per minute, as measured soon after waking up, oscillates plus-minus 8-10 beats, breathing plus-minus 4-6, systolic pressure plus-minus 10-15 mmHg, diastolic pressure plus-minus 5-10 mmHg; it means that on the same or on the next day the values of these indicators are going to increase significantly. Loss of weight reaches 0.5-1.5 kg. More stable numbers characterize athletes with a smaller proper weight because they have a greater ratio of lung volume to body mass. In the favorable meteorological conditions of workout, depending on the specifics of the sport, the weight after a day of rest may again increase by 0.5-1.5 kg.

With normal training loads, the body weight should be constant (a slight lowering at the beginning of the preparatory period of the macrocycle is OK). After a sudden drop, resulting from applying maximal loads in a workout, the weight should be regained within 1-3 days. A prolonged period of lowered weight in the competitive period may mean overtraining. A weight increase may accompany the increase of loads in strength training.

Grip dynamometry is also done in the morning, together with heart and breath rate measurement, to see the level of strength and excitability in the nervous system.

Nutrition: The athlete should have a detailed record of the hours of meals and the kind and amount of food eaten at each meal. An improper diet can weaken the organism, reduce resistance to infections, and cause overtraining.

All health complaints and pains should be noted in the athlete's diary and the coach should be notified. Feelings of fatigue, local infections, headaches, toothaches, stomachaches, as well as complaints that are more obviously connected to the training, such as muscular pains, joint pains, nervous pains, and any sensations concerning the heart, must be brought to the coach's attention. Initially, small discomforts may be early warning signs of an impending, more serious injury. Oftentimes, a predisposition to some types of injury is a result of neglected and accumulated microtrauma. The athlete should note what pains he/she had before the workout, or what pains or ailments intensified during and after the workout.

The pace of recovery or restitution after the workout varies from athlete to athlete, even in the same workout group. Depending on the degree of recovery (some not recovered yet, some recovered, and some already in the supercompensation phase), each athlete requires different loads.

Symptoms permitting an approximate evaluation of the degree of fatigue and the training load during workout according to D. Harre:

Fatigue: moderate, Load: moderate;
Perspiration: light or moderate– depending on temperature.
Breathing: accelerated but even.
Precision of movement: normal.
Concentration: normal, full attention during explanations.
Disposition: good, no complains.
Readiness for effort: good.
Mood: happy, lively.

Fatigue: high, Load: optimal;
Perspiration: heavy, above waist.
Breathing: very fast.
Precision of movement: flaws begin to appear, lowered precision.
Concentration: inattention during explanations, lowered ability to apply advice, lowered differentiation (ability to notice differences in the amount of strength applied in the movement).
Disposition: feeling of muscular weakness, lowered efficiency, increased overall weakness.
Readiness for effort: lowered activity, tendency to prolong rest breaks, but ready to continue the effort.
Mood: a bit subdued but happy if the results/effects of the workout are as expected.

Fatigue: very high, Load: ultimate;
Perspiration: very heavy, below the waistline.
Breathing: very fast, short, and irregular.
Precision of movement: big flaws, impaired coordination, lack of precision, uncertainty.
Concentration: clearly lowered, nervousness, elongated reaction time.
Disposition: great weakness, pains in muscles and joints.
Readiness for effort: none, longing for total rest.
Mood: fear of renewed effort, doubts about the purpose of a workout.

Load tolerance and symptoms of fatigue according to A. Soldatov:

Load tolerance	Attention	Sweating	Face	Technique
very easy	steady	none	normal	no changes
easy	steady	sweat	light red	no changes
satisfactory	weakened	considerable	more red	frequent mistakes
difficult	dispersed	profuse	strong red	basic mistakes
very difficult	very dispersed	very profuse	purple	uncoordinated movements

Control of planned loads in a microcycle

An evaluation of the immediate and delayed training effects of a workout can be done by measuring heart rate, weight loss, reaction time, purposefulness and precision of movements, and then, on that basis, corrections can be made within the microcycle.

For evaluation of the cumulative training effect on the level of the microcycle, standard (with strictly determined duration, intensity, and conditions of performance) effort tests are used. Changes of physiological and motor indicators in these tests, permit an evaluation of the course in the process of adaptation in a microcycle. For example, lowering the oxygen uptake, lung ventilation, or heart rate in subsequent tests indicates that the adaptation for the measured standard effort is proper. These standard tests must cause the same type of effort that the athlete is supposed to adapt to in a given microcycle. For example, the effectiveness of a microcycle designed to develop aerobic capability, may be measured by running, cycling or other aerobic activity and not by tests of speed, coordination, or strength. In a microcycle which has the task of developing speed-endurance in movements similar to those used in competitive activity, anaerobic capability, or the ability to maintain considerable speed in such movements for long time, will be measured— not the level of general abilities. Because the tests must be done at the end of each microcycle, they must be simple and easy to conduct.

The purpose of correcting the amount and type of loads in a microcycle, is to maintain the direction of adaptation planned for the mesocycle in which this microcycle belongs.

The corrections consist of either changing the total load in the subsequent repetitions of the microcycle, or of changing the type of microcycle. If the adaptation proceeds as planned, regulation of the loads consists of increasing the total value (absolute value) in subsequent repetitions of this type of microcycle.

For example, in a microcycle that has two days with very heavy workouts, one of the tasks may be to have increased work capability on the seventh day (which is the second day with a very heavy workout). This increased work capability results from supercompensation after the fourth day (first of the very heavy days). If it turns out that the period between the fourth and the seventh day of training is too long, and symptoms of supercompensation occur earlier, it is necessary to rearrange the microcycle. The very heavy workout from the fourth day can be moved to the fifth day, and on the second day, a heavy workout is done instead of the moderate one that was there previously.

(The microcycle used in this example originally looked like this:
first day: active rest
second day: moderate load
third day: active rest
fourth day: very heavy load
fifth day: active rest
sixth day: moderate load
seventh day: very heavy load.

After the changes it looked like this:
first day: active rest
second day: heavy load
third day: active rest
fourth day: active rest
fifth day: very heavy load
sixth day: active rest
seventh day: very heavy load.)

In cases of overworking, overstrain, or injury, it may be necessary to introduce a different type of microcycle for realization of the same training tasks. The differences in such case would be in the amount and type of workouts, sequence of types of workouts, and the loads.

The dynamics of oscillation of the functional state in a microcycle depend on the discipline of sports, current form and class of the athlete, and the period of training. The determination of poor recovery after a workout or a set of workouts by simple measurements is possible if accompanied by complaints from the athlete. These measurements are: an increase (above normal individual oscillation) of the heart rate, an increase of the difference between heart rate measured laying down and standing in the orthostatic test, a worsening of the atrial stability of the heart, an increase of the blood pressure (particularly diastolic), and an increased amplitude of muscular tremor. More accurate indicators of the degree of recovery may be obtained by recording the heart rate during the standard effort and during recovery, as well as by using more complicated medical methods.

Evaluation of the sufficiency of a load for a particular athlete, taking into consideration "sharp" changes, is possible by observing the behavior of the heart, blood pressure, breathing, and how the technique and efficiency are reduced in the additional effort. This additional effort, which is selected depending on the sports discipline and training period, is performed at the end of the workout, after 10-15 minutes of active rest. The information provided by this additional effort helps to evaluate the effect of the workout and to select an adequate amount and type of loads for the next day.

These additional efforts may be specific, for example, for wrestlers; the number and quality of throws of a dummy during 30 seconds, or nonspecific, for example, running in place for 15 seconds.

Control of planned loads in a mesocycle

Daily measurements of the pulse rate, temperature, frequency of breathing, grip dynamometry, weight, description of any pains or other complains, kind, amount, and time of meals, ability for work and state of mind, recorded for a few months, reveals the ascending and descending phases of the monthly cycle of changes in strength and rate of recovery. The changes of training loads in mesocycles have to be synchronized with this cycle.

Changes in the athletic form of female athletes may be related to phases of the menstrual cycle, so female athletes need to systematically conduct gynecological self-observation to find out exactly how phases of the menstrual cycle influence their individual ability to work.

Gynecological self-observation involves marking the date that begins the period and the symptoms that accompany it, such as pains, nausea, appetite, amount of bleeding.

Exercise induced amenorrhea may cause premature bone loss in women that have already begun menstruating.

There are situations where the athlete, because of insufficient preparation, or because of an unwanted type of adaptation, cannot fulfill the planned content of the mesocycle. Changes in the training tasks planned for the mesocycle entail changing the structure of the mesocycle and its microcycles, proportions of the training means, and an introduction of a means of regeneration, or in the worst case, excluding the athlete from training. In some cases, plans for starts in competitions have to be changed. When the general and directed preparation of the athlete is inadequate, it is possible to substitute the previously planned special preparatory mesocycle with one that has more general tasks (e.g., perfecting technique in endurance efforts).

To evaluate the cumulative effect of a mesocycle or a period, tests are used that determine the maximal level of effort abilities of the athlete, i.e. tests that cause full mobilization of the athlete, unlike the standard tests, in which the direction of influence of the effort is strictly limited.

Control of planned loads in a macrocycle

At the end of the preparatory period (especially in endurance sports, as well as in training with a great volume of loads), body weight is reduced, heart rate, blood pressure and breath rate are lowered, amplitude of tremor is decreased, the sum of heart beats during a standard effort, and during the recovery after it, is lowered, and the maximal lung ventilation and aerobic endurance are increased. In speed-strength sports, strength and strength-endurance are increased. In the period of immediate preparation for competition, the dynamics of the changes in the functional states of the athletes are less substantial (particularly for high class athletes). The greatest oscillations are observed among young athletes or if the habitual stereotype of training work was changed. At the end of this period and during the competitive period (period with principal competitions), indicators of efficiency and of functional states after specific, maximally intensive efforts are the most informative. During the last days before competition, an increase of the observed indicators may not reflect the true state of the organism because of the pre-start emotions and the regulation of body weight.

Measuring physical abilities

Physical (motor) abilities in their general form can be measured by nonspecific tests that are applicable to all sports disciplines. Specific forms of physical abilities are measured by specific tests reflecting the needs of particular sports. For example, the special speed of a boxer is measured by the frequency of his punches; a judoka or a wrestler by the frequency (number of throws per time) of throws of an unresisting partner or a dummy. The special speed of the soccer players is measured by 30 or 40 meters runs because these the typical sprint distances in soccer.

The following tests are for measuring physical abilities in their general form.

Agility. It is measured by a run on the "envelope" (a rectangle 3 meters/9.84 feet by 5 meters/16.4 feet).

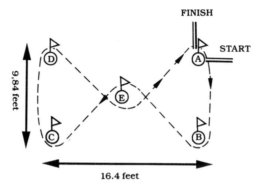

The athlete starts at the marker A and runs along lines B-E-C-D-E-A passing the markers without touching them. Markers are about four feet tall. The athlete completes three laps, and ends at marker A. The time of the whole run is the result.

Cardiovascular fitness. Two simple tests can be used to evaluate it— the Ruffier-Dickson test and the step-test.

The Ruffier-Dickson test consists of making 30 squats within 45 seconds. Heart beats are counted 15 seconds before test, for 15 seconds immediately after, and for 15 seconds after one minute of rest. Heart rate (in beats per minute) before (p), immediately after (p') and one minute after (p") the squats, is found by multiplying the heart beats by four. Next, these numbers are used in an equation:

$$\{(p' - 70) + 2(p" - p)\} \div 10 = \text{Ruffier-Dikson fitness index}$$

Index equal 0.0—very good, 0.1-5.0—good, 5.1-10.0—average, 10.1-15.00 poor.

The heart rate measured after one minute of rest should be close to the heart rate measured before squats. An ideal reaction of the heart is when the heart rate after one minute of rest is a bit lower than before squats.

Step-test: Rhythmically step up and down using a box 50.8 cm (20 inches) tall for men, 46 cm (18 inches) tall for women. Make 30 steps per minute. Start each step with the same leg. Continue for five minutes (men), four minutes (women). After the work, measure your pulse after the first minute (R1), after the second minute (R2), and after the third minute of rest (R3). Measure while sitting and count beats within 30 seconds (1min.-1min. 30 seconds, 2min.-2min. 30 seconds, 3 min.-3 min. 30 seconds).

Multiply total time of work (T—up to 5 min. men, and up to 4 min. women) by 100 and divide by two times the sum of the heart beats counted while resting (in three 30 second periods between 1 min. and 3 min. 30 seconds).

$$\frac{Tx100}{2(R1+R2+R3)} = \text{Step-test fitness index}$$

Sports	Athlete's shape according to the index			
	poor	sufficient	good	excellent
Basketball	94	95-110	111-125	126
Boxing	101	102-123	124-144	145
Fencing	80	81-92	93-103	104
Judo	94	95-109	110-123	124
Kayaking	84	85-104	105-123	124
Rowing	93	94-104	105-114	115
Running	92	93-109	110-125	126
(800-3000 m)				
Skating (speed)	101	102-119	120-136	137
Swimming	88	89-98	99-107	108
Volleyball	86	87-95	96-103	104
Wrestling	86	87-104	105-121	122

Cardiovascular fitness of athletes in various sports as measured by step-test.

Coordination. It is measured by the number of turns along the vertical axis of the body that one can perform during a vertical jump. The athlete stands, with feet at a hip width apart, in a circle 80 cm (31.5 inches) in diameter. The circle has degrees marked on its circumference. Then the athlete jumps up and turns either to the right or to the left. After a firm landing in this circle (other landings do not count), the total number of degrees of turns (or a turn) is recorded. The best one of three successful tries is the result. After performing the test with turns done in one direction, the athlete does it in the other direction. The rationale behind this test is that there are three levels of difficulty of movement coordination (see Chapter V), and that in this test, the ability to perform precise movements (maintaining balance while turning in the air, solid landing) in the short time of a jump, requires mastering the second level of difficulty in the development of coordination. Also, performing this test with turns in both directions, permits an evaluation of one's symmetry of movement control, which is important in achieving sports mastery.

Endurance. Results in endurance activity depend on other abilities such as speed and strength. Tests of the development of endurance can measure either its absolute value, not excluding the influence of speed and strength, or its relative value, through tests that exclude the influence of speed and strength. Such exclusion can be achieved in the following two ways:

— the task is performed by everybody with relatively (depending on maximal speed or strength of each individual) identical intensity. For example, a maximum number of lifts with 40% of the maximal weight, for an individual, in a given lift,

— the task is identical for everybody, but after completion, calculation accounting for strength, speed, weight, is made for each individual.

In cyclic sports, the following equations are used to find relative endurance:

1. Index of speed reserve (SR), which varies depending on the distances used to calculate it.

$$SR = (T_d \div n) - T_s$$

T_d— time on the control distance,

T_s— best time on a standard distance,

n— number indicating by what factor the control distance is longer than standard.

2. Cureton's endurance index (EI).

$$EI = T_d - n \times T_s$$

3. Lazaroff's endurance coefficient (EC).

$$EC = T_d \div T_s$$

4. INKF (Science Institute of Physical Culture, Poland) endurance index (300/60 EI).

$$300/60 \ EI = T_{300} \div T_{60} \times 5$$

T_{300}— time of 300 meter run,

T_{60}— time of 60 meter run.

This test is to be done only on athletes past puberty because for children, this effort is maximal. The results here depend mostly on anaerobic (lactacid) capability, which in children, depends on the stage of ontogenetic development in an individual, rather than on training.

To estimate general endurance in children, the following method, relying on measuring the duration of a run with constant speed equal to 60% of the maximal, is used. The time of a 30 meter run, from a flying start of 15 meters, is taken for each child. Then, by dividing the 30 meters by this time, the maximal speed is arrived at. After calculating 60% of that speed, the time of one 400 meter lap is figured out. Next the child runs laps. If the time of the lap falls 2 seconds below the calculated value, the test is over. The endurance is measured in the distance made with the assigned speed. For example, less than 800 meters— low, 800-900 meters— average, over 2000 meters— high.

Power. It is measured by the height of a jump. The athlete faces the wall, standing 4-5 inches from it. Standing on flat feet, he/she marks the highest point on the wall with an outstretched arm (using chalk). Then, turns his/her side to the wall, bends the knees, swings arms backward and jumps and touches the wall as high as possible. The distance between the first and the second point is the result. This test is done twice with a rest of 1-5 minutes between tries. The better try is measured.

Reaction time. It is measured by electronic instruments that give a sound or light signal and stop the clock at the moment of breaking the circuit by touching the target. If no such instruments are available, reaction time can be estimated by having the athlete grab a stick with strips (one strip— one centimeter or half inch), that is released by a partner without warning.

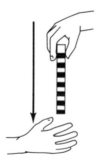

Reaction time test.

Speed. It is measured by a 60 meter run. The athlete starts from starting blocks. The tape is placed at the finish. At least two persons are taking the time. The athlete runs twice with a rest period of no more than 15 minutes between tries. The average of the time taken in the better try is the result.

Strength. There are direct and indirect methods of measuring strength. Direct methods measure strength using dynamometers and line measures. The amount of force that muscles can exert on a joint depends on a moment of force. Measurement of muscular strength must take into account the distance from the point where resistance is applied to the axis of the joint, and the angle at this joint. For the measurement to be accurate, the angle at which joint is held (in direct methods) should be standard.

$M = Fr$

M = moment of force of a given muscle group.

F = Force as measured by dynamometer

r = distance from point of resistance to the axis of the joint

Where such precision is not needed, strength can be measured by the maximum weight that can be lifted by the athlete. Since lifting such weight can be dangerous (injurious), we can estimate the maximum weight by using the following table, showing an approximate correlation between the external load and the maximal number of repetitions in strength exercises.

Approximate correlation between the external load and the maximal number of repetitions in strength exercises:

Number of repetitions	Percentage of maximum weight
1	100
2-3	99-90
4-6	89-80
7-10	79-70
11-15	69-60
16-20	59-50
21-30	49-40
31 and more	39-30

The correlation shown above is typical for weightlifters. The number of repetitions one can perform with a given percentage of maximum weight depends on the loads and repetitions used in training, as well as on one's ratio of fast to slow twitch muscle fibers. The athletes of other sports, especially those stressing endurance, may be able to move a given percentage of their maximum weight (which will be much lower than the maximum weight of a weightlifter in the same weight category) more times than the weightlifters.

Strength-endurance. A method for measuring the strength- endurance of selected groups of muscles, involves computing the kilogram force meters (kGm) of the athlete. For example, to measure the strength-endurance of elbow extensors, the athlete does bench presses to failure, then the weight of the barbell is multiplied by the arm's length and by the number of repetitions (load in kG × limb's length in m × repetitions = kGm).

Special tests of physical abilities.

Track and Field:

Sprints; 5 times 60 meters, rest 3 min.

Middle distance; 5 times 100 meters, rest 3 min.

Long distance; 3 times 400-1000 meters, rest 3 min.

Marathon; 3 times 3000 meters, rest 5 min.

Walking; 3 times walking 3000 metes, rest 5 min.

Throws; 3 sets of 3 throws in each set, rest 5 min.

Jumps (high and long); 3 sets of 3 jumps in each set, rest 5-6 min.

For runners and walkers, these tests are accompanied by measurements of heart rate, blood pressure, electrocardiogram, pulmonary diffusion of gases in lungs, etc. Throwers and jumpers should also be subjected to tests of the neuromuscular system: miotonometry, reaction time, electromiography (latent contraction and relaxation times), etc.

Wrestling:

To evaluate cardiovascular fitness, wrestlers do a test consisting of two periods of 30 seconds of throws (hip throws or shoulder throws) of a dummy, done with maximal speed and frequency. The coach times (chronometry) and counts the throws and evaluates their technical correctness. Only the throws that score 4 or 5 on the scale 0 to 5, are counted. The heart rate, blood pressure, and frequency of breathing are measured while the wrestler is sitting; at rest before the test, after a warm-up, after the first period of throws, and after the second period. The rest between the two periods is 3 minutes.

In mass testing of wrestlers, similar measurements are made but the wrestler throws the dummy for only one period of 20 seconds.

Wrestlers with high athletic class do dummy throws during two, three minute periods separated by 1 minute of rest. During the first 3 minutes, in each minute they do 5 throws during first 50 seconds and then a maximal number of throws during remaining 10 seconds. In the second period they do a maximal number of throws in the first 20 seconds of each minute, and then do only 4 throws in the remaining 40 seconds.

The speed of wrestlers is measured by the time it takes to perform 10 favorite throws with a dummy or an unresisting partner.

Cycling:

Test for sprinters—three repetitions of 400 meters.

Chasers (pursuit)—three repetitions of 1000 meters. Rest between repetitions is 5 minutes. During the rest, the same measurements used for wrestlers and runners are made. If the ergometer is used, work against resistance, that still allows for a maximal number of revolutions (sprinters), can be done, or work can be done until exhaustion while recording the heart rate. To evaluate the functional state and special endurance of the cyclist, a coefficient—a ratio of the sum of the pulse counted during 4 minutes of work to the sum of revolutions during the same time is used. A lower value of the coefficient indicates better special endurance.

Cross-country skiing:

Runs on distances of 800, 1000, 1500, 2000 meters 3-6 times at nearly maximal speed. Immediately upon finishing, heart rate during 10 seconds is measured. The measurement is repeated every minute until the heart rate lowers to 30% of its maximal value registered by radiotelepulsometry during the running.

Swimming:

Tests by additional efforts at the beginning and at the end of the workout. Test may consist of 2 times 25 meters or 2 times 50 meters at the top speed, or 100 meters with top speed, or 200 meters with submaximal speed, or 6 times 50 meters with 75% of maximal speed and rest breaks of 10 seconds. The best additional effort that can be included in every workout is a 200 meter crawl at 50% of the speed. Such a test, conducted at the beginning of the workout, may inform about traces of fatigue after the previous workout; and during or at the end of the workout (after a necessary, brief period of active rest), inform about the effect of separate exercises in the whole workout. The time of covering the distance (of the test) and heart rate during 10 second measured in water immediately after the swim, as well as at the end of the first and second minutes of rest, are measured. Fatigue increases the time of covering the distance and affects the reaction of the pulse.

Boxing:

Following tests are used:

Shadowboxing 3 rounds 3 minutes each recording heart rate and blood pressure during rest breaks.

Combined test consisting of two rounds of hitting the speed bag and one round on heavy bag. Rounds last 3 minutes each and rest between rounds is 1 minute. After these three rounds, heart rate and blood pressure is recorded during 5 minutes.

Test with a punch dynamometer: after a usual warm-up, boxer punches the dynamometer with an assigned force, at the rate of 150 punches per minute, during 2 minutes. Next, after 1 minute of rest, boxer punches the dynamometer with a maximal force for 3 minutes. After the test, the force of all punches is added up. The greater the sum, the better the special endurance of the boxer.

Ice hockey:

According to Dyeriabin S., the best tests for evaluating the form of young (11-18 years) hockey players are: long jump without pre-run, 30 meter run, 300 meter runs, skating 10 meters, skating 30 meters, and skating slalom with and without the puck.

In the following listing of various functional tests, I will tell you what the final results of measurements mean, but I will omit a detailed description of procedures because those who have the required equipment surely know how to use it.

Grip dynamometry: Turn needle-follower on dynamometer to zero before each test. Stand up, with feet about a foot apart, shoulders back, and look straight ahead. Extend the arm (holding the dynamometer) downward, 30 degrees from body. Squeeze quickly with full strength. Release grip and record value indicated by needle-follower. Repeat the whole procedure with the other arm.

An acceptable variation from the normal values is 1-2 kg. In overstrain, insufficient recovery, and in the initial phase of over-training, the values of a morning dynamometry go down.

Miotonometry measures the muscular tonus (elasticity, hardness of muscles) of relaxed, and of voluntarily contracted, muscles. In case of improving form, the difference between the tensed and relaxed state increases (the tonus in tension grows, and in relaxation lowers). In local fatigue, tonus in tension decreases, and in relaxation increases. The exact spots where measurements are to be made, depend on the specifics of the sport, period of training, and preceding workout. These measurements must be made on the muscles that are most affected by training.

Electromiography is used to find the latent times of contraction and relaxation of a muscle. On a signal, for example switching on a light, the athlete contracts as quickly as possible a muscle to which electrodes are attached and then, as soon as the light is switched off, quickly relaxes the muscle. The latent time of contraction is the time elapsed between switching the light on, to the beginning of the first signs of electric activity in the muscle. The latent time of relaxation is the time elapsed from switching off the light, to a sharp decrease of the amplitude of the bioelectric potential/current in the muscle. Measurement is made 3-5 times during 5 seconds.

The ratio of latent contraction time to latent relaxation time, decreases after workouts with high loads and a high level of fatigue. Both latent contraction and relaxation times decrease as the athlete's form improves, and increases as the form worsens. The latent contraction time changes most.

Electrothermometry is used to determine the functional state of an organism after a workout. After very intensive work, in a hot environment, temperature is raised. After a low training load or after rest, temperature is lowered. Temperature may be raised, and read- outs for both sides of the body may be different in overtraining, exhaustion, during acclimatization, and after brain damage.

Tremorgraphy is used to evaluate the emotional condition of an athlete by measuring the amplitude and frequency of muscular tremor. The measurement is done while athlete stands or sits, with dominant hand resting on a table, and a sensor attached to the end (last phalanx) of the index finger. After a few seconds, when the hand is relaxed, the registering mechanism is switched on and a record is made during 5-6 seconds. Amplitude and frequency is determined on the basis of the last two seconds of measurement. The character of tremor depends on the individual. Fatigue, excitement, pre-start fever, and illness increase the amplitude and frequency of tremors. Improvement of general and special athletic form is accompanied by a lowered amplitude of tremor.

Measuring sensitivity of muscles (kinesthesis) and joints. The minimal amplitude of active and passive movements that an athlete can detect in a given joint is measured in angular degrees. As a rule, such measurements are done on kinematometers. The sensitivity of muscles and joints depends on sports discipline, emotions, and fatigue.

Romberg's test measures sensitivity of the equilibrium organs. An athlete stands upright, feet together, arms outstretched to the front, eyes closed. In the more difficult version the feet are on one line, toes of one foot touch the heel of the other. The maximal time of maintaining the stance is determined as an average of three attempts. For trained athletes— divers, gymnasts, acrobats, and swimmers, the time increases with the improving athletic class and exceeds 120 seconds.

Yarocki's test is yet another test of balance. An athlete stands at attention, arms at sides, feet together, eyes closed. The head is turned from side to side at the pace 2 turns per second. The maximal time of maintaining position is recorded. Swimmers, divers, water polo players, gymnasts, and acrobats can maintain balance for 60-80 seconds. Superior equilibrium stability characterizes gymnasts, acrobats, divers, swimmers, and hammer throwers. In some sports, for example, in boxing, there are conditions for the occurrence of the pre-pathological states.

Pulsometry is the simplest means of evaluating the functional state of the cardiovascular system. Heart rate can be measured by instruments (electrocardiograph, seismocardiograph, telemetry, etc.) or by hand, sensing the pulse on arteries, or directly on the heart. Measuring the heart rate after an effort has to begin within 10 seconds after the end of exercise. The heart rate lowers significantly within the first minute after effort.

To ensure precision of measurement, the heart rate is taken as follows: After finding the pulse, stopwatch is started with the first beat (this first beat is not counted) and then, after counting ten beats, the stopwatch is stopped. Knowing the time of ten beats, the number of beats per minute can be calculated. To make it easier, I include here a table of heart rates based on a time of 10 beats and for even more precise measurement, a table of heart rates based on a time of 30 beats.

Sec.	B/min.	Sec.	B/min	Sec.	B/min	Sec.	B/min	Sec.	B/min
6.9	87	6.1	99	5.3	113	4.5	133	3.7	162
6.8	88	6.0	100	5.2	115	4.4	136	3.6	166
6.7	90	5.9	102	5.1	117	4.3	139	3.5	171
6.6	91	5.8	103	5.0	120	4.2	143	3.4	176
6.5	93	5.7	105	4.9	122	4.1	146	3.3	182
6.4	94	5.6	107	4.8	124	5.0	150	3.2	188
6.3	96	5.5	109	4.7	127	3.9	154	3.1	194
6.2	97	5.4	111	4.6	130	3.8	158	3.0	200

Heart rate (beats per minute) projected from duration (sec.) of 10 beats.

Sec.	B/min.	Sec.	B/min.	Sec.	B/min.	Sec.	B/min.	Sec.	B/min.
22.0	82	19.1	94	16.2	111	13.3	135	10.4	173
21.9	82	19.0	95	16.1	112	13.2	136	10.3	175
21.8	83	18.9	95	16.0	113	13.1	137	10.2	176
21.7	83	18.8	96	15.9	113	13.0	138	10.1	178
21.6	83	18.7	96	15.8	114	12.9	140	10.0	180
21.5	84	18.6	97	15.7	115	12.8	141	9.9	182
21.4	84	18.5	97	15.6	115	12.7	142	9.8	184
21.3	85	18.4	98	15.5	116	12.6	143	9.7	186
21.2	85	18.3	98	15.4	117	12.5	144	9.6	188
21.1	85	18.2	99	15.3	118	12.4	145	9.5	189
21.0	86	18.1	99	15.2	118	12.3	146	9.4	191
20.9	86	18.0	100	15.1	119	12.2	148	9.3	194
20.8	87	17.9	101	15.0	120	12.1	149	9.2	196
20.7	87	17.8	101	14.9	121	12.0	150	9.1	198
20.6	87	17.7	102	14.8	122	11.9	151	9.0	200
20.5	88	17.6	102	14.7	122	11.8	153	8.9	202
20.4	88	17.5	103	14.6	123	11.7	154	8.8	205
20.3	89	17.4	103	14.5	124	11.6	155	8.7	207
20.2	89	17.3	104	14.4	125	11.5	157	8.6	209
20.1	90	17.2	105	14.3	126	11.4	158	8.5	212
20.0	90	17.1	105	14.2	127	11.3	159	8.4	214
19.9	90	17.0	106	14.1	128	11.2	161	8.3	217
19.8	91	16.9	107	14.0	129	11.1	162	8.2	220
19.7	91	16.8	107	13.9	129	11.0	164	8.1	222
19.6	92	16.7	108	13.8	130	10.9	165	8.0	225
19.5	92	16.6	108	13.7	131	10.8	167		
19.4	93	16.5	109	13.6	132	10.7	168		
19.3	93	16.4	110	13.5	133	10.6	170		
19.2	94	16.3	110	13.4	134	10.5	171		

Heart rate (beats per minute) projected from duration (sec.) of 30 beats.

Immediately after waking up, the heart rate is close to its nightly value. Between 0800-1000 hours its value increases, around 1400 hours it slows down, around 1500 hours it starts increasing, and reaches its highest values between 1800-2000 hours. Heart rate measured while the subject is standing is 2-4 beats faster than when subject is sitting, and in a sitting position it is 6-8 beats faster than while lying down. Athletes of endurance oriented sports have a heart rate 60-40/min. or less. In speed oriented sports, the heart rate is higher.

40-60 minutes after the end of the workout, the heart rate is normally 10-20% faster than its value at rest.

Gradually lowering the values of heart rate after a workout, particularly after an endurance workout, means that the recovery proceeds normally. If such a gradual lowering of the heart rate is interrupted by a sudden jump to lower values, it may be a sign of overtraining.

A higher than normal heart rate occurs in overstrain and in illnesses with fever.

In pre-start states, of emotional excitation, the heart rate becomes faster and irregular. The behavior of heart rate in pre-start states depends on age, sex, and intensity of the effort ahead of athlete.

Sphygmomanometry/Blood pressure measurement. The blood pressure of healthy individuals is unstable and oscillates during the day by 10-20 mmHg. The amplitude of oscillations is lower during a night's sleep. A measurement of blood pressure done without special preparation and at a randomly chosen time, is called random. The value of this random measurement is a sum of the stable blood pressure and the additional pressure that changes depending on circumstances. The stable pressure can be determined after 10-15 minutes of rest. Additional pressure (systolic and diastolic) normally does not exceed 5-10 mmHg. The value of additional pressure and the time needed for returning to the value of the stable pressure increases in the early stages of disturbing the regulation of arterial blood pressure.

The basal arterial blood pressure is measured in the morning, lying down in bed, after a good night's sleep. Its value is, to a significant degree, a physiologic constant for the individual.

Horizontal position of the body, physical rest, and mental calm lower the arterial blood pressure. Eating, smoking, and physical and mental tension increase blood pressure.

The level of diastolic pressure, in considerable degree, reflects the level of basal pressure in the arterial system and the value of the vascular resistance. Changes of the diastolic pressure are often a more serious symptom than changes of the systolic pressure. Pulse pressure has great importance. It is the difference between systolic and diastolic pressure.

The normal average value of systolic pressure is between 100 and 140 mmHg, and diastolic pressure is between 60 and 80 mmHg. Lowering systolic pressure below 100 mmHg is called arterial hypotony. An increase of the values of systolic and diastolic above the normal values (shown above), is called arterial hypertony. Athletes staying in cold climates have a blood pressure 10 mmHg higher, warm weather causes a lowering of the blood pressure.

Frequency of breath ought to be measured in the morning, immediately after waking up. One should not increase the depth of breaths when taking the measurement because it reduces frequency. A frequency greater than normal for an individual, may indicate a problem in the cardiovascular and/or respiratory system. The longer the inhalation and shorter the exhalation, the better the gas exchange is. The average values: inhalation—from 0.3 to 4.7 seconds, exhalation—from 1.2 to 6 seconds.

Another measurement, that may be used for early detection of overtraining or a disruption in oxygen transporting systems, is the change in the normal time an individual can hold his/her breath. Average values are within 55-60 seconds at inhalation, 30-40 seconds at exhalation and depend on lung capacity, efficiency of pulmonary circulation, and oxygen carrying capacity of the blood.

An athlete has to be weighed in the morning after getting out of bed, as well as before and after the main workout of a day. With normal training loads, the body weight should be constant (slight lowering at the beginning of the preparatory period of macrocycle is OK). After a sudden drop resulting from applying maximal loads in a workout, the weight should be regained within 1-3 days. A prolonged period of lowered weight in the competitive period may mean overtraining. A weight increase may accompany the increase of loads in strength training.

Measuring technical and tactical skills

The results of sports competition depend (in equal measure) on mastering the technique and on the physical abilities of the athlete. This means that results in sports are a sum of technique and physical abilities. When testing technique, we do not know if we measure only technique or the sum of technique and physical abilities. Certain techniques are impossible to perform without a sufficient amount of strength, speed, or flexibility.

In games, individual non-contact sports, and in individual contact sports, it is impossible to measure technical and tactical proficiency separately.

The technical proficiency of an athlete is determined by the ratio of sport result to energy expended on achieving it. The greater the technical proficiency, the less effort it takes to achieve a given result.

Technical proficiency (mastery) has three components:

a) Technical versatility of the athlete, which means the skill in using widely differing techniques (amount of techniques an athlete can perform.).

b) Technical efficiency, which is the ability to get the best results using a given technique.

c) Technical reliability, expressed by the ratio of successful attempts to total number of attempts.

Technical efficiency can be judged by using subjective and objective methods. Objective methods are used in weightlifting, swimming, and in track and field. In the high jump, one of the indicators of technical efficiency is the distance from the center of the athlete's gravity to the bar at the moment of clearing it (passing over it). The smaller this distance the more efficient the technique, and the greater the technical mastery. In weightlifting, the lower the height of the barbell at the moment of squatting, the more technical the lift. In swimming, technical efficiency is judged by the degree of variation from the average speed. Smaller variation means greater efficiency. In acrobatics, the smaller the difference between the time spent in the air performing simple evolutions and the time spent performing complicated evolutions, the better the technique. Subjective methods are used in gymnastics and similar sports.

The efficiency of the technique, in sports that cannot be objectively measured, is determined by the difference between the athlete's motor potential and the actual result (potential to result ratio). Technique is evaluated by looking at, and mentally comparing, the performed technique to the ideal technique. The technique can be evaluated as a whole, or its elements can be evaluated separately (rhythm, speed, precision). The points can then be summed up. The motor potential is found by special tests and calculations.

In basketball, the reliability of a free throw can be judged by the percentage of made shots. In individual contact sports, like judo or boxing, technical reliability can be measured by dividing the number of scoring techniques; for example, landed blows or good throws; by the total number of attempts (attempted techniques).

Not only the general technical proficiency in a fight or a number of fights (bouts, encounters) can be measured this way, but also the reliability of a particular technique, for example, a given punch in boxing, or any of the techniques in judo.

The technical reliability of a player in team ball games is calculated by dividing number of times (P) the player properly handled the ball (passing the ball to the opponent is improper) by the total number (C) of his/her contacts with the ball.

$$T_R = P \div C$$

Absolute reliability equals one.

The activity of the player is calculated by multiplying the total number (C) of contacts with the ball had by this player, by the number of players in the team; for example 11 in soccer, and then divided by the total number (C_t) of contacts with the ball made by his/her team.

$$A = (C \times 11) \div C_t$$

A result greater than one means that the player was very active in the game.

The technical efficiency (T_E) of the player can be calculated on the basis of his/her reliability (T_R) and activity (A)— multiplying the number of times (P) the player properly played the ball by the number of players in the team (11), and then dividing the result by the total number (C_t) of contacts with the ball had by his/her team.

$$T_E = T_R \times A = P \div C \times (C \times 11) \div C_t = (P \times 11) \div C_t$$

To get a better idea of the efficiency of the players, additional points should be awarded for directly scoring points (goals) and for passing the ball to a player that scored. For example, in soccer, the additional points are awarded as follows:

first goal— 8 points, co-author— 4 points,

second goal— 6 points, co-author— 3 points,

third goal— 4 points, co-author— 2 points,

fourth goal— 2 points, co-author— 1 point,

each following goal— 1 point, co-author— 0.5 point.

In individual contact sports, an athlete's "competition value" can be calculated for each competition by adding the following ratios together: the ratio of points scored in fights to the maximal number of points available in these fights, the ratio of minimal number of attacks needed for victory in each fight to the total number of attacks, and the ratio of number of fights the athlete had to the total number of possible fights in this competition. Comparing this value to the maximal possible value tells how far from an ideal performance the athlete is, and allows for an objective comparison of the performance of athletes.

IX. NATURAL MEANS OF RECOVERY

Presented here are a means of enhancing the recovery that do not require complicated equipment and/or special licenses to operate.

Nutrition. Proper nutrition is essential in maintaining good health. It is especially important in athletic training, where the food has to provide energy and building materials for the organism subjected continuously to great loads. Athletes in physically demanding sports generally need more animal protein, vitamins, and minerals than non-athletes. Dr. Galina Shatalova from the USSR Research Institute of Physical Education has proven by several experiments that the number of calories is less important than than the biological value of food.

During several long-distance races (several days of running 30 to 50 kilometers per day) athletes, participating in these experiments, taking less than 1000 calories daily, were able to continue the race, and some even gained up to 1/2 lb. (500 grams). The athletes that were on a conventional diet, eating up to 6000 calories daily, felt tired and lost up to 6 pounds.

Shatalova explains that "...the most important factor is the proper supply of energy... It is believed that energy losses are compensated by food exclusively. It is said that a person burns a certain amount of calories and to restore them he/she needs to eat food containing the same amount of calories. Actually, the whole thing is much more complex. Our food is no firewood, and nutrition cannot be compared with burning. The facts show that the human body can restore energy losses which are far greater than the [mere] caloric content of the food we eat.

The traditional belief that losses of energy must be compensated by the appropriate amount of food makes people include in their diet [too much] animal proteins and fats. But man must be one with nature using everything it has to offer to the best advantage. Vegetables, fruits, beans, edible greens, nuts, seeds, and honey are what one needs."

Shatalova recommends that people eat the most nutritionally valuable foods of a season. In spring— edible greens, in summer— fruits and berries, in fall— fruits and vegetables, in winter— cereals and peas and beans (legumes).

She believes that spicy, fatty and roasted foods make one too aggressive, and that eating "yesterday's food"— soft, overboiled and stale— makes one passive and sluggish.

In endurance sports, such as long- distance running, skiing, cycling, rowing, and in other sports where athletes sweat profusely for long periods of time, replenishing the lost water and chemicals is a priority after a workout or a match, or even during the work. Loss of water by perspiration is usually accompanied by a decrease in the amount of electrolytes, which impairs the function of muscles and of the central nervous system. To make up these losses, athletes increase the amount of salt in food, and drink mineral waters, fruit juices, and vegetable juices.

The fluids should be drunk slowly, in small sips, and normally, only after the circulatory system has recovered from the effort. In case of great dehydration, this rule can be broken. The complete replenishment of the lost fluids should take a few hours. The temperature of the drinks in summer should be more than 20 degrees Celsius, and in winter should be no higher than the temperature of the body. Proper temperature facilitates the passage of fluids through the digestive system, and speeds up their arrival to dehydrated tissues. Sweet drinks can irritate stomach lining and can slow down the recovery process by lowering the blood sugar level (secondary hypoglycemia). One should not eat right after drinking lots of fluids. Only after the organism is completely calm, which may take up to 2-3 hours after a workout, can one eat.

Each sports discipline has its specific detailed nutritional guidelines which would take too much space to present here.

Sleep. Lack of sleep causes irritability and an increased feeling of fatigue. It impairs attention, creative thinking, and the ability to deal with unfamiliar situations. If sleep deprivation is frequent, the efficiency of physical work is also impaired. Minimum amount of nightly sleep is 7-8 hours. One should not eat for a few hours before going to bed. Immediately before going to sleep one can drink a glass of warm water. Coffee and tea are stimulants that interfere with getting a good sleep. The peak of stimulating action of tea is long after we have ingested it. It does not prevent falling asleep, but the most precious phase of deep sleep (fourth stage non-REM), occurring in the first hour after falling asleep, is shallow and ineffective. Taking vitamin B-15 has similar effects.

The bedroom must have fresh air, and be dark, silent, and cool (17-19 degrees Celsius). The body has to be under warm cover. The head is cool, the feet warm. The bed surface has to be even and sufficiently hard. Long, hot baths stimulate. Cool baths followed by vigorous rubbing with towel, induce sleep in up to 20 minutes. Athletes with a dominating parasympathetic system become sleepy after a warm bath. To induce sleep after intensive workouts or before competitions, drink one big glass of warm beer with lots of sugar.

Sleep during the day, before a workout or competition, is not recommended. The ability to work is lowered after waking up, which prolongs the warm-up.

Environment. Swimming in natural (open) waters improves the functioning of the nervous system (mainly of its vegetative part), and the skin, as well as the thermo-regulation of organism. Frequent swimming in the summer, prevents the intensification of arthritic pains of the joints and spine that normally occurs in fall and winter.

Sea air with its high content of iodine and salt (NaCl), improves the function of breathing passages.

Sunshine improves blood circulation in the skin and lung ventilation, soothes pain, lowers the blood pressure, and stimulates the nervous system and metabolism (particularly, management of calcium and phosphorus). Amount of exposure to sunshine should start from 30-60 minutes depending on the season and time of day, and then can be gradually increased.

On cloudy days, exposing the body to air improves lung ventilation, the function of the cardiovascular system, and regulates the vegetative nervous system. The influence on these systems is more intensive with lower temperatures.

Music can be used as a means of psychotherapy. Music pieces with simple tonal construction, with agreeing harmonies, and little changes of tempo, calm down, relieve anxiety, relax muscles, reduce resistance in the respiratory tract, and deepen the breath.

After intensive effort, calming music should be listened to for up to 30 minutes in the evening before going to sleep.

Light, pleasant music at a maximum loudness of 40 dB, can be used during the workout to improve mood, and invigorate athletes.

The colors of the environment influence emotions and the ability to concentrate. Each color has a psychophysiologic characteristic, which should be taken into account when decorating gyms and recreation rooms. Walls in rooms used for recreation or relaxation should be lighter at the top, and get gradually darker at the bottom. The light, higher part of the wall gives the impression of free space, and the darker bottom creates feeling of security. In the gym, big contrasts in lightning (illumination) and colors can cause difficulties in estimating space relationships. The amount of light should be in the medium range with good visibility provided by the proper arrangement of colors. The fixed, immovable apparatus should be painted in various shades of low intensity, medium light, green color. It suggests stability. The moving equipment, such as dumbbells, ought to be painted in more active colors: reds, oranges, yellows—of high intensity and lightness.

Colors, probably through the vegetative nervous system, influence the human organism. The kind, and the amount of influence depends on the color and its intensity. Red increases the blood pressure, heart rate, muscular tonus, and the frequency of breathing, but in the long run is tiring. Blue lowers the blood pressure, slows down the heart rate and the breathing. Green increases the ability to perform long lasting muscular efforts. White suggests lightness and pleasant coolness. Yellow is uplifting, suggests spaciousness, warmth, increases heart rate, stimulates the central nervous system, and may increase aggressiveness. Orange increases heart rate, invigorates, and warms up. Crimson induces an elevated mood. Purple tires, causes a feeling of heaviness and confinement. Blue calms down and saddens, blue interiors seem cool and confined. Light blue calms down and enlarges space. Blue with white cools and calms. Green lowers pressure in the eye balls and sharpens vision, normalizes blood circulation, causes a feeling of light coolness, and is soothing. Brown causes a feeling of stability and calm. Gray tires, causes apathy and boredom. Brown-gray causes anxiety. Black lowers muscular tonus, and is depressing. Surfaces painted black seem heavy.

Massage. Massage or auto-massage is beneficial for skin, muscles, and ligaments. It removes dead cells from the surface of skin and brings more blood to it. In muscles, it speeds up removal of the products of metabolism, and improves blood circulation. The elasticity and strength of ligaments is improved by massage.

Besides these local influences, massage affects blood and lymph circulation, as well as the central nervous system. The blood and lymph circulate faster. Massage improves cardiovascular adaptability, and the blood flow in coronary vessels. Through reflexive mechanisms, it regulates the central nervous system.

Massage complements or precedes the warm-up because it stimulates the neuromuscular system. Massage during the workout ought to be mild and applied on the primary working muscles. After the workout, massage is done only after the athlete has calmed down, and quite a while after a meal. It improves blood circulation, speeds up the biochemical processes in tired muscles, and relieves tension and excitability.

Classic massage improves the strength of muscles and point massage relaxes nervous system; both types of massage can be done together.

An article by Birukov, Kafarov, and Lukyanov, describes an experiment on the effect of massage on the performance of wrestlers. The authors reached the following conclusions:

Massage done after the warm-up and before 30 second test of throws and bouts, improved the number and quality of throws in the 30 second test and the effectiveness of actions in a bout. Muscle tonus after the bout when the massage followed the warm-up, was lower than when no massage was done and when the massage was done before the warm-up.

The effect of massage conducted prior to the warm-up was slight.

There are several kinds of sports massage; workout massage, preventive massage, recovery/regenerative massage, and therapeutic massage.

Workout massage, whole body or local, has to speed up the process of recovery after the workout. It is done after 1.5-2 hours after the end of the workout. If the workout ends late in the evening, it may be followed by a short session of local massage or a recovery/regenerative massage lasting no more than 20 minutes. The whole body massage should be done the next morning. In the microcycle of intensive training, a local workout massage can be done on the first, third, fifth, and seventh day, and a whole body workout massage on the second, fourth, and sixth day. On days with two workouts, a light recovery/regenerative massage is done 20-30 minutes after the first (morning) workout and a more intensive massage, lasting up to one hour, is done 1.5-6 hours after the evening workout. Workout massage can be done in the sauna.

Its duration then is about half that of a massage done in normal conditions (not in the sauna).

The duration of whole body and local massages, depends on the athlete's weight.

Athlete's weight	Duration of massage in minutes			
	In normal conditions		In sauna	
	General	Local	General	Local
up to 60 kg (132 lb.)	40	20	20	5-10
61-75 kg (134-165 lb.)	50	25	25	6-12
76-100 kg (167-220 lb.)	60	30	30	7-14
over 100 kg (over 220 lb.)	over 60	35	35	8-18

Athlete's weight and duration of massage.

Preventive massage is done immediately before an effort. It is used to relax the body, warm-up and prevent a cooling down of the body, and regulate the pre-start emotions. Relaxing massage lasts 15-25 minutes and ends 5 minutes before the start in competition. In endurance sports, massage is done slower, longer and deeper. In speed-strength sports energetic massage is performed on those muscles that are most stressed. Warming up massage is to be done before workout, starts in competitions, and in the breaks between starts if it is cold and there are long breaks during the competition. The massage should last 10 minutes. It is done energetically, at a fast pace. After completing the massage of any body part, it should be covered and kept warm, and after the whole massage, the athlete should put on a warm-up suit (sweatsuit). A massage regulating emotions, has to calm down the athlete in the case of pre-start fever and energize him/her in the case of pre-start apathy. For pre-start fever, usually 4-6 minutes of stroking, followed by up to 2 minutes of light, superficial kneading, and up to 2 minutes of shaking is done. For pre-start apathy: 5-8 minutes of kneading, pressing up to 2 minutes, and hitting up to 2 minutes. All actions are done energetically and end 5-7 minutes before the start of competition.

Recovery/regenerative massage is done during breaks between heats (running or swimming), between bouts (wrestling, boxing), before a change of apparatus in gymnastics, and to speed up recovery after workouts or competitions. Actions used: stroking, rubbing, kneading, shaking. Initially, massage is light, and then it gets deeper and more energetic. The massage may begin as soon as the heart beat and breath are back to normal (20-30 minutes after effort). Massage lasts 7-12 minutes. If the rest break during competition is going to be approximately 1.5 hour, the recovery/regenerative massage is done immediately after the start and lasts 7-15 minutes. In case of considerable fatigue, this massage is done after 1-2 hours for 15-20 minutes. In cases of great fatigue, as observed in marathon runners or cross-country skiers after 30 or 50 kilometer runs, recovery/regenerative massage is done 2-3 times per day. First session—30 minutes after the effort, lasts 7-15 minutes. Second session—2-3 hours after the effort, lasts 20-30 minutes. Third session—5 hours after the effort or on the next day. Vibrators are an effective means of speeding up recovery, especially in the case of local muscle fatigue. Massage with vibrators should last 3-5 minutes, with a frequency of vibration—150-170 per second (150-170 Hz); 5-10 minutes after the effort and in cases of repeated starts, immediately before each start. Hydromassage (water massage) is done by a stream of water under pressure. The athlete is immersed in the bath tub (water temperature 35-38 degrees Celsius) and rests for five minutes. Next the stream of water, directed toward the center of the tub, massages the limbs at a pressure of 3-4 atmospheres. Following that, the pressure is reduced to 1-1.5 atmosphere and the stream is directed at the trunk and abdomen. The heart and genitals are not to be massaged.

Therapeutic massage is prescribed by a physician in the case of some illnesses and various sports injuries.

Sports massage for female athletes, on days preceding menstruation, has to be shortened to 20 minutes. Strong, deep kneading, hitting, as well as massage of the abdomen, is not done on these days. One or two days after the end of the cycle, the massage session increases gradually to 35-40 minutes. Milk glands are not to be massaged but the chest (pectoral) muscles can be massaged.

<u>Water.</u> A shower is taken after every workout. After a heavy workout that raised temperature, a shower should begin with 2-3 minutes of cool water, and then gradually get warmer. It should end with cool water. While in the shower, one should rub the fatigued muscles with a sponge or a brush.

A warm wet compress is applied on muscles with "fatigue pain". To intensify its action, one can use salt water in the wrap.

A warm bath (35-37 degrees Celsius) is recommended after strength or speed-strength workouts, in cases of increased muscular tension, and fatigue pains. After the bath, cool down and rest.

A hot bath should start with 37 degrees, with the temperature gradually raised to 39-42 degrees Celsius. After 3-5 minutes at this temperature, one should gradually cool down under a shower. During the bath, the head has to be kept cool with a cold compress to prevent the dilation of blood vessels in the brain. After a short cooling off under the shower, one should rest lying down for 30-50 min. This recommended after (but not immediately after) intensive muscular efforts resulting in acidosis. (The best times are after-noons or evenings in days of rest.) A hot bath speeds up the removal of tocsins and by-products of effort.

A jacuzzi (whirlpool) combines the massaging action of streams of water with a high temperature that warms up the body. It is recommended after intensive workouts because it relaxes muscles, reduces pain, and improves blood circulation.

In a steam bath the temperature of the air reaches 60-70 degrees Celsius, with a humidity of 20%-70%. In the sauna, the tempera-ture of the air reaches 100-140 degrees Celsius, with a humidity of 10%. When using the sauna, it is more comfortable to enter it 3 times, for 5-7 minutes each time, than it is to stay a long time once. Each time after leaving the sauna, one should take a shower (13-15 degrees Celsius) for 20-40 seconds, and then take another shower or bath at 37-39 degrees, lasting 1.5-2 minutes. This is followed by another cool shower for 10-15 seconds and another hot shower (or bath) for 1 minute. After these showers, one should sit or lay down for 5-7 minutes. The above procedure can be followed after the evening workout or competition if there is to be more work on the next day. If a heavy workout is to be followed by a day of rest, or during breaks of over 20 hours between workouts or starts, the sauna is used in a different manner. Namely, the athlete enters the sauna 3-4 times, for 5-7 minutes each time. The air temperature in the sauna reaches 100-120 degrees. After each stay in the sauna, the athlete takes a cool shower (or bath) for 10-15 seconds, and next a warm shower (or bath of temperature 30 degrees) for 2.5-3 minutes. The rest between the stays in the sauna is 7-10 minutes. At the end of a training cycle or after competitions followed by a lowering of the training loads, the sauna is recom-mended for the morning of the next day. The number of stays in the sauna depends on how the athlete feels. It may be up to 4 times. The duration of each stay is 5-7 minutes. Temperature of the warm bath is 26-30 degrees.

If the above recommendations are not followed, as well as in cases of illness or overwork, overheating (heat stroke) in the sauna may occur. Symptoms of the initial stage of overheating are: excitation, nausea, dizziness, headache, and frequent urination. In the later stages, sleepiness, heavy breathing, salivation, a lack of perspiration appear. If the athlete has the above symptoms, he/she has to be removed from the sauna, covered with warm blankets and placed in the stream of fresh air. Next, let him/her smell ammonia and drink hot sweet tea with lemon. Further steps are to be decided by a physician.

A steam bath (sauna) the regulates circulatory system by dilating peripheral blood vessels and increasing the heartstroke volume per minute. It also speeds up the removal of the products of metabolism. After washing off and drying, one should get into sauna and sit on a lower bench until sweating begins. Then pour half liter (one pint) of water on the stones, and after a while get out; take a cool shower for 1-3 min., dry the skin and get into sauna again, this time on a higher bench; when warm, pour water on the stones, use the birch twigs, and remain in sauna until sweating begins again. After this, one should leave the sauna and cool down under a shower or in the snow. After a good rubbing with a towel, rest for 20-30 minutes. Do not stand in sauna. Head can be cooled with cold water. No food or drink (even water) immediately after. Athletes should use a sauna once or twice a week (in the afternoons), on days with one workout done earlier. Adolescents younger than 16 years stay in a sauna for a shorter time and at a lower temperature (60 degrees Celsius). Swimmers occasionally warm themselves up, during rest breaks between swimming exercises, in a sauna.

The use of a steam bath disrupts metabolic processes in the athlete's body. Even on the second day after having the steam bath, the athlete's organism has not completely recovered. For this reason, the steam bath should be done after (but not immediately after) a workout, and not on a day of rest. This will allow the athlete to have a day of complete rest.

According to an article by Shiyan and Nevzorov in *Sportivnaya Borba*, after the steam bath, the urea level in the bloodstream rose substantially for the athletes that spent three hours in the steam bath room and were in the actual steam 4-5 times for 10 minutes each time.

Because of the increased level of urea, it was concluded that a steam bath disrupts the metabolic processes in the athletes' bodies. Even on the second day after the steam bath, researchers observed an incomplete restoration in the athletes. This occurred when the athletes used the steam room on their rest day. No such thing occurred during the actual working day when the athletes used the steam room a few hours after the workout and for shorter periods of time.

All over body heating, such as a hot bath or sauna, should not be done immediately after an intensive workout because it further strains thermo-regulation. Water or steam make the evaporation of sweat impossible. The body may reach 39-41 degrees Celsius, which disturbs tissue metabolism (especially in the nervous system) and can cause cramps or even fainting.

Young athletes (children) should use only warm baths and auto-massage. As an athlete ages and uses a more intensive means of training, a more intensive means of recovery such as massage, sauna, ultrasound, etc. are used.

An organism adapts to the means of recovery similarly as to the means of training so the medical supervision is necessary.

Means of recovery in a macrocycle.

In the general preparatory period, cool or lukewarm showers are taken in the mornings. After strength workouts, warm-cool showers; after workouts with overheating (mainly endurance), cool-warm-cool showers. Twice or three times a week, use warm baths and massage after a workout. Use a sauna or hot bath once a week, or even less often.

In the special preparatory period, when the work stresses more of the muscular and nervous system, more local measures such as local massage, heating, and compresses are used (in addition to the above means). Hot baths or sauna are used 2-3 times a week if the athletes do not sweat too much during workouts.

In the competitive period, due to the specific character of the psychological and physical loads, the means of recovery have to specifically suit the needs of the sport.

Endurance sports: general, mildly toning treatments and local heating and relaxing treatments are used (baths, massages, overheating 2-3 days before contests).

Speed sports: use local treatments 1-2 times a day, and overheating twice a week with profuse sweating (sauna, hot bath).

Technical sports (gymnastics, diving, shooting): use gentle showers, mineral baths, and underwater massage. Young (less than 18) gymnasts: use warm salt (0.5-1%) half-baths with auto-massage.

Individual contact sports: use local treatment, for example, massage, every day; one day salt bath before sleep, followed the next day by a whole body warm bath with rubbing; or an underwater massage. Since workouts cause great fluid losses, overheating (sauna) should be used carefully, 1-2 times a week, and not immediately after workout.

Speed-strength sports (weightlifting, jumps, ski jumps): use warm baths (normal or mineral), with rubbing followed by massage. Use hot bath or sauna 1-2 times weekly.

Games: use cool-warm-cool shower immediately after workout or match, or a warm bath (normal or mineral) with underwater massage or auto-massage (max. pressure 3-3.5 atm.). Once a week, use a sauna or warm bath. For local overloads, massage, wraps/compresses, local baths are used.

BIBLIOGRAPHY

1. Batashev A. "The Shooter's Daughter." Sport in the USSR number 3, 1989.
2. Bergh U. "Physiology of Cross-Country Ski Racing." Human Kinetics Publishers, Inc., Champaign IL, 1982.
3. Birukov A. A., Kafarov N. A., Lukyanov A. G. "Some methodological aspects of using warm-up massage for wrestlers." Tieoriya i Praktika Fizicheskoy Kultury number 11, 1986 (quoted in Soviet Sports Review, June 1989).
4. Blakeslee S. "Hormone fluctuations affect women's abilities, study shows." The Orange County Register, November 18, 1988.
5. Bompa T. O. "Theory and Methodology of Training", Kendall/Hunt Publishing Co., Dubuque IA, 1985.
6. Bosco J. S., Greenleaf J. E., Bernauer E. M., Card D. H. "Effects of acute dehydration and starvation on muscular strength and endurance" Acta Physiologica Polanica number 25, 1974.
7. Breit N. J. "The effects of body position and stretching technique on the development of hip and back flexibility" Dissertation for degree of Doctor of Physical Education. Springfield College, 1977
8. Bullock J., Boyle J., Wang M. B., Ajello R. R. "Physiology." Harval Publishing Co., Media, 1984.
9. Burkett L. N. "Causative factors in hamstring strains." Master of Arts thesis. San Diego State College, 1968.
10. Cherepanova N. "Harnessing Emotions." Sport in the USSR number 5, 1989.
11. Chrominski Z. "Metodyka sportu dzieci i mlodziezy/Methodology of youth and children's sports." Sport i Turystyka, Warszawa, 1980.
12. Dawson J., Perry S. "The Secrets Our Body Clocks Reveal." Rawson Associates, New York NY, 1988.
13. deVries H. A. "Physiology of Exercise for Physical Education and Athletics." Wm. C. Brown Company Publishers, Dubuque IA, 1980.
14. I. P. Digtyaryev I. P. Getke L. P. "Fundamental means of strength training for boxers of different ages and qualifications." Tieoriya i Praktika Fizicheskoy Kultury, number 12, 1984 (quoted in Soviet Sports Review, December 1989).
15. Douglis C. "Humankind bops along in time to the rhythm of life." The Orange County Register, January 26, 1988.
16. Drabik J. "Wybrane zdolnosci koordynacyjne osob w roznym wieku z uwzglednieniem symetrii i asymetrii ruchu/Selected coordination abilities of persons in different age taking into account symmetry and asymmetry of movement." Zeszyty Naukowe AWF in Gdansk, number 7, 1983.
17. Dyeriabin S. "Struktura fizicheskoy podgotovlennosti yunyh hokkeistov/Structure of physical preparation of young hokey players." Tieoriya i Praktika Fizicheskoy Kultury number 12, 1981.
18. Farfiel W. S. "Fizyologya Sporta/Physiology of sports." Fizkultura i Sport, Moskva, 1960.
19. Farfiel W. S. "Metody niezwlocznej informacji w treningu sportowym/Methods of immediate feedback in sports training." Sport Wyczynowy numbers 1-9, Warszawa, 1964.

20. Filin W. P. "Vospitanye fizicheskih kachestv u yunyh sportsmyenov/Development of physical qualities in young hokey players." Fizkultura i Sport, Moskva, 1974.
21. Georgiev N., Semov K. "Metod za opredeljane na natovarvaneto v trenirivkata po basketbol" in Vaprosy Fizicheskoy Kultury number 5, 1975 (quoted by Naglak).
22. Giesielievich B. A. "Medicinskii spravochnik trieniera/Medical manual for the coach." Fizkultura i Sport, Moskva, 1976.
23. Goleman D. "Put on a smile and the rest follows" The Orange County Register, August 24, 1989.
24. Grochmal S. "Teoria i metodyka cwiczen relaksowo-koncentrujacych/Theory and methodology of relaxing and concentrating exercises." PZWL, Warszawa, 1979.
25. Halberg F., Johnson E., Nelson W., Runge W., Sothern R. "Autorhythmometry—Procedures for Physiologic Self-Measurements and Their Analysis" Physiology Teacher number 4, January 1972.
26. Handelsman A. B., Smirnov K. M. "Fizjologiczne podstawy treninigu sportowego/Physiological foundations of sports training." Wydawnictwo PKOL, Warszawa, 1972.
27. Harre D. "Trainingslehre. Einführung in die allgemeine Trainingsmetodik." Sportverlag, Berlin, 1971, 1985.
28. Harris N. "The stress that drives athletes to illness." The Independent, November 7, 1989.
29. Hettinger T., Mueller E. A. "Die trainierbarkeit der musculatur", Arbeitsphysiologie 16, 1955 (quoted by deVries).
30. Holley D., DeRoshia C., Winget C. "Circadian Rhythms and Athletic Performance" Medicine and Science in Sports and Exercise volume 17, pp. 494-516, 1985 (quoted by Dawson and Perry).
31. Houston M. E., Marrin D. A., Green H. J., Thompson J. A. "The effect of rapid weight loss on physiological functions in wrestlers." The Physician and Sportsmedicine number 9, 1981.
32. Ikai M., Steinhaus A. H. "Some factors modifying the expression of human strength." Journal of Applied Physiology, 1961.
33. Israel S.,"Das Akute Entlastungssyndrom." Theorie und Praxis Der Körperkultur, number 12, 1963.
34. Jeffries S. C. "Sport Physiology Study Guide" Human Kinetics Publishers, Inc., Champaign IL, 1986.
35. Kano J. "Kodokan Judo" Kodansha International, Tokyo/New York NY, 1986.
36. Katin A. "Athletes' Menu" Sport— USSR and World Arena number 8, 1990.
37. Krumm J. E. "Kids' Load Limits" Muscle & Fitness page 13, September 1988.
38. Kukushkin G. I. "Sistiema fizichieskovo vospitania v SSSR/System of physical education in the USSR." Raduga, Moskva, 1983.
39. Kurz T. "Stretching Scientifically, A Guide to Flexibility Training" Stadion Publishing Company, Cypress CA, 1987.
40. Leighton J. R. "A study of the effect of progressive weight training on flexibility." American Corrective Therapy Journal 18 (4):101, 1964.
41. Matvyeyev L. P. "Fundamentals of Sports Training", Progress Publishers, Moskva, 1981
42. Matvyeyev L. P. "Osnovy sportivnoy trienirovki/Fundamentals of sports training." Fizkultura i Sport, Moskva, 1977.
43. Matvyeyev L. P. "Zasady planowania treningu w okresie bezposredniego przygotowania startowego/Principles of planning training in the period of immediate start preparation." Sport Wyczynowy number 7, 1979.
44. Maugh, II, T. H. "Studies tie sex hormones to women's level of skill." Los Angeles Times, November 17, 1988.
45. Mika T. "Fizykoterapia/Physical therapy." PZWL, Warszawa, 1987.
46. Moritani T., DeVries H. A. "Neural Factors vs. hypertrophy in the time course of muscle strength gain." American Journal of Physical Medicine number 58, 1979.
47. Mountcastle V. B. Ed. "Medical Physiology", C. V. Mosby, St. Louis MO, 1980.
48. Myedvyedyev A. S., Gulianc A. J., Rodinov W. T., Rogozyan W. N. "Vliyanye napravyennosti sodierzhanya trenirovochnego processa tyazhelo-atletov v podgotovlyennom peryodie na resultat/Influence of directing the content of training process of weightlifters in the preparatory period on the result." Tieoriya i Praktika Fizicheskoy Kultury number 12, 1981.

49. Naglak Z. "Trening sportowy—Teoria i praktyka/Sports training—Theory and practice." PWN, Warszawa, 1979.
50. Nikiforov J. B. "Badania oddzialywania obciazen treningowych przy budowie treningu wedlug zasady 'wahadla'/Study of effects of training loads when conducting training according to the 'pendulum' principle." Sport Wyczynowy number 8, 1972.
51. Ozolin N. G. "Sovriemiennaya systiema sportivnoy trenirovki/Contemporary system of sports training" Fizkultura i Sport, Moskva, 1971 (quoted by Bompa).
52. Platonov V. N. "Teoriya i metodika sportivnoy trenirovki/Theory and methodics of sports training". Vyssha Shkola, Kiev, 1984.
53. Puni A. C. "O diagnostyce niedociagniec w stanach psychicznych gotowosci do zawodow/On diagnostics of deficiencies in psychological preparation to competitions" Kultura Fizyczna number 5, 1968 (quoted by Naglak).
54. Ratov I. P. "Some results of analysis of the system of complex control in sports and perspectives of its development/Niekatoryie itogi razrabotki sistiemy kompleksnego kontrola w sportie wysshych dostizheniy i perspectivy yeye razwitiya" Tieoriya i Praktika Fizicheskoy Kultury number 11, 1984.
55. Raven J. C. "The R.E.C.I. Series of Perceptual Tests: An Experimental Survey" British Journal of Medical Physiology volume 18, number 1, 1939.
56. Repin L. "What's behind stress." Sport in the USSR number 12, 1988.
57. Rudy D. M. "The relationship of fatiguability and flexibility to hamstring injuries in sprinters".
58. Shcherbina Y. V. "Changes in electrical activity and muscle strength after physical exertion performed at different times of the day." Teoriya i Praktika Fizicheskoy Kultury number 4, 1987 (quoted in Soviet Sports Review, June 1988).
59. Schröder W. "Cechy specjalistycznego treningu silowego/Features of special strength training." Sport Wyczynowy number 9, 1973 (quoted by Naglak).
60. Shiyan V. V., Nevzorov V. M. "Steam Bath." Sportivnaya Borba, 1986 (quoted in Soviet Sports Review, March 1989).
61. Siek S. "Relaks i autosugestia/Relax and autosuggestion." KAW, Warszawa, 1986.
62. Sklarenko A. "Strongest of The Strong" in a compilation by Snegirev V. "How Stars Are Born" Novosti Press Agency Publishing House, Moskva, 1980.
63. Soldatov A. "Oddzialywanie roznych obciazen a planowanie treningu/Effects of various loads in planning athletic training" Sport Wyczynowy number 10, 1969 (quoted by Naglak).
64. Spasov A., Todd T. "Bulgarian Leg Training Secrets" Muscle and Fitness, December 1989.
65. Strojnowski J. "Psychoterapia/Psychotherapy." IWPAX, Warszawa, 1985
66. Theiss G. "Jak czesto nalezy startowac w sporcie dzieciecym i mlodziezowym/How often one should start in children's and youth sports." Sport Wyczynowy number 9, 1966.
67. Ulatowski T. "Teoria i metodyka sportu/Theory and methodology of sports." WAWF, Warszawa, 1979.
68. Ulatowski T. "Teoria i metodyka sportu/Theory and methodology of sports." Sport i Turystyka, Warszawa, 1981.
69. Volkov N. J. "W poszukiwaniu naukowych podstaw teorii treningu/In search of scientific foundations of theory of sports training." Sport Wyczynowy number 2, 1971.
70. Wazny Z. "Zasady przygotowania silowego zawodnikow reprezentujacych wysoki poziom sportowy/Principles of strength preparation of high class athletes." Materialy z Konferencji Szkoleniowej PKOL i INKF, "Podstawowe elementy wspolczesnego treningu cech motorycznych", Wydawnictwo PKOL, Warszawa, 1972.
71. Wickstrom R. L. "Weight training and flexibility." Journal of Health, Physical Education and Recreation 34(2):61, 1963.
72. Wilmore J. H. "Athletic Training and Physical Fitness." Allyn and Bacon, Boston, 1983.
73. Zaciorski W. "Ksztaltowanie cech motorycznych sportowcow/Developing motor abilities of athletes." Sport i Turystyka, Warszawa, 1970.
74. Zaton M. "Niektore aspekty kontroli zdolnosci wysilkowej w treningu sportowym/Some aspects of control of the changes of work ability in sports training." Sport Wyczynowy number 12, 1987.
75. "Endurance and Pubertal Development." Running and Fitness, 1984 vol. 16, #4, July/August.

76. "O niedostatkach i nowym podejsciu do kontroli treningu/On insufficiencies of and on the new approach to control of sports training" in Sport Wyczynowy number 12, 1987.

77. "What is this thing called sleep." National Geographic, December 1987.

INDEX

coordination, 91
Isotonic contraction
  definition, 84

J

Jacuzzi
  benefits, 238
Javelin throw
  analytic method, 154
  flexibility, 140
  max. results age, 189
  resistance, 99
  special exercises, 45
Judo
  analytic method, 155
  contact sports, 41
  directed exercises, 46
  overstrain, 33
  speed test, 214
  sports selection, 49
  tactical training, 166
  technical reliability, 228
Judoka
  stretching, 143
Jumping
  children's training, 190
Jumping (ski)
  first starts, 189
  max. results age, 189
  selection age, 188
Jumping ability
  definition, 93
Jumps
  directed exercises, 45
  max. results age, 189
  overstrain, 33
  special endurance, 120
  special test, 220
  speed-strength sports, 41

K

Kinesthesis
  emotions, 224
  measuring, 224
Kinesthetic sensations
  ideomotor exercises, 154
  technique, 43
Kinesthetic sense
  balance, 134
  technique, 49

L

Laboratory tests
  sensitivity, 195
Lactacid capability
  children, 217

Lactic acid
  adaptations, 115
  aerobic capabilities, 115
  boxers, 203
  fatigue, 32
  internal load, 31
  sprinters, 40
  threshold speed, 204
Ligaments
  children, 97
  massage, 234
  steroids, 12
  strength exercises, 98
  stretching, 139
Load
  critical value, 26
  internal, 32
  standard, 17
Loads
  adaptability, 16
  adaptation, 17, 99, 205
  before competition, 54
  body weight, 209, 227
  changes, 23, 213
  changing, 18, 54
  children, 187
  competitions, 132
  competitive period, 76, 78
  correction, 207
  decreasing, 18
  evaluating adaptation, 206
  general edurance, 120
  general preparatory period, 74
  immune system, 37
  long-term training, 192 - 193
  low intensity, 18
  macrocycle plan, 194
  menstrual cycle, 69
  mesocycle, 69
  mesocycle plan, 211
  microcycle, 64
  microcycle control, 203
  microcycle plans, 195
  mountain training, 118
  ordinary microcycle, 67
  overstrain, 33
  overtraining, 33 - 35
  period plan, 194
  periodization, 53
  physical, 172
  planning workouts, 206
  preparatory period, 214
  psychological, 172
  recovery, 17
  reduction, 71
  results, 26, 192, 197
  shock microcycle, 67
  special preparatory period, 75
  stabilization, 70
  training effect, 39
  volume vs. intensity, 54, 73

standard exercises, 40
tactical training, 166
technical proficiency, 228
technical training, 164
Weightlifting exercises
  runners, 20
Weightlifting workouts
  planning, 96
Whirlpool
  benefits, 238
Will
  competitive exercises, 171
  components, 169
  endurance training, 117
  maximal weight, 89
  re- acclimatization, 119
  training ability, 49
Will developing
  exercises, 173
Will qualities
  physical exercises, 172
  sports, 170
Will to win
  developing, 172
Will training
  coach and, 173
  competition, 171
  competitions, 172
  macrocycle, 183
  physical training, 170
Will-power
  aerobic endurance, 112
Women
  aerobic capability, 115
  bone loss, 213
  strength, 87
Work
  athletic form, 54
  external load, 31
  internal load, 31 - 32
  recovery, 39
  training and, 67
  training plans, 193
  volume and intensity, 16
Work capability
  menstrual cycle, 69
  periodization, 54
  rest, 37
  workout frequency, 62
  workout structure, 55
Work capacity
  competitive period, 77
  rest period, 104
Work duration
  continuous training, 125
  oxygen consumption, 114
Work efficiency
  ideomotor exercises, 180
  microcycle, 23
  sleep deprivation, 232
Work intensity

athletic form, 25, 73
competitive period, 78, 132
continuous training, 125
definition, 26
endurance training, 117
general preparatory period, 74
heart rate, 28, 200
intensive training stage, 192
interval training, 126
introductory mesocycle, 70
max. results stage, 192
microcycle, 65
mountain training, 118
ordinary microcycle, 67
preparatory stage, 187
progress, 28
re-acclimatization, 119
repetitions, 113
restorative microcycle, 68
semiannual cycles, 73
special endurance, 122
special exercises, 74
special form, 54
special preparatory period, 75, 131
transitory period, 79, 132
variable training, 125
Work volume
  accumulation period, 80
  athletic form, 25, 73
  competitive period, 78, 132
  definition, 25
  endurance training, 116
  general exercises, 74
  general preparatory period, 74, 101,
131
  intensive training stage, 192
  introductory mesocycle, 70
  max. results stage, 192
  mountain training, 118
  Olympic cycle, 82
  ordinary microcycle, 67
  overtraining, 36
  parasympathetic system, 207
  preparatory stage, 187
  progress, 28
  record results, 197
  recovery, 113
  restorative microcycle, 68
  results retention stage, 192
  semiannual cycles, 73
  special endurance, 123
  special form, 54
  special preparatory period, 75, 132
  strength training, 100
Workout
  agility exercises, 137
  auxiliary, 61
  best time for, 60
  children, 190
  circuit training, 128
  continuous, 43

Stretching Scientifically,
A Guide to Flexibility Training

Published in 1990
ISBN: 0-940149-26-5 hardcover, 0-940149-28-1 softcover
Library of Congress Catalog Card Number: 87-61431
Page count: 128
Illustrations: 124 photographs plus 106 drawings
Back matter: Appendix, bibliography, index

Stretching Scientifically, A Guide to Flexibility Training is a unique exercise manual based on East European scientific research. This manual gives **new** information on flexibility training. Thomas Kurz's knowledge of both the coach's and of the athlete's perspective makes this manual more helpful than most others. His demonstration of incredible strength and flexibility resulting from isometric stretching should convert all athletes to this method of developing flexibility.

April 14, 1986
"A friend of mine loaned me Stretching Scientifically. I started to read it, and could not put it down! I feel like maybe there is a chance for me now. I am 40 years old and have been involved in Tae Kwon Do for six years—I work very hard but after six years, my kicks are still low—gut high—with fair power. But I have been doing much of my hard work backwards! Thank you so much for writing your book."—Victor Roggio, St.Peters, Pennsylvania.

September 26, 1986
"I have been using your technique consistently. Yours is the only technique that has actually increased my stretch, that I have tried in the last four years."—Victor Roggio, St.Peters, Pennsylvania.

"I had the old book, now I have the new. I can do a front split on chairs, the side split should be done by the end of summer. (This letter was written in the summer of '88 and the above picture was taken in the fall of '88.) I am pleased with this system, why wasn't the book written 15 years ago."—George Patnoe, Jr., Brockport, New York.

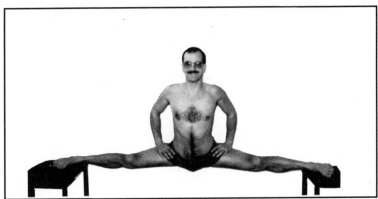

George Patnoe, Jr.

"... I have never been able to display my maximum range of motion without thoroughly warming up, a process lasting some 30 to 45 minutes, and muscles would always be limited in mobility early in the morning. Using your method, I am able to achieve the same stretch in only five minutes, and perform with maximal range of motion even in the morning! ...Stretching is no longer a tedious task. Stretching Scientifically is, without doubt, the most effective, efficient and safest method of stretching..."— Mr. H. D. Palfrey, Karate instructor, Gillingham, England.

Stretching Scientifically, A Guide to Flexibility Training tells you how to work out, what the common mistakes are, and gives you the information on the "whys" of "do's" and "don'ts", so no one will be able to mislead you any more. You will know how to make your muscles grow longer and stronger, how to determine your potential flexibility (there are tests that tell if you will be able to do front and side splits), and what exercises are "no-no's" if you want to stretch your muscles. Do you know that it takes only eight weeks to attain maximum dynamic flexibility? If you work on it longer than that it means that either you or your instructor is doing something wrong. **NOW YOU WILL BE AN EXPERT!**

"Your book Stretching Scientifically is excellent. It gives the scientific basis for your techniques and then a good description of each exercise."—Steven Gerrish, university professor, Sault Ste. Marie, Michigan.

"Prior to buying your book I had spent long periods using traditional type stretching i.e. sitting on the floor in a 'box split position' stretching from side to side (none bounce). Before kicking I had to spend 20 to 30 minutes stretching. This I had to do 2 or 3 times a day. Using your method this situation has improved. Now after warming up and leg lifts I can kick reasonably well."—M. Richardson, Karate instructor, Stafford, Staffordshire, England.

"Your book has given me a new life in TaeKwon-Do. Before I got the book I would have to go down to the gym 45 min. before the black belt class, but now it takes 15 min. to warm up. I have not had one injury since I got the book."—Thomas R. Phoenix, Jr., TaeKwon-Do instructor, Republic of Ireland.

"I am writing this letter to thank you for the tremendous help your book, 'Stretching Scientifically' has been to me in achieving long time flexibility goals.
I have always had flexibility but could never attain full splits. Additionally, I needed to warm up for a minimum of 45 minutes before attempting any serious kicking. However, after reading your book and implementing your techniques I now have better stretch with less pain and injury than I thought was possible.
I co-own a TaeKwon-Do school with approximately 90 students. Because of my rapid progress, we instituted many of your exercises within our normal class structure and not surprisingly, almost all of our students have also realized increased flexibility in just a few short months.
The ad said 'It could be your picture...' Well, enclosed is actual photo shot in July of this year [1990] with proof positive that your method does produce results."—Stephen N. DiLeo, Altoona Academy of TaeKwon-Do, Altoona, PA.

Stephen N. DiLeo, Altoona Academy of TaeKwon-Do

"I received your book 'Stretching Scientifically' and I'm glad because in just one week I had some gains"—Amilton A. M. Allcantara Jr., Saquarema, Brazil.

"Two month ago I ordered your book 'Stretching Scientifically', which really improved my flexibility tremendously.
...in about a month I will have completed my task [of achieving full splits]. Thanks to your help my muscles not only became loose, but strong as well. Your method truly works."—Eagle Mathis, Clifton NJ.

Stretching Scientifically, A Guide to Flexibility Training will be useful to athletes, instructors, and coaches. It describes the systems and organs of the body that determine one's flexibility. But that's not all. The theory is illustrated with practical examples and then followed by a detailed practical guide to the safest and fastest stretching methods.

Every stretching method is carefully explained, then recommended ways of application are suggested. Every exercise is shown and clearly described. Exercises are grouped by body part (arms, legs, etc.) and accompanied by listings of sports in which they can be applied.

Tom Kurz's Secrets of Stretching, Exercises for the Lower Body

Produced in 1990
System: NTSC, PAL, SECAM
Format: Color, VHS or BETA
Length: Part I— 64 minutes, Part II— 34 minutes.

This video will make you an expert on flexibility and strength training. First, you will learn all about conditioning for "out-of-shape" athletes so you can safely increase your or your students' flexibility, and prepare yourself or your students for intensive, but not difficult, strength and flexibility training shown later on this tape, leading eventually to Tom Kurz's results. You will learn:

• What determines how flexible you are;

• How to test your potential flexibility;

• How to choose your stretching method;

• How to arrange your strength training and stretching routine;

• How the results shown in our ads were achieved;

• How to have your full flexibility (normally available only after a warm-up) even without a warm-up.

Now you can have the know-how that should enable you to achieve ultimate flexibility and strength.

Tom Kurz's Secrets of Stretching (Part I & Part II) is the only video that you need to achieve ultimate flexibility and strength. Apart from showing and explaining exercises for general conditioning it shows **FOUR EXERCISE ROUTINES** (one for beginners, one for intermediate, and two for advanced athletes) that you can do along with Tom Kurz. All these routines were used by Tom Kurz and his students for the results that could be yours too... Just dedicate 4-15 minutes (more for beginners and less for advanced) every morning to dynamic stretches and twice a week spend 23 minutes on strength exercises and static stretches for your legs during your strength workout. Our isometric stretches are improved versions of exercises tested by Holt, Travis and Okita, and later by Tanigawa, which have been shown to cause **267% greater increase in flexibility** than any other kind of stretches.

Thanks to following our program you will be able to display your full flexibility even with no warm-up!

"The book is fantastic! Please send 'Tom Kurz's Secrets of Stretching' in VHS format. Thanks!"—Dr. Martin P. Marcus, Marcus Chiropractic Clinic, St. Petersburg, FL.

"I am a martial artist, and have always spent 45 minutes to an hour stretching before my kicking routine which usually last an hour itself. Since I have began using your methods, I begin my kick routine after a brief warm-up using dynamic stretches. My kicks seem to have more snap, and my amplitude has remained about the same [as with the 45 minute warm-up]."—Richard Parker, Cresson, PA.

"I have ordered your video tape. I must say, within the two months that I have been following your program my flexibility has improved a great deal. In the side split I am lower than I have ever been in all my years of training.
...I have been doing karate for over five years; and I am also proud to say that I am good at it. In order for me to do the splits, especially side ways, it would take me like most people forty five minutes to an hour, but since I got your tape the time has decreased drastically."—Antoine Christopher, Laval, Quebec, Canada.

"I am a practitioner of Tae Kwon Do and have been for 8 years. For the past 3 years I have experienced a plateau in my stretching program. I make same gains, but only with great pain and with a much decreased rate of gain. Recently my teacher, man of seemingly superhuman flexibility, revealed to me that he once suffered from similar obstacles and surmounted them through application of your principles. I am thus understandably interested in purchasing a copy of your video tape."—Andrew Johnson, Toronto, Ontario, Canada.

"Thank you for the prompt and fast handling of my VHS tape order. I found your concept fascinating. It certainly gives me hope. I found the video presentation excellent. The quality of picture outstanding. Overall, a first rate job." – Lawrence M. Lynch, Chicago, IL.

ORDER FORM

TO: Stadion Publishing Company

P.O. Box 447-F1

Island Pond, VT 05846

I understand that I may return the book in good condition within 30 days or tape within 10 days for a full refund of your purchase price.

Here is my check/money order in the amount of $_____. Please send the book/videotape.

Foreign orders, please pay by International Money Order in US dollars only!

___**Stretching Scientifically,**
A Guide to Flexibility Training (softcover) . . . . @$15.95

___**Stretching Scientifically,**
A Guide to Flexibility Training (hardcover) . . . .@$21.95

___**Science of Sports Training:**
How to Plan and Control Training for Peak Performance (softcover) . . . . . .@$26.95

___**Science of Sports Training:**
How to Plan and Control Training for Peak Performance (hardcover) . . . . .@$33.95

___**Tom Kurz's Secrets of Stretching,**
Exercises for the Lower Body (videotape 98 min.) . . . . @$69.95

Please circle video system and format: VHS BETA PAL (Europe) SECAM (Asia)

Shipping:

SURFACE MAIL (Book rate): $1.50 for the first book and 25 cents for each additional book. Surface shipping may take three weeks.

AIR MAIL: $3.00 per book. Videotapes: $4.00 for each tape (foreign orders: $6.00). Tapes are shipped via AIR MAIL only.

PLEASE PRINT

Name _____

Address _____

City _____

State/Zip_____